The Shell Book of
COUNTRY PARKS

The Shell Book of
COUNTRY PARKS

Mary Waugh

DAVID & CHARLES
Newton Abbot   London   North Pomfret (Vt)

(overleaf) The Afan Valley in Afan Argoed Country Park, West Glamorgan. *West Glamorgan CC*

Shell U.K. Limited while sponsoring this book would point out that the author is expressing her own views.

British Library Cataloguing in Publication Data

Waugh, Mary
    The Shell book of country parks.
    1. Parks − Great Britain − Directories
    I. Title
    914.2   SB484.G7

ISBN 0-7153-7963-1

Library of Congress Catalog Card Number 80-68695

Typeset by Typesetters (Birmingham) Ltd
and printed in Great Britain
by Butler and Tanner Ltd, Frome and London
for David & Charles (Publishers) Limited
Brunel House   Newton Abbot   Devon

Published in the United States of America
by David & Charles Inc
North Pomfret   Vermont 05053   USA

Contents

Appendices

Maps

Introduction: Our Country Parks

How many people realise that almost 200 country parks have opened in Britain since 1969? It is an achievement we can be proud of, and one which can add to the pleasure and interest of exploring the countryside. There is a wealth of opportunity on offer at the parks, which have usually been developed by a local authority. Partly because at least half of the initial cost has been covered by government grants, admission is free in all but a few special cases. In size and character these parks fit somewhere between the typical town park, established fifty or a hundred years ago, and the ten National Parks of England and Wales, developed in the last thirty years. But their purpose is different; country parks set out to attract visitors, to be what planners call 'honeypots'. However if your preference is for solitude in the countryside, you can escape from the crowd—except perhaps on the very busiest summer Sundays.

At the very least you can be sure of space to walk or picnic without the fear you may be trespassing, and there will be adequate car-parking and toilet facilities. Most country parks offer much more than this; there are sixty where you can get a ticket for a day's fishing, thirty-five where you can sail a dinghy, launch a canoe or hire a rowing boat, and others which offer golf, putting or riding.

A number of country parks are in magnificent hill and coastal settings. There are also ancient forests, deer parks, lakes and landscaped gardens. In many cases much of the attraction is man-made; there are castles and great houses, but also farms and watermills, a complete slate-working complex, restored canals and a railway station. All but the smallest country parks provide an information service, with park staff to answer queries, and self-guided trails or waymarked paths to suggest what you might wish to explore. The larger parks have visitor centres and may have exhibitions or film shows.

I first became involved with country parks when beautiful places I already knew suddenly acquired car parks, toilets and picnic tables. Intrigued, I

sought information about other country parks. The two Countryside Commissions, which have overall responsibility for the parks, issue free summary lists of the sites, but without precise instructions on how to find them. Indeed, for those in England and Wales, the main clue is a grid reference to the mathematical centre of the park (not helpful, for example, at a reservoir site!). The aim of this book is to help everyone to find the country parks, and to provide a summary of the interesting features of each. To this end, much of the book is a gazetteer of all our country parks, arranged regionally. In all but the most awkward instances, anyone should be able to find a selected park with no more than a road atlas and the instructions given, but for people with large-scale maps I have added a grid reference to the park entrance.

In the course of discovering which parks had opened, and how to get in, I had adventures up narrow mountain lanes on the Welsh border, where a green strip up the middle is the prelude to being decanted into a farmyard. It is equally harrowing, in heavy traffic, to be carried inexorably past one's destination (I recall a desperate U-turn at the aptly named Waterloo outside Oldham, while searching for Daisy Nook). My one plea to all local authorities responsible is for adequate and clear road signs to help intending visitors; sometimes also better signs are needed inside the parks, and a map of the layout should be a normal feature. I can claim to have visited every country park listed here, and my particular problem was finding out about those still incomplete. In the end the best way was to approach *all* the likely sources. These include local tourist information centres, the regional offices of the Countryside Commission for England and Wales, and the national office in Scotland (the addresses are at the back of this book), and the planning departments or recreation services of all the local authorities.

When Essex County Planning Department sent me the name of Cudmore Grove, a park on which the Countryside Commission in Cheltenham were silent, and which no one in Colchester then appeared to have heard about, it was with a degree of fatalism that I drove out across the salt marshes and down to the eastern tip of Mersea Island. Pursuing the narrow, rough and twisting lane at the finish, I emerged to my astonishment in one of the largest assemblies of parked cars I have yet seen at a country park. If ever I saw a 'honeypot', Cudmore Grove was it! And later, escaping against the

---

(previous page) The Home Farm, built by Robert Adam in 1777 beside Culzean Castle on the coast south of Ayr, and now converted to form the visitor centre in the country park. This magnificent coast faces the mountains of Arran across the Firth of Clyde. *National Trust for Scotland*

incoming tide of further eager visitors, I reflected on the monumental traffic jam likely to develop when everyone went home again.

Every country park has something to offer to the keen naturalist, and a number include a Site of Special Scientific Interest (or SSSI) or a local nature reserve. Others include important archaeological sites or historic buildings, and the range of these interests is indicated in the chapters which follow. Anyone familiar with a number of our country parks is likely to be intrigued by the way they have been developed, and I have taken examples to show how a stately home and its surrounding deer park has been adapted to give pleasure to a wider public, or how a wasteland of derelict collieries has been turned into a watersports complex. The reasons which led the government to pass the necessary legislation and make money available to help develop the country parks are described in Chapter 7. It is too soon to pass judgement on the success of these policies, but we can enjoy looking at what has been achieved.

The Parks in this Book

All the country parks listed by the two Countryside Commissions have been included in the gazetteer starting on page 57. The commission for Scotland distinguishes between fully recognised country parks and schemes that are incomplete and are provisionally registered. There are no privately developed country parks in Scotland, although Finlaystone in Strathclyde and Hopetoun House in West Lothian are examples which have received help from the commission and are comparable with the private country-park schemes of England and Wales. The official list of the parks in England and Wales lags behind events, however, and for complete coverage one must add information supplied by the regional offices of the Countryside Commission or the local authorities directly concerned.

Confusion can arise from two sources: a very small number of country parks which appeared on earlier lists have now been deleted (Westwood and Howell Wood in South Yorkshire are cases in point), and there are some comparable schemes which are not called country parks. Thus Bristol City developed what amounts to a country park at Ashton Court, without seeking Countryside Commission aid or recognition. Then, both the Forestry Commission and the water authorities have developed a number of countryside recreation schemes; some of these have country park status, but most do not. The Forestry Commission provides good regional maps and lists of its picnic and camping sites, scenic drives and other facilities (obtainable from Tourist Information Offices or its headquarters).

11

Accordingly Forestry Commission sites are referred to only where these border on, or are part of, established country parks.

Important water-authority sites comparable to country parks are briefly referred to in the gazetteer under 'Other Schemes'. Into this category also go schemes like Studley Royal Park, developed and termed a country park by North Yorkshire CC, but which may not receive Countryside Commission recognition, and also schemes which are still at the planning stage.

Anyone interested in exploring all the new opportunities created in the countryside over the past decade should inquire at a Tourist Information Office. For example there are now various medium and shorter distance walking routes, not as well known as the longer South Downs or Pennine Ways. It is also a good idea to check on special events in the countryside such as farm open days, the Easter Fair at Hollingworth Lake Country Park or the County Show at Elvaston Castle for example; and because established country parks add to their activities, do not be surprised to find features not mentioned here!

At the end of the day, country parks are about enjoyment. The short chapters that follow show what the parks are all about and the kinds of countryside and facilities they can offer. The gazetteer, beginning on page 57, aims to give practical help on each park, showing what is available there and how to find it. If the country parks give you as much pleasure as I have had in exploring them, the book's preparation will have been well worthwhile.

1

The Choice in One County

Visiting the countryside is the most popular outdoor activity in Britain. A recent national opinion survey showed that three out of every four people in England and Wales enjoy trips of this kind, though only a small fraction of their expeditions take in one of our country parks. Most country lovers already know one or two of the parks, but few so far have any idea of the scope of what is on offer. No two country parks are alike, so it may be helpful to indicate the range by looking at those in one English county.

Hampshire County Council was one of the first to seize on the chance to use the grants made available after 1968 to improve countryside facilities. This was mainly because areas such as the New Forest, Old Winchester Hill and stretches of local coast were visibly suffering under the impact of too many visitors. The earliest schemes were simple, and involved no more than improving car-parking, picnic and toilet facilities on popular stretches of open land. Yateley common on the A30 trunk road is rolling heathland, popular for walking and riding, and well frequented by local residents. Those who live further afield may find it a pleasant picnic site, and an ideal escape from the noise and pressures of driving. There are some sixteen small and unpretentious country parks of this kind in England and Wales, but none in Scotland, where planning policies have been rather different. Hampshire has two other simple country parks, again developed in the early years and primarily for local people, but which holidaymakers would find worth visiting. The first is a chain of sites along downland west of Winchester, called Farley Mount. This will appeal to those who want a picnic or barbecue at an excellent viewpoint, or who enjoy walking on chalk downland and through woods. The other is Lepe and Calshot, two separate stretches of undeveloped Solent coast and foreshore, where you can swim or fish, and watch seabirds or all manner of craft in one of the world's busiest shipping lanes.

Hampshire already has two big country parks, and a third is being developed; it is these that give the best idea of what the parks are all about.

The Queen herself opened Queen Elizabeth Country Park in 1976, on a site where the London to Portsmouth road cuts deeply through the chalk escarpment at Butser Hill. This is a large park in an area of fine natural scenery, designated an Area of Outstanding Natural Beauty, or AONB.

The best starting point is the information desk at the visitor centre, where literature is on sale and exhibitions or an audio-visual programme in the lecture theatre give an indication of what can be enjoyed. There is a café (a feature generally found in the larger parks only) and local craftsmen give demonstrations of their work at weekends in the main season. The eastern side of the park is developed on Forestry Commission land, where grassy clearings among beech plantations provide picnic and barbecue sites. Those

The Butser ancient farm demonstration area in Queen Elizabeth Country Park near Portsmouth. The Pimperne House, reconstructed from archaeological evidence, stands beside plots where crops in use 2,000 years ago are being cultivated. *Queen Elizabeth Country Park Centre*

2

Making the Most of the Parks

We are not very adventurous when it comes to visiting the countryside. Most of us go back repeatedly to places we have been to before, but there is plenty of opportunity to try out new ones, not only country parks but a number of other schemes, often linked to the parks, which deserve to be better known. An obvious starting point is to discover just what is available within a reasonable distance of home or holiday base. In addition to any special interests you may wish to follow up, you can decide whether you want to enjoy the fun at a popular 'honeypot' site, or escape into quieter places.

Many country parks offer both kinds of experience. The parks are generally quiet on weekdays and out of season, but some on well-established sites draw large numbers at peak times. A warm summer Sunday may bring over 14,000 visitors to the popular parts of Cannock Chase, but this is exceptional. Bradgate Park in Leicestershire, a beautiful and interesting site, has about 900,000 visitors a year and, in addition to extending the country park, Leicestershire CC have developed a number of other comparable sites and a farm trail nearby. A park such as Queen Elizabeth can absorb its 350,000 visitors a year without many problems. However at Sherwood Forest a smaller number of visitors—probably 300,000 a year—are more difficult to accommodate because almost all want to walk along the same paths to one particular tree. Coastal parks in holiday areas (Hastings, Seven Sisters or Berry Head, for example) and favourite National Trust sites such as the Clent Hills, Frensham Common and Box Hill are also very popular and best avoided at peak times by anyone looking for solitude!

In contrast, a lot of country parks are under-used, I suspect largely because little has been done to promote them or indicate how to find them. A few newly developed reclaimed sites are still raw, but have the space for sporting, and especially watersports, facilities. Water in its various forms fascinates most of us, and a third of all trips to the countryside are to a waterside site of one kind or another. Watersports are one of the most rapidly growing types of recreation. Sailing, like the newer sport of hang-gliding, is fun to watch. So, while only four out of every hundred people who visit the countryside take part in an active and organised sport, very large numbers go to watch.

It is perhaps useful to indicate what country parks do *not* provide. A few include facilities for team games, but this is uncommon. None of the parks provides a fun-fair atmosphere, nor are they suitable for noisy activities—stock-car racing or motor-cycle scrambling, for instance. Though more appropriate sites are provided in some areas, in the absence of more adequate facilities it is not altogether surprising that a young motor-cycle enthusiast should be spending Sunday afternoon roaring round the ramparts of the hill fort at Barbury Castle, something the byelaws are intended to prevent.

Opening Hours and Admission Charges

The majority of country parks on publicly owned sites are open throughout the year during daylight hours and make no admission charge. Car-parking may be free, or there may be a charge at peak times and occasionally this is by meter. Sandringham and Goodwood apart, the privately developed

The new visitor centre among the ancient oak trees of Sherwood Forest Country Park. *East Midlands Tourist Board*

country parks must pay their way and charge for admission. They are open during the main season only, and for more limited hours. Since these arrangements are apt to change, a telephone number has been given so that details given in the gazetteer section can be checked. Some of the more elaborate parks managed by local authorities also have limited opening times and may charge for admission. As might be expected, visitor centres, cafés and other facilities may be closed outside the main season. Queen Elizabeth is one of the parks which charges for admission; others include Culzean in Scotland, Margam in Wales and Tatton and Lyme in Cheshire. Three (Culzean, Tatton and Lyme) are National Trust properties, but the country park is administered by the local authority, so all must pay, including National Trust members. Anyone making regular visits would be wise to get a season ticket.

It is worth adding that when the BBC radio programme, 'It's a Bargain', took a light-hearted look at the stately homes business, several of the more elaborate country parks came out as the top bargain in their respective regions. Tredegar House in Gwent and Knebworth were instances selected.

Using the Interpretative Services

One of the main differences between visiting a country park and going to any unmanaged part of the countryside is the chance to find out more about what there is to see. All but the very smallest and simplest parks provide additional information for the visitor, and larger park centres offer all sorts of interesting and visually exciting exhibitions, slide shows and talks. The park ranger or warden is the best source of information, and the one most generally appreciated. The larger parks depend on a number of people, from tea ladies and parking attendants to countryside interpreters (and sometimes, alas, security guards); but it is the park warden or ranger in his Land-Rover with whom visitors are most frequently in touch. In the past these were usually called wardens, and they still have the job of keeping an eye on visitors, to see that the byelaws are observed and that no one gets into difficulties on a tidal foreshore or steep hillside. But the job and usual title have now changed; it is the park ranger who must enlist the support of the local community, who may become involved in a public relations exercise to reassure local residents and farmers, or who may be asked to talk to a local conservation society. This book owes a great debt to many park wardens and rangers for their enthusiasm and generous help.

Interpretation means more than merely providing background information; it implies developing a theme, elaborating a story or explaining relationships. Perhaps for this reason some of the best displays and trails are those which portray a historical event or the story of a great house and its family. To the unaided eye, the hillside where knights in armour fought the battle of Bosworth in 1485 is a pleasant but unremarkable stretch of Leicestershire farmland. But watch the film and slide shows at the centre, look at the models explaining what happened and replicas showing how the combatants were armed, and the experience gains a new dimension. Then go outside and stand beneath King Richard's standard, and later go to the place where he was killed. Few will forget the scene.

The natural history of the countryside is the most typical subject of exhibitions and trails. Almost all country parks have marked out some form of self-guiding nature trail. The approach they adopt varies greatly; some are essentially designed to help children to identify plants, to notice telltale signs of a fox or a badger; others treat a theme at some depth. A glance at the trail leaflet will give some idea of what is involved and of the length and strenuousness of the trail. I have seen babies in pushchairs being manhandled round some distinctly unsuitable nature trails! The leaflet may be available from the park centre, or from a dispenser near the car park; if not, you may have to contact the offices of the council which manages the park.

3

Fine Scenery and Wildlife

Country parks in the very best natural scenery tend to be in the more remote areas or on the fringes of the National Parks. Some, but not all, are sites popular for many years.

Take first the exhilaration which comes from a sense of being on top of the world. Anyone with a car can experience something of this sensation with minimum effort at a surprisingly large number of country parks but, for those able to explore further, the pleasures are enhanced. Moel Famau on the North Wales border is particularly fine. The narrow chain of the Clwyd Hills is crowned by prehistoric hill forts, linked by an ancient routeway which is now the line of Offa's Dyke Path.

There are other good viewpoints in the Pennines. At Beacon Fell near Preston you can drive much of the way up this isolated summit and circle round to take in the view in all directions, before climbing on foot to the top. Tegg's Nose on the Cheshire border above Macclesfield is another good viewpoint. At another former quarry site on Penistone Hill, above Haworth, there is the added attraction of exploring the moorland which inspired the Brontë sisters. Two National Trust properties in the Pennines have now become country parks, the Longshaw estate, west of Sheffield, and well known by rock climbers for the gritstone crags above, and the weirdly shaped Brimham Rocks, on moorland above Pateley Bridge. Outside Stockport are two country parks now linked by a footpath. Werneth Low is on a ridge below the main Pennine summits, and Etherow in the deep valley below.

Several of the Scottish country parks have excellent views extending northwards towards the Highlands and if the hilltop country parks of the Midlands and southern England lack height and a sense of isolation, even modest summits like Burton Dassett Hills in the West Midlands provide an excellent view. Box Hill in Surrey is certainly the best known, but the small park at Trosley in Kent, Butser Hill in Hampshire and Barbury Castle in Wiltshire have many of the same features. All these, with Ham Hill in

Somerset and the two Cotswold parks at Crickley Hill and Broadway Tower, are in excellent walking country, quite apart from the importance of the archaeological sites at Barbury Castle, and Butser, Crickley and Ham Hills. The Clent Hills are the most attractive of several similar country parks in the West Midlands, but reaching the summits requires rather more effort. Moreover this is a very popular recreation area, and because of the particular rock formation which underlies it, one which shows the damaging effects of over-use.

Rivers and lakes greatly enhance the natural beauty of many country parks. Among the most interesting is Ilam, where the river Manifold comes boiling up to the surface through fissures in the limestone. Craig-y-nos in the Brecon Beacons (and the unlikely setting for Madame Patti's private opera house) and the River Dart in Devon are particularly attractive. The view up Loch Lomond from beside Balloch Castle, or a similar view along Windermere from the small park at Fell Foot, are justly celebrated. The antics of fishermen and sailing boats add to the enjoyment of the lakeside scene at Castle Semple in Scotland, Talkin Tarn in Cumbria or the old reservoir at Hollingworth Lake near Rochdale. The beautiful and popular Frensham Ponds in Surrey are also man-made, though less obviously so.

Unspoilt stretches of sea coast have an irresistible appeal for many of us, especially where there are cliff-top paths to be explored, and interesting plants or seabirds. I would rate Mount Edgcumbe in Cornwall and Culzean near Ayr as the most beautiful of all, but Berry Head in Devon, Durlston in Dorset, Seven Sisters and Hastings in Sussex and John Muir in East Lothian are all excellent and (of course) popular coastal country parks.

At Northam Burrows, beside the great pebble ridge at Westward Ho! in Devon, and at Pembrey in South Wales, the country park facilities are not yet complete, but both have great unspoilt stretches of sand. For those who enjoy bird-watching on tidal mudflats and sands, I would recommend Upton Park in Dorset, sections of the Wirral park, and Bardsea in Cumbria. A more boisterous scene with shipping is provided at Loirston, Aberdeen, Eastham Woods on Merseyside (another popular park), or on the Solent at Fort Victoria and Lepe and Calshot.

Wildlife Habitats and Geological Sites

Few parts of Britain remain as wilderness areas, but the higher and wilder stretches of moor and coast are relatively undisturbed. Typical moorland has a cover of heather, moor grasses, and such plants as tormentil, heath bedstraw and bilberry (or blaeberry), developed on an acid soil, and boggy hollows characterised by sedges, sphagnum moss, cotton grass or bog asphodel, or scattered rowan, birch and alder trees. Small animals, such as the mole, shrew, vole, stoat or weasel, live here, as well as hares and foxes, and sometimes badgers and roe deer. Heather moorland is a favourite habitat for various butterflies and moths, and the variety of birds is too numerous to list. For example, over a hundred bird species breed within the Clyde Muirshiel Regional Park in Scotland, and well over 200 species frequent the coastal country park at Dunbar called John Muir. Cold northern waters at Loirston, Aberdeen, or at John Muir are the place to watch Arctic skua, eider duck and shearwater, and here or at Berry Head in Devon there are colonies of gannet, shag, kittiwake and guillemot. Berry Head is a magnificent headland of Devonian Limestone and a local nature reserve. Five rare plant species survive here, as well as the more plentiful pink thrift, autumn squill and varieties of rockrose and stonecrop. The orchids and other beautiful flowers which are typically found on chalk and limestone slopes have already been mentioned. At Seven Sisters the less

The coast in John Muir Country Park, a view through the ruins of Dunbar Castle, where Mary Queen of Scots twice took refuge. *Ian Fullerton, East Lothian Planning Department*

common round-headed rampion can be seen, as well as the yellow horned poppy on the shingle. Both Durlston and Seven Sisters are excellent sites for the bird-watcher; each illustrates aspects of the physical evolution of the landscape and is interesting to the geologist. For this reason both parks, like Box Hill, have been used for field studies by generations of students. Both Seven Sisters and Durlston are within what are now defined as Heritage Coast areas. This is the term given to the finest unspoilt coasts of England and Wales, areas where by definition the needs of conservation take precedence. The way this sort of coastal country park is managed is discussed later in more detail.

A number of lowland heaths and fen communities have survived, and some of these (usually designated SSSIs) are within country parks. Most of such sites are more interesting to the naturalist than to other people. The most popular are on Cannock Chase and Kinver Edge in the West Midlands, but other sites are at Waldridge Fell in Durham, at Holt Woodlands in Norfolk, on Knettishall Heath in Suffolk and Ditchling Common in Sussex. There is an important bogland site at Colemere in Salop, and more recently developed fenland plant communities at Hardwick Hall, Durham, and Cosmeston in South Wales.

Of all our natural habitats the richest is ancient oakwood, which may support over 500 plant and animal species. Very little, if any, of our primary woodland survives, but there are remnants of ancient forest in various places. Some are what remains from royal hunting forests, now preserved within later estates. Sherwood Forest is certainly the best known of these ancient oakwoods. Some of the oak trees within the park are probably more than 300 years old and grow among birch trees in a tangle of bracken, willowherb, foxgloves and harebells. Other fine oaks survive in the great deer park at Bradgate, along with more recent introductions like the cedars of Lebanon, which were planted here more than a century ago. Bradgate is in any case exceptionally interesting for its geology, a place where some of the oldest rocks in Britain come to the surface, as displays at the visitor centre make dramatically clear. Three country parks near London (Stockgrove in Bedfordshire, Bayhurst near Hillingdon and Great Wood near Potter's Bar) also include important oakwoods (these tend to be wet underfoot!). Northaw Great Wood, to give it its full name, is another remnant of hunting forest and the dense woodland is composed of mixed stands of oak with birch, hornbeam and sweet chestnut. There are three other interesting woods of a different type. One at Porthkerry in South Wales is a local nature reserve. Sea Wood at Bardsea is a mixed woodland of oak, ash and wild cherry, growing among a tangle of ice-transported

24

Inside the Poached Egg Chamber of Poole's Cavern at Buxton in Derbyshire, a show cave once visited by Mary Queen of Scots, now reopened to all and accessible to those in wheelchairs. *Buxton and District Civic Association Ltd*

boulders (and now designated an SSSI). Grin Low Wood, outside the limestone cave which forms the centrepiece of Poole's Cavern at Buxton, shelters other unusual plants, and here again the visitor centre provides a good introduction to the interesting geology and wildlife of the park.

Hatfield Forest in Essex gives the most complete picture of the way medieval foresters managed a typical deer park. Here, as in many other estates, the woodland acts as a refuge for wildlife in what is otherwise open farmland. Pollard oaks from a former deer park can also be seen at Langley Park in Buckinghamshire and Weald Park in Essex.

Trees planted to provide shelter are particularly important in creating reservoirs of wildlife outside the Midlands and south of England. Forestry Commission plantations act in this way, but the best examples are woodlands on estates which are now country parks at Haughton House, Aden House and Haddo in Grampian.

Wooded valleys in an otherwise open countryside act in the same way, for example at Plessey Woods in Northumberland, or Almondell in West Lothian. Wooded estates are equally important refuges for wildlife in city areas, as in Trent Park in London.

4

Great Estates, Deer Parks, Gardens and Farms

The country houses of Britain disappear at the rate of two a week, and have been doing so for the past eighty years! In the past a number have been transformed into offices, hospitals or colleges, while their surrounding parkland and gardens (in Scotland known as the policies) might form the basis of a municipal park or playing fields. This pattern continues, and over the past decade similar country estates on sites all over Britain have become country parks. In strict terms this transformation involves the gardens and parkland only; the house is generally managed separately. Where a house is in adequate repair, and not too large, it may be used by the local museum to mount displays.

The fate of larger houses is a more uncertain one. Any lengthy period of neglect leads to a situation where the main house becomes a ruin, or must be demolished, although the stables and outbuildings quite frequently survive. In these circumstances the outbuildings may be restored to provide a visitor centre. The landscaped parkland of these country estates is both a refuge for wildlife and a source of pleasure to visitors.

The really magnificent house, given good fortune, passes into the hands of the National Trust or to an enterprising local authority, which must then obtain grants through the Historic Buildings Council towards the necessary restoration work. In this category come the Scottish properties of Haddo House and Culzean Castle, Erddig in Clwyd, Cragside in Northumberland and Hardwick Hall in Derbyshire. In these cases the country park is a separate development from the main house. At the great Cheshire estates of Tatton and Lyme the county council now manages both house and grounds for the National Trust, while at Croxteth in Liverpool, Elvaston Castle in Derbyshire and Tredegar House in Gwent the local authority owns both house and grounds. Finally there are those great houses still in private hands, but where a country park has been developed on part of the estate, as

27

at Sandringham, Goodwood, Knebworth and Burton Constable.

There are two very good country parks of this type beside the M4 motorway in South Wales, and both are now tourist attractions. Tredegar House, outside Newport, is a fine building which dates mainly from the seventeenth century, but incorporates older structures. This has now been restored.

Margam Park, close to Port Talbot, was bought for the people of South Wales by Glamorgan County Council in 1973. What the county acquired was almost 800 acres (321 hectares) of landscaped deer park and mountainside (with its herd of fallow deer), various ancient monuments from the past 4,000 years, the empty shell of a Victorian castle, an eighteenth-century orangery and the ruins of a twelfth-century Cistercian abbey. The whole estate had already suffered years of neglect, following its sale in 1942. The job of restoration and adaptation was a formidable one, and has involved much voluntary help.

The estate at Culzean Castle on the Ayrshire coast must surely be the finest country park in Britain. The castle with its policies (the surrounding gardens, woods and clifftop) was given to the National Trust for Scotland in 1945 by the family who had owned it since 1744. The site is a magnificent one on cliffs which look out across the sea to the islands of Arran and Ailsa Craig. Here the architect Robert Adam redesigned and extended the castle buildings two centuries ago. Before the castle could be opened to the public, painstaking renewal of the stonework and careful restoration of the interior decorations were needed. The necessary money was raised by national appeals, and grants were made available through the Historic Buildings Council for Scotland.

The gardens at Culzean and the whole setting needed preservation as well as the castle, so as soon as the Countryside Act for Scotland made this possible in 1967, Culzean was proposed as the first country park. The castle continues to be owned and managed by the National Trust for Scotland, but the trust joined with the three local authorities most directly concerned, so that the country park could be grant-aided through the Countryside Commission for Scotland. The country park was established in May 1969, but its great feature, the park centre, did not open until 1973.

At Culzean the creation of the country park saved Robert Adam's Home Farm for posterity as the park centre, and contributed to the beauty of an estate which attracts visitors from Britain and overseas. At another of the great National Trust estates, Tatton Hall in Cheshire, new and fascinating aspects have been developed for the same reason. The Countryside Commission has invited expert groups to report on ways of interpreting some of our major assets, and in 1973 an experienced team from the American National Parks Service came to study Tatton Park. Several features have been developed as a result. The aim is to recreate living history from what remains there from the period before the deer park and present hall were established.

Deer Parks and Landscaped Gardens

The story of ten years' progress in such parks as Tredegar House, Margam Abbey, Culzean Castle and Tatton Hall represents some of the greatest achievements, but all the sixty estates and gardens which are now country parks have much to offer. The finest deer parks are still graced by their herds of red or fallow deer. The descendants of medieval herds still roam the wilder parks at Bradgate and Lyme Hall, and the more elegantly landscaped parks at Tatton, Knebworth, Normanby Hall and Dalemain form an appropriate setting for other impressive herds. Elsewhere the deer park itself remains, but the former herds have escaped, and shy wild roe deer, or sometimes ancient breeds of cattle and sheep, have taken their place (as, for example, at Hardwick Hall in Derbyshire).

The greatest of the landscaped parks date from the eighteenth century and were designed to complement the Palladian mansions of the day. Lancelot ('Capability') Brown was responsible for the most celebrated of these. At Clumber, though the house has gone, all the other ingredients of landscaping in the grand manner remain. There are magnificent avenues, and the beautiful combination of a specially created lake, set off by terraces, a temple and a bridge in the classical style. The avenues and gardens beside the lake at Coombe Abbey are another example of his work, and he may have had a hand in the landscaping of the deer park at Bretton in West Yorkshire. In northern Scotland, where shelter was as essential as fine design, the park at Haddo House is a tribute to what could be achieved in an initially hostile environment. The gardens and park at Elvaston have been restored and are now beautiful in a different fashion. The other great landscape designer, Humphrey Repton, was responsible for shaping the eighteenth-century deer park at Tatton Hall, created after Tatton village had been destroyed. The famous gardens at Tatton, with an orangery, fern house and authentic Japanese garden, were partly the work of Paxton. The gardens and park at Cannon Hall, near Barnsley, are among the finest surrounding lesser eighteenth-century mansions, and there are instances at Weald and Thorndon Parks in Essex, and still more at Hardwick Hall in Durham, where one has to turn detective to uncover traces of the original grand design. The magnificent trees at Goodwood and the fine plantations at Sandringham belong to later and less formal designs.

When it comes to enjoying the beauty of a garden, I would put those at Mount Edgcumbe in Cornwall first, with the range of formal and informal settings, and the marvellous collection of a thousand camellias. The great gardens at Culzean Castle and Lyme and Tatton Halls are well known; the wonderful rhododendron and azalea collections at Cragside in Northumberland and Cefn Onn, outside Cardiff, perhaps less so. I can also recommend the gardens at Balloch Castle in Strathclyde, Haigh near Wigan, Normanby Hall on Humberside, Langley Park near Windsor and those beside Fritton Lake in Norfolk.

Several gardens illustrate important horticultural techniques. The walled garden at Croxteth Hall shows the range of glasshouses and walls heated by flues which enabled delicate crops to be harvested in a northern climate, and the elaborate pruning techniques employed when garden labour was abundant. At Erddig House, outside Wrexham, older varieties of fruit trees are being trained according to traditional methods. Of the many fine collections of specimen trees, the most interesting arboretum is that established at Gelli Aur in Dyfed over a hundred years ago, but the new collections at Queenswood near Leominster, and at Greenway Bank in Staffordshire deserve to be mentioned. The effort and care now being put into planting trees and shrubs in our country parks, and especially those on reclaimed sites, is a particularly encouraging development, though the full beauty of these schemes will not be attained for many years.

Working Farms, Farm Animals and Wildlife Collections

A working farm is an economic unit, and its daily and seasonal routines cannot be halted to show to the casual visitor. However many of us derive great pleasure from watching what goes on; modern mechanised farming is an impressive spectacle, especially during the harvest, and can be seen from a respectful distance.

Anyone interested in farm machinery will find a selection ranging from ancient tools to recently pensioned tractors at a number of country parks, especially the privately developed ones, such as Dalemain, Erddig or Burton Constable and also at Elvaston Castle. A number of parks feature a pets' corner for children. A more serious purpose underlies the rearing of ancient or unusual breeds of farm animals.

At Easton Farm Park, near Wickham Market in Suffolk, everyone can see part at least of the daily round on a modern dairy farm. Two other country parks which feature farm trails are Trent and Langley parks, in the London area, and it is hoped to provide demonstrations of farming activities at Croxteth in Liverpool and Marsh Farm in Essex.

At Farway in Devon the main interest lies in the extensive collection of different breeds of farm animal, especially the more ancient and unusual breeds. Farway also features paddocks where native species of deer are reared, as does another privately developed park, at Broadway Tower in the Cotswolds, where it is hoped to breed representatives of many species of British wildlife. This last idea is the central feature of Palacerigg, near Cumbernauld in central Scotland.

Two of the privately developed parks, Robin Hill on the Isle of Wight and the Suffolk Wild Life Park, also have extensive collections of native British species and act as refuges for local wildlife in the same way. However they have, in addition, collections of exotic species (tropical birds, lions, reptiles and monkeys, for example). Both of these parks provide an opportunity to see animals at close quarters and in attractive countryside settings.

At this point we have moved some way from the enjoyment *of* the countryside towards entertainment *within* it, an equally important element in many country parks, and one more fully discussed in Chapter 6.

5

Links with the Past

Anyone interested in the development of building styles can find examples which date back over the last thousand years among structures associated with (though not necessarily a part of) our country parks. Beyond that, there are prehistoric sites stretching back into the New Stone Age. The first farmers of the Neolithic period lived on Crickley Hill, though the more obvious structures on this Cotswold summit belong to the Iron Age. Again, there is a display to help interpret what has come to light in excavations which take place here each summer. There are other important sites from a similar period on the summit ridges at Barbury Castle and Moel Famau, as well as the experimental Iron Age farm at Butser Hill in Queen Elizabeth Park. At Ham Hill in Somerset, a hill fort was reoccupied in the Roman period, and the foundations of a Roman villa are featured at Robin Hill, on the Isle of Wight. In Suffolk at West Stow there is evidence of settlement over a long period. Just to the west is the site of a Roman villa, and as the Roman legions withdrew, early Anglo-Saxon groups penetrated up the valleys of eastern England and established a settlement here which lasted approximately from AD 400 to AD 650, a period for which archaeological evidence is generally scanty. Some of the Anglo-Saxon buildings have been reconstructed, using evidence derived from excavations.

The earliest of the surviving buildings from the historic period is the celebrated Saxon church of St Lawrence at Bradford on Avon, a short walk from Barton Farm, a small country park surrounded by a fine collection of medieval and later buildings. The great fourteenth-century tithe barn, which belonged to Shaftesbury Abbey, is the most famous. The finest castle and abbey buildings of Britain passed into the care of the Office of Works (and now the Department of the Environment) many years ago, but there are some examples in country parks. The best castle ruins are at Caldicot in Gwent, Hadleigh in Essex and Dean, at Kilmarnock in Scotland. At Clare in Suffolk the Norman motte and bailey remain, but little else. Fragments remain from three of the great Cistercian abbeys, the most impressive being

The newly-restored orangery and gardens at Margam Park in South Wales. Ruined arches from the Chapter House of the Cistercian Abbey can also be seen; the orangery, with its citrus trees, stands on part of the former cloister. *Wales Tourist Board*

at Margam. At Coombe Abbey, in Warwickshire, part of the chapter house is incorporated in the later building, and at Rufford in Nottingham the monastic structure underlies parts of the later, and now ruinous, great house; it cannot at present be visited. The ruins of the little St Fittick's church at Loirston, near Aberdeen, are a link with the much older Celtic church.

From this point on the story is mainly taken up by the architectural history of the great houses, but three country parks give a clearer idea of how yeoman farmers and some of the poorer families lived during the last four centuries. At Mapledurham in Oxfordshire the Elizabethan great house, the church, the estate cottages and the watermill are grouped together beside the Thames, and provide an idealised and picturesque version of English village life. A more realistic view, both of the lack of comfort and of the consummate skill of the craftsmen responsible, comes from a visit to the Weald and Downland Open Air Museum near

Chichester. Here various houses and farm buildings, rescued from sites in south-east England, have been re-erected, but shorn of later additions and restored as nearly as possible to their original condition. In a harsher Pennine landscape stands the stone-built Lancashire hamlet of Wycoller. Here, on the site of a medieval cattle-rearing farm (a vaccary), a community developed during the eighteenth century which depended on the handloom-weaving of woollen cloth, and subsequently decayed. The ruined great hall, like its counterpart at Oakwell in West Yorkshire, is associated with Charlotte Brontë.

The Old Hall at Tatton is the finest representative building from the fifteenth century. The ruins of the great house in Bradgate Park, once the home of Lady Jane Grey, and the shell of the Tudor building at Mount Edgcumbe are also from this period. Of the three outstanding examples of Elizabethan great houses, Mapledurham, Burton Constable on Humberside and Hardwick Hall in Derbyshire, the last is the most famous. This magnificent building on its hilltop has remained almost unaltered since it was erected by Bess of Hardwick in the late sixteenth century. It contains an outstanding collection of contemporary embroidery, furniture and decorations. Much of Lyme Hall in Cheshire is also Elizabethan, although this has been masked by later extensions. In the same way the Georgian front at Dalemain in Cumbria masks an earlier Tudor hall and still older pele tower. There are signs of the older structure behind the Georgian front at Lydiard Tregoze (but the greater interest here lies in the astonishing collection of seventeenth-century memorials in the neighbouring church).

Tredegar House in Gwent, Erddig in Clwyd and the main front at Croxteth Hall in Liverpool are fine examples of Jacobean buildings, and in each case the story of the great house and its life above and below stairs is now displayed. The great houses at Knebworth near Stevenage and Goodwood in Sussex also date mainly from this period, but have later additions.

The finest buildings of all date from the eighteenth century. Haddo House in Grampian is a magnificent Palladian building from the 1730s (although the interior is largely Victorian) and Cusworth and Cannon Halls in Yorkshire are impressive lesser Georgian buildings. The orangery at Margam is recognised as one of the most beautiful buildings in the classical

---

(opposite page) The Old Hall at Tatton Park in Cheshire, which dates mainly from the fifteenth and sixteenth centuries. The oldest section of the building is now open to the public, and restoration of other parts continues, with the help of contemporary documents. Old Hall is the focus of the historical trail at Tatton Park. *Cheshire CC*

manner. Robert Adam's magnificent rebuilding of Culzean Castle, and the Home Farm there, are the supreme examples of later eighteenth-century architecture. Tatton Hall and Haigh Hall illustrate wealth and solidity around 1800. The more flamboyant neo-Gothic style of the early nineteenth century is illustrated by Elvaston Castle at Derby, and Balloch Castle in Strathclyde, and the dramatic ruins of Margam Castle date from the 1830s. Normanby Hall on Humberside is one of several houses from the Regency period. Finally there is Cragside, built by the Victorian architect Norman Shaw on a Northumbrian hillside, which still contains most of its original furnishings and some of the scientific inventions of its first owner, Lord Armstrong.

Industrial Archaeology Sites

About a dozen country parks provide anyone interested in industrial archaeology with relatively complete experience of a past activity, and there are a number of others where detective work will uncover intriguing clues. A working watermill is an object lesson in the skills of an earlier technology, and the best of these stands close to the M1 motorway. The watermill at Worsbrough near Barnsley was probably built about 1625, and stands on the site of one recorded in the Domesday Book. It remained at work into the 1960s, and has now been fully restored. Every process can be followed, and the mill can still turn out wholemeal flour. The only surviving watermill on the Thames has also been restored and may now be seen at work beside Mapledurham Country Park, and other working mills have been re-erected at the Weald and Downland Open Air Museum. At Rufford the mill machinery is missing, but the buildings, mill race and mill pond remain, while water power to work an early cotton mill is the main feature of an industrial site at Styal in Cheshire. The Apprentice House, school, chapel and other buildings of a complete eighteenth-century community associated with this mill can also be seen.

At Padarn on the lakeside below Snowdon, part of the largest slate-working complex in the world is now displayed. The buildings and machinery remain and now include a national museum collection. Two country parks taken together tell something of the story of coal-mining in South Wales. At Afan Argoed in West Glamorgan the signs of former mining activity have almost disappeared, as new forests mask old colliery sites. But at the park centre there is a miner's museum, set up by former miners, and incorporating a collection of mining equipment. Over the mountains at Dare Valley, above Aberdare, the legacy of coal-mining and iron-working is much more evident in the landscape, and an industrial trail traces the significant sites.

Several other country parks on reclaimed colliery sites betray something of this activity. For example at Plessey Woods in Northumberland there are bell pits from old iron workings, as well as signs of former coal-mining. A miners' museum is likely to be established at Lochore Meadows in Fife.

Another extremely interesting mining site associated with early industry lies hidden in woodland below Haigh Hall in Lancashire; it includes an astonishing feat of early engineering, an 1,100yd tunnel started in 1652 to drain the coal workings, the Haigh Sough. Here you need to work with the trail guide to gain an understanding of what has happened. No other country park can boast such a variety of evidence of former industry, though several in central Scotland (which are still incomplete) may prove to include interesting sites. At Muiravonside, near Falkirk, a deep valley is crossed by an aqueduct on the Union Canal, completed in 1822, and there are limekilns and other evidence of former industry. Almondell and Calderwood Country Park is also linked to the Union Canal by an aqueduct and feeder canal, and has an unusual series of bridges. The most interesting of these, built by Alexander Nasmyth about 1800, is unfortunately likely to be demolished. The proposed country park site at Roslin Glen includes the deeply cut valley of the North Esk, a river which has provided power for gunpowder mills and a succession of other early industrial sites. Finally, Durham County Council intend to create a country park beside Beamish Hall and the Beamish North of England Industrial Museum and this is likely to include the estate home farm.

Canals, Railways and Fortifications

Several country parks incorporating canals have already been mentioned. Devon's scheme at Tiverton (not so far recognised by the Countryside Commission) features the Grand Western Canal, which opened in 1814 and was intended as part of a system to link Exeter to the Bristol Channel, via Taunton and Bridgwater. The canal and towpath have been restored and horse-drawn barges operate from the Tiverton Basin during the summer. Restoration of a different kind has been employed at Daisy Nook, near

(overleaf) The Quarry Museum and part of the Dinorwic slate quarries at Padarn Country Park in North Wales. Slate working ended here in 1969, but the equipment and even the quarry hospital wards have been preserved. *Wales Tourist Board*

Oldham, where branches of the former Manchester and Ashton-under-Lyne Canal became derelict. Old lock sections have been converted into a cascade, but the reservoir at Crime Lake remains, and the aqueduct over the Medlock Valley is the central feature of the country park. Various other canals in the Greater Manchester area and in the Sankey Valley at St Helens have also been cleared and tidied up. Some provide routeways linked to country parks—for example parts of the Peak Forest system run close to Chadkirk and Lyme parks. Moreover several storage reservoirs intended to serve the former canal network are important features in country parks at Hollingworth Lake near Rochdale, Daventry in the Midlands, and Pen-y-Fan Pond in South Wales.

However the most interesting canal to explore is the section of the Kennet and Avon which runs along the edge of Barton Farm Country Park in Wiltshire. The building of this canal began in 1794, and John Rennie designed the aqueduct at Avoncliff, at the western end of the park. There are interesting mill buildings here also (but privately owned), and you can follow the towpath towards Bath, and the even finer Dundas aqueduct.

One of the very first country parks was created from a 12-mile stretch of disused single-track railway, on the western side of the Wirral peninsula. This has now been preserved and converted into riding and walking trails. From the point of view of the industrial archaeologist, the most interesting section is at the southern end, between Hooton and Neston. This is also the oldest part (it opened in 1865), and includes the deep cutting near Neston, and Hadlow Station, preserved virtually as it was about 1950, with displays which explain how country stations of this type were run.

Derwent Walk, on the line of the North Eastern Railway Company's single track from Swalwell beside the river Tyne to Consett in County Durham, is a more exciting route because of the depth of the river valleys. Much of the line was at a continuous gradient of 1 in 66 (1·5 per cent), and the most impressive engineering feats are the huge cutting north of Rowlands Gill, and four viaducts, of which the tallest is 120ft (37m) above the Pont Burn at Hamsterley Mill. The railway opened in 1867, and ran for almost a century. The steel industry at Consett is the direct descendant of earlier steel-making sites. Sword-makers from Solingen in Germany fled from religious persecution to settle at Shotley Bridge in 1687. A very early form of steel-making furnace survives in the Derwent Valley at Derwentcote, east of Hamsterley, where wrought iron was converted into steel in a small stone building. Derwent Walk also provides views across the Gibside Estate, a park landscaped to eighteenth-century designs, and containing the beautiful Gibside Chapel.

Berry Head in South Devon, a magnificent limestone headland and local nature reserve. Once crowned by a prehistoric hill fort, it was fortified in Napoleonic times (the old magazine building stands beside the flagstaff). Brixham harbour is visible in the distance. *Herald Express, Torquay*

The two other country parks on sections of former railway are pleasant, but less impressive for the industrial archaeologist. At Clare, in Suffolk, the park centre is in the station buildings, and there is a walk along part of the old line. Forest Way in Sussex runs for almost 10 miles and passes several former station buildings (now converted to private houses). This was a branch line built by the London, Brighton and South Coast Co in 1866. For much of the way the line ran on level ground in the Medway Valley, and the most interesting section is where it climbed up from Forest Row towards East Grinstead.

For those who enjoy old steam locomotives, there are three country parks where these may be seen (although it is important to check when these privately run railways operate): Ferry Meadows on the Nene Valley Steam Railway, Llyn Padarn on the Llanberis Lake Railway and Knebworth Park, where the narrow-gauge line is just part of the entertainment complex.

A totally different subject for investigation is provided by two early nineteenth-century fortifications. Berry Head forms a magnificent defensive site at the southern end of Torbay in Devon, and was formerly crowned by fortifications dating back to the Iron Age. In 1794, when invasion from France was expected, the government bought part of the headland (the broad arrow symbol of the Board of Ordnance still marks the boundary), and two forts were built a few years later. A lot of the stonework survives; there are ramparts and gun emplacements, a sentry box, artillery store and magazine. The fortifications on the Isle of Wight at Fort Victoria are later structures, but the strategic importance of the site is even greater. Fort Victoria was built in 1853 on the site of an earlier gun battery, established in Napoleonic times. The ruined gun emplacements are worth exploring, and the view of shipping from the ramparts is excellent.

6

From Gravel Pits to Watersports

Country parks on reclaimed sites are in some ways the most interesting of all, because they offer new scope to develop sports facilities and nature reserves. Large areas can be provided for the sports which need space, at the same time as dereliction and eyesores are banished, though this can be an expensive undertaking. The very best watersports facilities are nearly always either on reclaimed gravel pits or on reservoirs. Of the sixteen country parks developed on reclaimed sites, half are on gravel-working sites, and the remainder on former mining and quarrying sites. Some of these schemes are on a very large scale. In the Upper Thames Valley between Cirencester and Swindon, a new English Lake District has come into existence, now called the Cotswold Water Park. The total area involved is about 14,000 acres (or 5,666 hectares), a quarter of which will soon be open water. Keynes Country Park is one small section of this complex, and all is now under the joint control of the Gloucester and Wiltshire County Councils. The gravels, so vital to the construction industry, lie on top of clay, and the high water-table means that all excavations fill with water as soon as working ceases. The new lakes are quite shallow and readily colonised by marsh plants, fish and birds, and parts of the Cotswold Water Park are protected as nature reserves. There is space to accommodate a variety of watersports.

Ferry Meadows, outside Peterborough, is another country park on a gravel-extraction site, and the centrepiece of a planned regional development known as Nene Park, which is designed to serve the expanded city of Greater Peterborough.

There are major watersports facilities on former gravel workings on both sides of the river Trent at Nottingham. South of the river the county, with the Sports Council, have developed Holme Pierrepont, the National Watersports Centre, with a 2,000m rowing course, and a smaller water-ski training area. The country park, which surrounds the rowing course, includes a nature reserve and is popular for fishing. Across the river at

Colwick, Nottingham City Council are developing a marina with moorings for 200 boats, and there is already provision for sailing, boating, fishing and riding. The other major centre on a similar site in the West Midlands is at Kingsbury Water Park.

At Emberton, near Olney, gravel-working ceased in 1962, and it is interesting to see the effects both of natural regeneration of the vegetation and of careful landscaping. The much smaller site at Barnwell near Oundle provides fishing, and has made special stands for disabled fishermen, while Dinton Pastures, near Reading, is newest of all and still incomplete.

The biggest reclamation schemes of all are aimed at attracting new employment through providing a massive clean-up and face-lift operation. A country park is a part of this, and again it can be planned to provide for a variety of sports. Schemes of this type cost large sums, but most of the reclamation costs (normally 85 per cent) can be covered by grants under either the Local Employment or Industrial Development Acts. The largest schemes in the country have been undertaken in Fife. The county council began with a relatively modest scheme in 1963, and turned 23 acres (9 hectares) of disused colliery land, marsh and bings (tip heaps) into agricultural land grazed by sheep, within six months. There have since been five individual schemes, and the six phases of the Lochore Meadows scheme, centring on what is now a country park. It is an impressive story. Almost two-thirds of what is now parkland round a loch was totally derelict; burning material at temperatures up to over 1000°C had to be cleared, and a mere 3 inches (75mm) of topsoil was available to spread over the reshaped landscape.

The reclaimed site of Strathclyde Country Park is even larger (1,600 acres or 650 hectares), and the problems here included frequent flooding of the Clyde Valley on the edge of Hamilton, accentuated by subsidence following the closure of the last colliery in 1958. In reviving Patrick Abercrombie's original ideas, the Scottish Development Department had three aims: to control flooding, to provide recreation facilities and to improve the region's image. Putting a weir across the Clyde proved impracticable. Instead the artificial loch with its 2,000m rowing and canoeing course is fed from a tributary, while the silt-laden river Clyde is diverted round it. Except during special events the general public can use the watersports centre and sail on the loch. A large number of sports pitches, tennis courts and a golf course are available. There is also a camping site and an extensive area of nature reserve. The total cost of the scheme was £11,000,000, which must be set against the needs for flood control and major regional improvement. The only comparable scheme in England is still at an early stage in the

Rother Valley, on the borders of South Yorkshire and Derbyshire.

Reclamation schemes are not all on a very large scale or backed by a regional authority. Dare Valley in South Wales is an early instance of the successful reclamation of a coal-mining site initiated by a rural district council with help from several sources and the involvement of the local community. (The details are given in the gazetteer section.) Wansbeck Riverside Park in Northumberland is a more recent instance and, like Dare Valley, an award-winning scheme. Here an unsightly tidal estuary has been converted into an attractive watersports and camping complex.

Of the other country parks on reclaimed sites, those at Parkhall in Staffordshire and Cosmeston in South Glamorgan are still incomplete, but Irchester, an old Northamptonshire ironstone quarry, is now well clothed by grass and trees. At Shipley the National Coal Board cooperated with Derbyshire County Council to clear and reshape the land, after winning 1,500,000 tons of opencast coal between 1970 and 1973. The country park provides fishing and sailing on the newly contoured lake.

It is not only the newly created country parks that offer sports facilities, though sailing and fishing, the most rapidly growing outdoor activities in recent years, are the ones most widely available. Nearly sixty country parks in fact provide facilities for fishing—indeed it has been developed at almost all waterside sites. In a few cases it is restricted to club members, but generally day tickets are available, and sometimes the fishing is free. Thirty-five country parks cater for sailing, canoeing or boating (and several are used by sub-aqua clubs).

Many country parks provide separate riding trails, and pony trekking is a feature of several in the Midlands and southern England (Clent Hills, Ferry Meadows and Queen Elizabeth in particular). There are riding schools attached to the country parks at Elvaston Castle, Trent Park and Wellington. Golf enthusiasts are catered for at Lochore, Strathclyde and John Muir in Scotland and in or beside the parks at Pennington Flash, Haigh, Lickey Hills, Ferry Meadows, Cefn Onn and Dinton Pastures in England and Wales. Putting courses are found in a dozen parks, particularly those which have been privately developed. Swimming is recommended at a small proportion of waterside sites: there is a pool at Normanby Hall, lake swimming at Fell Foot, Burton Constable, Tatton Mere and Black Park, and sea bathing at Pembrey, Porthkerry, Northam, Lepe and Calshot and Hastings. The growing sport of orienteering is featured at several parks, from the small one at Tandle Hill to the large Lyme Park, and a few cater for less usual sports, such as sand-yachting at John Muir, or hang-gliding and grass-skiing at Queen Elizabeth. Country parks in Scotland and northern England become impromptu wintersports centres whenever conditions allow.

Nineteen country parks provide facilities for touring campers and caravanners, and the number will grow as sites like that at Pembrey are developed. At present there are camp sites at Aden House, Haughton House, Palacerigg, Strathclyde, Culzean and John Muir in Scotland, and at Fell Foot, Wansbeck, Burton Constable, Hartsholme, Ferry Meadows, Lonely Farm Leisure Park, Elvaston Castle, Wirral, Emberton, Wellington, Goodwood, Tredegar House and River Dart in England and Wales. Most country parks provide at least some facilities for family entertainment; at its simplest this means an adventure playground for children and open grass for impromptu ball games. It may also include an obstacle course or trim trail, where adults can try out their agility. The privately developed country parks generally put more emphasis on entertainments, which range from donkey rides to gift shops and restaurants.

7

The Planning Behind the Parks

Country parks were conceived as part of a strategy to help reconcile the conservation of natural beauty in the countryside with the need to secure public access for recreation. The National Parks Commission was established in 1949, with overall responsibility for defining and establishing the National Parks and Areas of Outstanding Natural Beauty in England and Wales, and had the task of striking this difficult balance. Recreation in the countryside was then largely confined to a privileged minority and the implicit difficulties were not fully appreciated. Both the commission and the planning authorities directly responsible for the National Parks remained starved of funds, and without many of the powers needed to meet the rapidly growing number of visitors, at least until 1974; so conflicts arose between local residents, especially local farmers, and the rising tide of visitors. These were also the years when ideas of conservation gained popular support. One example is enough to show the nature of the problem. The summit of Snowdon attracts so many visitors that the tracks and summit area are literally worn away. Experts called to report on this in 1973 estimated that over 200,000 reached the summit each year, and that the maximum number possible might be some 15 per cent more than this. More recent estimates put the number of visitors to the summit at over 400,000, of whom over three-quarters walk up.

In varying degree this type of pressure applied to other stretches of coast and countryside in England and Wales, though less marked in Scotland. The reasons are well known; the most important single factor was the growth of private-car ownership, a reflection of the general rise in living standards and the effects of motorway construction. The reduction in hours of work and an increase in the total population have been contributory factors. During the 1960s the number of visitors to the countryside was believed to be rising at a rate of 15 per cent a year. It is not surprising that this was seen as an apparently inexorable threat to the survival of our heritage of natural beauty, and indeed to the viability of agriculture in the most vulnerable areas.

It was against this background that a White Paper on 'Leisure in the Countryside' in 1966 put forward the idea of country parks, places largely in public ownership where visitors should have the space and facilities to enjoy themselves, and where informal countryside recreation would be the main activity. The two Countryside Acts which followed (for Scotland in 1967, and for England and Wales in 1968) defined a country park as 'a park or pleasure ground in the countryside which by reason of its position in relation to major concentrations of population affords convenient opportunities to the public for enjoyment of the countryside or open-air recreation.'

In England and Wales the Countryside Commission was established, taking over the responsibilities of the former National Parks Commission, and a parallel body was created for Scotland. Each commission had responsibility for the conservation of natural beauty and the need to secure public access to the countryside for recreation, and had powers to carry out research and provide information services. Local authorities were given the power to acquire land (by compulsory purchase if necessary), to carry out the necessary development, to make byelaws and to appoint park wardens. The two commissions could make grants from national funds to cover up to three-quarters of the costs of acquiring land, and constructing roads, car parks or necessary buildings, on all approved schemes. In England and Wales (not in Scotland) the National Trust and some private bodies were also encouraged to develop country parks.

Essentially, therefore, the task of proposing and developing country parks fell to the local authorities, while the two Countryside Commissions could give advice, carry out related research and channel grants to approved schemes. In Chapter 1 we saw how Hampshire CC responded to this opportunity. Other councils, and especially those with experience of the problems in the National Parks, had already surveyed likely sites for country parks. The new county (or in Scotland regional) structure plans incorporated these ideas, the main objectives differing according to where the country parks were situated. Thus East Sussex saw the Hastings Country Park as being essentially for public enjoyment and recreation, whereas at Ditchling Common (which includes an SSSI) the first aim was to protect it from unsuitable development, and to repair damage done by unrestricted parking. At Seven Sisters, on what is now defined as a Heritage Coast and one of the most precious stretches of cliff and shore, the needs of conservation were to predominate. In South Wales the first real attempt to coordinate country parks into a regional plan for recreation took place at a conference in 1973. As a direct result, South Wales has probably the most varied and interesting collection of country parks in the kingdom, and all have been developed with an eye on the projected line of the M4 motorway.

The Changes since 1974

For various reasons, circumstances altered around 1974. The major reorganisation of local government caused some interruption to planning, and led to the abandonment of a few country park schemes. To the newly created Greater Manchester Council, however, it gave an opportunity to tackle the cleaning-up and reclamation of former industrial sites in the valleys which radiate from Manchester itself, and at the same time to provide a series of linked facilities for outdoor recreation. Existing country parks were integrated into this overall pattern, and new ones were added.

A typical event at the National Watersports Centre, Holme Pierrepont near Nottingham. *By kind permission of G. S. Dibley, Centre Director*

Greater Manchester Council did not attempt this single-handed; all the bodies concerned participated on joint committees, and this meant cooperation across county boundaries, and the participation of the water and canal authorities, the National Trust and the Civic Trust.

The joint management of country parks has now become a normal feature. Since the Forestry Commission, water authorities, sports councils and tourist boards were all directly involved in providing for outdoor recreation, there was a need to ensure effective coordination of plans. The two Countryside Commissions were well placed to do this, and research is coordinated through CRRAG, the Countryside Recreation Research Advisory Group. New regional councils for sport and recreation are now producing strategies for each region in England and Wales. In Scotland STARPS, the Scottish Tourism and Recreation Planning Studies, are carrying out a similar review of needs and existing resources. (Anyone who finds initials exasperating is offered the thought that a STARPS committee sat down and played a recreation and tourist game called RATPAK!) The Scottish commission has proposed a park system for Scotland, ranging from urban and country parks up to what would in effect be National Parks, though without that title for fear of arousing too many expectations. While there is no immediate prospect of National Parks for Scotland, there is a move to create regional parks, broad areas in which country parks, picnic sites and similar facilities can be linked together. The Clyde Muirshiel Regional Park already exists, and the Pentland Hills should be the next example. The idea of regional parks is not new; the Lee Valley Regional Park has been developed as a result of legislation in 1966, and a similar idea is behind the more loosely linked country parks and other recreational sites in the Colne Valley, west of London.

Country parks developed in England and Wales since 1974 have tended to be larger, more often on reclaimed sites, and particularly at points on the edges of cities accessible by public transport. Grants for approved country-park schemes are now on a sliding scale, based on a system of priorities. A scheme is eligible for a grant up to half its cost in one of the high-priority areas, that is, in a Tourist Growth-Point Area, a Green Belt or in a buffer zone between a city and a National Park or Heritage Coast. A lower rate of grant is available elsewhere. Since tourism now employs three times as

---

(opposite page) Creating a country park at Stover near Newton Abbot in Devon. Men recruited under STEP, the Special Temporary Employment Programme, building a bridge across the stream which flows into Stover Lake. *By courtesy of Mid Devon Newspapers*

many people and earns three times as much foreign exchange as the car industry, fostering it is seen as one way of combating unemployment. The three Tourist Growth Points so far defined by the English Tourist Board are the North Pennines, Scarborough, and part of north Cornwall. In Scotland the grant system has remained unaltered, and the commission has given further encouragement to local authorities to embark on country-park schemes. In the present economic climate, however, less can be spent on recreation schemes of all kinds, and we need to look for cheaper and more cost-effective ways of protecting the countryside.

We know from surveys that visiting the countryside is our most popular year-round outdoor activity, and that a typical trip is a drive of 15 to 20 miles which centres round a family picnic on a summer Sunday afternoon. Numbers visiting the countryside are still increasing, but not at the rate anticipated in the 1960s. Catering for this demand means taking account of different preferences; while the majority of visitors do not move far from their cars, a minority follow special interests or seek relative solitude whenever possible. Country-park plans are devised to meet this variety of preferences, as the recently published plan for Cannock Chase Country Park makes clear.

Among the achievements of country-park policies during the 1970s is the creation of more than 70 new sites not previously accessible to the public, and the reclamation of some 8,650 acres (3,300 hectares) of derelict and damaged land. Another undoubted achievement has been the expertise developed. Both Countryside Commissions have sponsored a variety of essentially practical research projects leading to better land management for recreation, and our visits to the countryside can be enriched by the new interpretative service. The various job-creation schemes involve teams of young people on reclamation and conservation work in parks all over Britain, with benefit both to the countryside and to those involved.

Another achievement is the links developed between the country parks and the wider community, a two-way process, with volunteers working in the parks and park staff giving lectures, taking guided walks or otherwise becoming involved beyond the park boundaries. The British Trust for Conservation Volunteers have contributed to projects throughout Britain, and in 1976 alone worked in eight country parks. Many other groups and private individuals have contributed in unskilled tasks such as litter collection or footpath maintenance, or more demanding jobs like rebuilding stone walls, planting trees or acting as part-time rangers.

The Conservation Issue

The essential idea behind the creation of the country parks was to give us all areas of pleasant country where we can enjoy ourselves without worrying that we may be trespassing. The two Countryside Commissions have overall responsibility for conservation of the countryside, that is for protecting its wildlife and natural beauty and at the same time providing us with better chances to explore and enjoy our rural heritage. It was because these twin aims came into conflict within the National Parks that the idea of creating alternative properly managed sites for recreation in the countryside was first proposed some fifteen years ago. It has since been decided that, at least in the National Parks and on Heritage Coasts, when all other ways of resolving this conflict have proved unsuccessful, the needs of conservation must prevail. Future generations would otherwise have little countryside or wildlife to enjoy. The same problem of course arises in a number of our most beautiful and interesting country parks; indeed, some lie within National Park and Heritage Coast areas.

Box Hill on the South Downs has given pleasure to millions over the years, as well as providing object lessons in field study for generations of students and school parties. We owe this opportunity to the generosity of philanthropists who gave the land to the National Trust. When Box Hill was recognised as a country park, government grants became available to tackle the problems of erosion caused by the constant wear and tear of innumerable feet across steep slopes, on top of thin downland turf. Various experiments have been carried out to repair the gulleys washed out of the chalk and to allow grass and other plants to recover and reclothe the damaged areas.

On another National Trust site in Surrey, the very popular Frensham Ponds, a similar problem arose. In this case the underlying rock was not hard chalk, but a soft and unconsolidated sandstone. The result of driving cars or riding horses across this rolling heathland can be loose sand, devoid of vegetation. Even greater damage has been done here by forest fires. The only answer is to stop the rapid downwash on steep slopes by using local timber to build steps, to fence and reseed some areas, and to control car-parking and horse-riding on others.

Too many people on a thin topsoil not only damage existing vegetation, but prevent natural regeneration. Sherwood Forest Country Park inherited a legacy from generations of former visitors; the legend of Robin Hood had become centred on one tree, the magnificent Major Oak. By the time the country park was established, it was estimated that 1,000 pairs of feet an hour trailed from car park to tree and back, on summer Sundays, and that as many as 500 people might be queuing to stand inside the hollow tree. Such intense use destroyed the surrounding vegetation and compacted the soil, causing damage to the rooting system of the Major Oak, and of course Sherwood Forest is a Site of Special Scientific Interest. In an attempt to tackle the problem, a new car park and new paths to the tree were developed. A new visitor centre was opened so that visitors might have a better understanding of the importance of Sherwood Forest, and the steps being taken to protect it.

The answer to the conservation problem in most country parks is careful management of the site, so that the load of eager visitors is spread and the most sensitive areas can be adequately protected. Just how this is tackled can be seen by looking at the country park on a beautiful and scientifically important stretch of coast just west of Dunbar in East Lothian. The park is named after John Muir, who grew up in Dunbar and later became a pioneer of conservation ideas, and played a major role in the creation of Yosemite National Park in America.

The most important natural features on this 8-mile stretch of coast are concentrated towards the two ends. The ruins of Dunbar Castle, twice visited by Mary Queen of Scots, stand at the eastern limit of the park. Here the sea is actively eroding cliffs in which sandstone rocks alternate with those of volcanic origin. Beyond the sands and seabird communities in Belhaven Bay is another site particularly interesting to the specialist. Whitberry Hill is formed of a very unusual volcanic rock and rises above a rocky platform cut by the sea. An inlet here, known as St Baldred's Cradle, is associated with an early Celtic saint who died on Bass Rock in AD 607. Beyond lie Ravensheugh Sands, where the coast is backed by dunes under attack by wind, and therefore in particular need of conservation.

Parts of this coast have been popular for some time and there is a clifftop path, camp sites, and various tourist facilities on the outskirts of Dunbar, but of course most people are particularly attracted by the beautiful sands of Belhaven Bay. Accordingly, the local council has centred the development of the country park at a point where these sands can be reached with minimum disturbance to local residents or bird communities. Efforts are being made to control the wind erosion on the dunes. Road signs and good publicity attract everyone towards fields where the grass is managed so that it will stand up to intensive use. There is no visitor centre, but the picnic, barbecue and toilet facilities are all grouped here, and local traders have concessions to provide refreshments. So far as the cliffs at Dunbar are concerned, a very good booklet has been produced which helps all who are interested to get the most out of walking along the clifftop trail. The western end of the park is left as far as possible undisturbed. No reference to this area is made in publicity material and there are no road signs. There is a very small car park, set back from the coast, and anyone who penetrates as far as this can follow the webbed-feet signs—surely the most attractive form of waymarking. (I can vouch for the undeveloped character of this part of the coast: it was here that I was temporarily lost *inside* a country park!)

Gazetteer

Arrangement

The country parks have been grouped into the regional divisions adopted by the Countryside Commission, each regional section having a map. Where schemes are incomplete or not yet officially recognised as country parks, they have been added to the end of the regional list.

Finding the Parks

With the directions in this gazetteer and a road atlas, there should be no difficulty in reaching each park. A larger-scale map is of course useful and for those who have one, six-figure grid references are given, pinpointing the park entrance or another important feature. Where a reasonably frequent bus service passes near a park, accessibility by bus is noted; in other cases an infrequent or local bus service may serve the park, and it is essential to check this locally.

Opening Hours

Details of opening hours given here are as up-to-date as possible, but inevitably they may change. At privately developed country parks in particular the dates and hours of opening vary seasonally, and here telephone numbers are given so that these may be checked.

Facilities

All country parks provide car-parking space. It may be free and any charge is usually small, but may be by meter. Refreshments are not necessarily available in, or even near, a country park; where they are provided this is indicated. At other parks it is of course possible that a local trader may have a concession to sell light refreshments from a van at busy times. All fully completed country parks have toilet facilities and most have toilets for the disabled; small and remote country parks often have Portaloos.

Guidebooks

In the larger parks, informative, well-produced leaflets on the park or its nature trail, etc, are usually available on site for a small charge. Otherwise it is best to contact the park's managing authority, often the local council.

Abbreviations in the Gazetteer

Two abbreviations used here require explanation. Additional protection against development is given when an area is designated an Area of Outstanding Natural Beauty, or AONB. And the Nature Conservancy list a Site of Special Scientific Interest, or SSSI.

Northern England

1 CRAGSIDE
National Trust 692 acres (280 hectares)
At Rothbury 12 miles (19km) SW of Alnwick. The entrance (well signed) is from B6344 Rothbury to Morpeth road at NU 072015. Country park open daily 1 April to 30 September 10.30–18.00 and October weekends 14.00–17.00. Admission charge. Hall open 1 April to 30 September daily except Mondays (but open Bank Holiday Mondays and closed the following Tuesdays) 13.00–18.00. Also open Wednesdays and weekends in October 14.00–17.00. Admission charge.

The hall and country park at Cragside were fully opened for the first time in 1979. Both house and estate are the creation of the first Lord Armstrong, begun in 1864. William Armstrong was the epitome of the successful Victorian industrialist, an inventor, engineer and armaments king who achieved enormous wealth and power. Cragside was both his country retreat and a suitable place to entertain clients; in its creation he could indulge the romantic side of his character, and the hall is a unique example of the Victorian romantic country house.

The visitor enters at Dunkirk Lodge and must then decide whether to drive some 4 miles through the country park on a single-way road, or to take the shorter route up to the hall. In either case he will leave by an exit on B6341 (the Rothbury to Alnwick road) and can then return to Dunkirk Lodge to try the other option.

At present the great attractions of the country park are the landscaped grounds and views across the Coquet Valley to the Simonside Hills. It is intended later to provide a visitor centre with interpretative displays, a nature trail, restaurant and shop. Lord Armstrong planted millions of trees to convert rough moorland into the richly wooded pleasure grounds we now enjoy. The magnificent rhododendrons and azaleas are at their best in early summer; another particularly colourful season is September when the heather blazes on the surrounding moorland. An exciting, well-surfaced road takes visitors up to car parks near the lakes. There are paths round the lakes or to the hall and viewpoints, and the park has long been a sanctuary for wildlife.

2 WANSBECK
Wansbeck DC 143 acres (58 hectares)
The Wansbeck valley S of Ashington. Main approach from A1068 1 mile (1½km) SW of Ashington centre, along Wellhead Dene Road to entrance at NZ 257866. Also accessible from A196 at Stakeford Bridge. Freely open at all times. Accessible by bus.

The tidal section of the Wansbeck Valley has now been converted into a fine stretch of water available for boating and sailing. Boats may be hired, or visitors may launch their

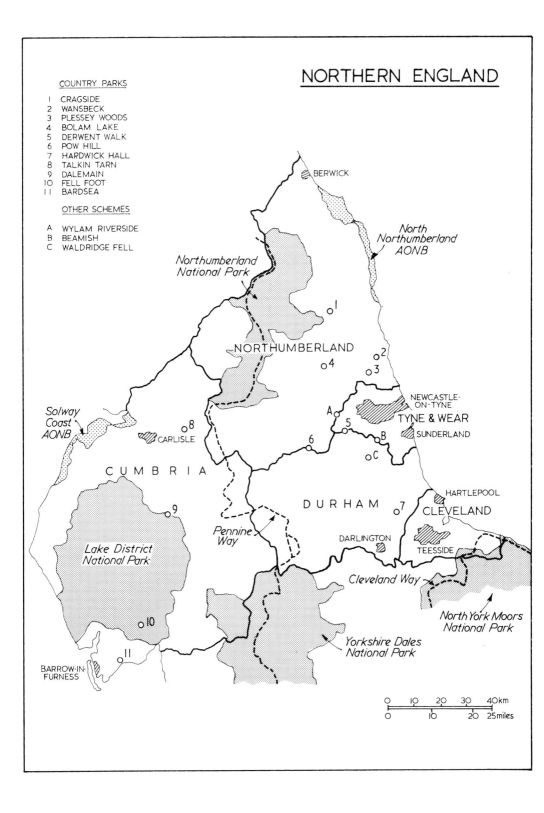

NORTHERN ENGLAND

COUNTRY PARKS

1 CRAGSIDE
2 WANSBECK
3 PLESSEY WOODS
4 BOLAM LAKE
5 DERWENT WALK
6 POW HILL
7 HARDWICK HALL
8 TALKIN TARN
9 DALEMAIN
10 FELL FOOT
11 BARDSEA

OTHER SCHEMES

A WYLAM RIVERSIDE
B BEAMISH
C WALDRIDGE FELL

BERWICK

North
Northumberland
AONB

Northumberland
National Park

NORTHUMBERLAND

NEWCASTLE-
ON-TYNE
TYNE & WEAR
SUNDERLAND

Solway
Coast
AONB

CARLISLE

C U M B R I A

HARTLEPOOL

CLEVELAND

D U R H A M

Lake District
National Park

Pennine
Way

DARLINGTON

TEESSIDE

Cleveland Way

North York Moors
National Park

Yorkshire Dales
National Park

BARROW-IN-
FURNESS

0   10   20   30   40km
0   10   20   25miles

own from a slipway near the main riverside picnic area. A weir at the river mouth maintains the water level and there is a lock large enough to allow boats up to 30ft (9m) long to reach the sea. An attractive and sheltered caravan and camping site has been developed above the river, with its own facilities and a shop. The site is open from 1 April to 30 September (tel Ashington 812323 for bookings). There is also a large and well-equipped children's playground.

The riverside walk runs along the north bank from Sheepwash Bridge to the sea. (It is intended to provide additional facilities on the S side, in conjunction with a licensed restaurant to be developed beside Sheepwash Bridge.) A nature trail has been laid out, featuring birds and woodland plants. The sheltered and partially tidal water attracts a variety of birds. The valley sides are steep and attractively wooded at the western end. Nearer the sea the banks have been raised (to avoid flooding) and planted with shrubs and young trees, and the county council have carried out extensive reclamation on a former colliery waste tip. Two impressive viaducts cross the valley, one carrying a mineral railway and the other the new Northumberland Spine Road. Purists may argue that since the walk is asphalted and lit at night it is not a true countryside amenity. However it represents a striking example of local initiative, which has improved the quality of life for local residents and is increasingly popular with tourists.

3 PLESSEY WOODS
Northumberland CC 101 acres
(41 hectares)

1½ miles (2½km) SW of Bedlington. On A1068 N of Hartford Bridge at NZ 238805. Freely open at all times. Accessible by bus.

Like the river Wansbeck further N, the Blyth has cut a deep winding valley into the low plateau of this part of Northumberland. The surrounding countryside is open farmland, interspersed with mining settlements, and the car park is on land reclaimed from former colliery workings. The sheltered valley woodlands are totally different, a natural wildlife refuge where more than 200 species of plants flourish. The winding river, brown from its moorland origins, flows over rocks and through inviting pools. Fishing is managed by the local angling club, and day permits are restricted to those coming from a distance (tel Bedlington 822011 for details). There is a small display and information centre, attractive sites for picnics and a riding trail through woods. Facilities are available for transit campers (not caravans). A nature trail is being laid out which will feature, in addition to the variety of plants and wildlife, some of the evidence of former mining activities. Rocks of the Middle Coal Measures underlie Plessey Woods, and there is evidence of old bell pits and former quarry workings.

4 BOLAM LAKE
Northumberland CC 91 acres
(37 hectares)

3 miles (5km) NW of Belsay. Approach along A696 to Belsay, and then by signed minor roads. There are three car parks. The main entrance is at NZ 084820. Freely open at all times.

This small lake, surrounded by mature woodland, lies between the open upper valleys of the Wansbeck and Blyth rivers, in a landscape of scattered farms. The lake itself is man-made (by John Dobson in 1817) and very shallow. It is unsuitable for swimming but a popular and attractive setting for picnics, boating and canoeing. Permits are available for coarse fishing. There is a small visitor centre, with display space, and a nature trail has been laid out. The embankments of a hill fort lie partly within the NW corner of the park (the line of the Devil's Causeway, a Roman road, runs a short distance further W). A wildlife sanctuary has been established in mixed woodland, reed beds and shallows at the remotest end of the lake.

5 DERWENT WALK
Durham CC and Tyne and Wear Met CC 287 acres (116 hectares)

The old railway line from Consett to Swalwell (E of Blaydon). Accessible wherever paths, roads and bus routes cross the former railway. Best initial approach is from A694 in Rowlands Gill, by signed minor road down to Derwent Park on the riverside. Freely open at all times.

Derwent Park at Rowlands Gill is the best starting point for new visitors. It is managed by Gateshead Met BC, and most attractively set out with flowers and shrubs. In addition to a riverside picnic site and children's play area, there is a site for touring campers and caravanners, a bowling green and tennis courts. More important, however, is the information centre where new visitors should pick up the excellent Derwent Walk Country Park guide. This combines a large-scale map of the walk and its surroundings, with invaluable information on bus routes and places of interest on or near the walk. (There are other guides on farming and trees seen from the walk.) The Swalwell station site is not yet complete, but two obvious

access points at the W end are at the former Shotley Bridge and Ebchester stations. (Both are on steep hills, and it is useful to know that the car park entrance is in each case on the lower side of the old railway bridge.)

The railway itself was opened by the North Eastern Railway in 1867 and finally closed to all traffic in 1962. Its route lies for the most part high above the river Derwent on the S valley side. There are impressive viaducts and deep cuttings, but the track is grass-covered, well graded and suitable for walking, cycling or riding. The Derwent Valley is attractive and wooded, despite the proximity of heavy industry on the Tyne and at Consett. Extensive areas, both within the country park and outside it N of the river, are now open to visitors and provided with car parks, picnic sites and walks. Moreover there are a number of historic buildings and surviving portions of the landscaped Gibside estate. The most interesting range from the remains of the Roman fort at Ebchester and the ruins of the thirteenth-century Old Hollinside Manor, to the eighteenth-century Gibside Chapel (now maintained by the National Trust) and Derwentcote, a furnace building used in an early form of steel-making.

6 POW HILL
Durham CC 44 acres (18 hectares)

Adjoining B6306 on S side of Derwent Reservoir. 1 mile (1½km) W of Edmundbyers at NZ 010513. It is suggested that visitors join the Derwent Reservoir Country Trail via Carterwayheads (on A68) to the N end of the dam. Freely open at all times.

Pow Hill is a small area of moorland at around 800ft (244m) by the shores of Derwent Reservoir. Worth visiting in itself,

Hamsterley Mill Viaduct on the former North Eastern Railway Company's line, which opened in 1867 and climbs up from the Tyne valley to Consett in County Durham. The viaduct is near the centre point of Derwent Walk Country Park. *Durham CC*

it is better viewed as one of a series of attractions round the reservoir. Here, as at Derwent Walk, it is most helpful to collect the relevant leaflets, published by the Derwent Valley Advisory Committee (available locally or from Durham CC Planning Department, County Hall, Durham). What is suggested is a drive round the reservoir, with stops for short walks or to picnic and admire the view. In addition to Pow Hill, there are two picnic sites with toilets and six scenic parking places beside the road. The drive starts at the dam (which must be approached at the N end) and continues round the N and W of the reservoir, finishing at Pow Hill. Visitors will enjoy a short diversion at the W end to see the beautiful village of Blanchland.

Construction of the reservoir began in 1960, and since 1966 the water has gone to industrial users and a million residents in areas between the Tyne and Tees. Because this is drinking water, swimming and paddling are not allowed, nor are dogs permitted at the Carricks and Millshield picnic areas. Dogs are allowed at Pow Hill if kept under control. Sailing is popular and is controlled by Derwent Reservoir Sailing Club (inquiries to the club, c/o Hadaway & Hadaway, Alliance House, Hood Street, Newcastle). Day permits are available for trout fishing from the water authority building at the dam, and boats can also be hired here. The W end of the reservoir is a nature reserve and not open to the public. One of the attractions is the number of waterbirds which now frequent the area, and there is a bird hide at Pow Hill. Other features of the country park are a sheltered picnic site by a stream and newly planted trees (important at this height), as well as more exposed viewpoints for watching birds and sailing on the reservoir.

7 HARDWICK HALL
Durham CC 40 acres (16 hectares)
On the W edge of Sedgefield. Entrance at NZ 347292 (also a hotel entrance) from A177 just N of the roundabout at its junction with A689. Freely open at all times. Accessible by bus.

Not to be confused with Hardwick Hall, Derbyshire! Hardwick Hall at Sedgefield is a relatively modest eighteenth-century mansion, incorporating parts of an earlier manor house. It remained a private house until 1923 but is now a hotel. The country park is the greater part of what were once magnificent pleasure gardens, created to the design of the architect James Paine in the 1750s. In its heyday this landscaped garden was regarded as in exquisite taste. All the characteristic features of the period were present: a lake, a cascade, a grotto, a gothic bridge, a temple and even a specially built ruin. But whereas in larger and more fortunate gardens (such as Stourhead, Wiltshire) these conceits have survived, at Hardwick Hall everything is changed. Some of the buildings, however, can still be found, and fine trees from the original scheme make this a secret woodland world. A nature trail, raised on a wooden walkway, winds through the interesting fencarr vegetation, rich in wildlife, which was originally the main lake. The smaller serpentine lake still survives and is the focus of attention where children try to catch minnows. Serious angling, however, is left to the herons. The park has a small information centre and there are picnic sites situated at the waterside. Many new specimen trees have been planted. Hardwick is one of a number of centres from which guided walks have been organised (and there is also a guided push for disabled people in wheelchairs).

Talkin Tarn in Cumbria, a small lake below the North Pennines which is popular for sailing and canoeing.

8 TALKIN TARN
Cumbria CC 166 acres (67 hectares)

2 miles (3km) SE of Brampton. Approach along B6413, following signs from Brampton. Entrance at NY 540590. Freely open at all times.

This is a popular and attractive small lake, fringed by woods and lying immediately below the North Pennine fells. The tarn is natural and the result of glacial action. It nestles among spreads of glacial gravels, and is on top of a major geological boundary between the Carboniferous rocks of the Pennine moorlands and the softer, younger rocks of the Vale of Eden. Water is the great attraction, whether for swimming, sailing or fishing. Visitors may launch their own boats (power boats are not allowed), and rowing boats may be hired. Two sailing clubs and a rowing club use the tarn, and their activities provide added interest for those who picnic on the shore. Coarse fishing is free. A footpath and riding trail circle the lake, and a nature trail is being laid out. Facilities are now available for transit campers with tents. A kiosk serves refreshments, and there is a hotel at the S end of the tarn. During the winter Talkin is popular for tobog-ganing.

9 DALEMAIN
Dalemain Estate 176 acres (65 hectares)
3 miles (5km) SW of Penrith, Cumbria. From Penrith or M6 Junction 40 take A66 towards Keswick, turning left on A592 towards Ullswater and Patterdale, to entrance at NY 478267. House and park open Easter to 30 September, daily except Friday, 14.00–18.00. Admission charge. This is a privately developed country park. Tel Pooley Bridge 450.

Dalemain stands surrounded by its gardens and deer park, close to Ullswater and on the edge of the Lake District. At first sight the house is a fine Georgian mansion in pink sandstone, but in fact the buildings are more interesting than this. Oldest part is a Norman pele tower, part of a line of defensive strongholds along the Scottish marches. Later a medieval hall was added, with a solar above, and later still a Tudor apartment, panelled in oak from the estate, and a priest's hole, originally approached up the chimney. The Georgian front was added about 1750 to what was by then an Elizabethan manor house.

Teas are now served in the medieval hall. The Norman pele tower contains the museum of the Westmorland and Cumberland Yeomanry, and the local militia which preceded these regiments. In the great sixteenth-century barn is a collection of old agricultural implements and household equipment, and a countryside museum and a gift shop are in the former stables.

Much of the surrounding estate is now farmed, but the herd of fallow deer in the deer park are the direct descendants of those which once roamed Martindale Forest. There are opportunities to explore the gardens, to climb up to Lobb's Wood or to picnic in the wild garden by the Dacre Beck.

10 FELL FOOT
National Trust 17 acres (7 hectares)
At the SE corner of Lake Windermere and on A592 near Newby Bridge. Main entrance at SD 382872. Freely open at all times.

Fell Foot is the smallest country park in Britain, but a popular one by virtue of the facilities it provides and its position on the lake shore within the National Park. It includes fine trees and open parkland, the grounds of a former mansion, with good opportunities for picnics and swimming. From the lake shore and slopes behind, the view extends the whole length of Lake Windermere to the distant peaks. The boathouse has been converted to provide an information centre, shop and café. Rowing boats can be hired here, and there is a dinghy park and slipway for launching sailing craft and canoes. South Windermere Yacht Club is based here. There is a caravan site for touring campers. A number of wooden chalets for holiday accommodation have been built (with help from the English Tourist Board) on an unobtrusive site. Railway enthusiasts will note that Fell Foot is close to the Lake Side Steam Railway.

11 BARDSEA
Cumbria CC 84 acres (34 hectares)
On the coast south of Ulveston, below Bardsea village. Approach along A5087 to main car park and information board at SD 302743. Freely open at all times.

This country park is a strip of coast extending from Wadhead Hill, in the east, to Sea Wood. Its main feature is the magnificent view across Morecambe Bay to Heysham and the Lancashire coast. It is a good place to watch seabirds. The beach at

Bardsea is backed by a low pebble bank from the foot of which the tidal sands stretch away towards Lancashire. When Bardsea was first recognised as a country park it, too, was part of Lancashire, a reminder of the ancient link across the sands to Cartmel. The Countryside Commission noted that any development of facilities at Bardsea must await a decision on the Morecambe Bay Barrage Scheme. Few facilities have been developed, but there is a café at the roadside. Sea Wood was bought as part of the country park. Visitors can walk through this attractive woodland, characterised by oak, ash and wild cherry, growing among ice-transported boulders, and now designated an SSSI.

Above and behind Sea Wood is Birkrigg Common, a very different world, a landscape of old quarries, ancient earthworks and stone circles. This common is not within the country park, but visitors can reach it by minor roads running W from Bardsea village or S from Ulveston.

OTHER SCHEMES
A WYLAM RIVERSIDE
Northumberland CC
At Wylam beside the river Tyne, 8 miles (13km) W of Newcastle. Accessible by bus.

A country park is to be developed here but is in its earliest stages.

B BEAMISH
Durham CC
At Beamish Hall and adjoining Beamish Open Air Museum. Approach from Gateshead on A692 or from Chester-le-Street on A693 following signs to the museum. Accessible by bus.

Woodland round Beamish Hall has been acquired to create a country park. Footpaths will lead from the hall to the Open Air Museum. The museum aims to recreate a regional way of life in the late 19th century. There is a station with steam trains, a colliery and row of pit cottages, the nucleus of a small town and Beamish Home Farm.

C WALDRIDGE FELL
Durham CC 285 acres (115 hectares)
1 mile (1½km) SW of · Chester-le-Street. Crossed by minor roads from Chester-le-Street through Waldridge to Edmondsley and from Waldridge to Chester Moor. Accessible by bus. Freely open at all times.

Waldridge Fell is a fully recognised country park. However, in deference to the known wishes of the county planning department, I have removed it from the main list. This is a case where an area of open heathland, important for educational purposes and designated an SSSI, was first proposed as a country park to qualify for a grant badly needed to clear rubbish and the relics of former industry. Initially it was intended that recreation facilities be concentrated at the N end. All that is now envisaged is management of the fell so that the public can enjoy its moorland landscape. Limited car-parking is available beside the two roads which cross the area. Every effort will be made to maintain what the Nature Conservancy defines as 'wet and dry lowland heath within bog and alder-ash carr: very rich entomologically'.

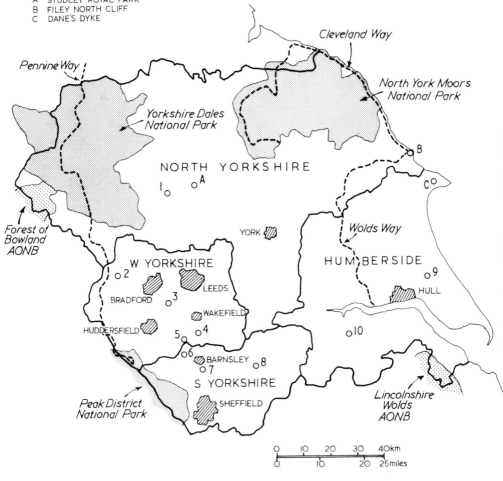

YORKSHIRE AND HUMBERSIDE

Cleveland Way

Pennine Way

North York Moors
National Park

Yorkshire Dales
National Park

NORTH YORKSHIRE

B

1 A

Forest of
Bowland
AONB

C

YORK

Wolds Way

W YORKSHIRE

HUMBERSIDE

2

LEEDS

9

BRADFORD 3

HULL

HUDDERSFIELD

WAKEFIELD

5 4

10

6 BARNSLEY 8

7

S YORKSHIRE

SHEFFIELD

Peak District
National Park

Lincolnshire
Wolds
AONB

0   10   20   30   40km

0   10   20   25miles

Yorkshire and Humberside

1 BRIMHAM ROCKS
National Trust 363 acres (147 hectares)
3 miles (5km) E of Pateley Bridge. The approach along minor roads is well signed from both B6265 and B6165. Main car park at SE 208643. Freely open at all times.

The strangely shaped rock formations at Brimham have been popular with visitors for 200 years. When the Brimham estate was given to the National Trust by Mr R. R. Ackernley in 1970, the immediate problem was to restore damage done by indiscriminate parking and litter, and to further public enjoyment and understanding of this unusual site. To this end the main car park is some 400m S of the park centre at Brimham House. The shop and information centre are open daily from April to late October, 10.30–12.00 and 13.00–18.00, and an exhibition with tape and slides explains the local geology and history. A refreshment kiosk and toilets are nearby.

The crags, isolated pinnacles and tumbled masses of rock at Brimham are the result of the natural processes of weathering (particularly during the severe conditions of the Quaternary Ice Age) acting on the vertical joints and horizontal bedding planes of coarse sandstones in the Millstone Grit series. Individual rocks have acquired names, descriptive or fanciful, and they occur over a wide area of moorland at around 900ft (275m) or on the edge of the W-facing escarpment above the Nidd Valley. Most of the area is now acid heathland dominated by ling, bilberries and bracken. It is particularly colourful in early autumn, with the rowan-berries red and heather (ling) in flower. Because of grazing animals, dogs must be kept under control.

2 PENISTONE HILL
West Yorks Met CC 177 acres (71½ hectares)
Immediately W of Haworth village. Approach from Haworth along West Lane and Cemetery Road to parking and picnic sites at SE 024373. Alternative approach along minor road, Moor Side Lane, between Stanbury and Oxenhope (which passes Lower Laithe Reservoir). Toilets and additional parking at the SW corner of the park at SE 018362. Freely open at all times.

Penistone Hill is the prominent moorland summit immediately W of Haworth village. Because of its fine views and close proximity to the Brontë Museum and Worth Valley Steam Railway, this has been a popular picnic site for many years. It is common land, grazed by sheep and cattle from surrounding farms, the E limit of a ridge extending out from the main Pennine range. The Pennine Way long-distance footpath is 1½ miles (2km) to the W, and a series of footpaths tempt the more energetic visitor to explore these wider possibilities and a

69

number of sites associated with the Brontë novels. Higher Withins is equated with 'Wuthering Heights', Ponden Kirk with 'Penistone Crag', Ponden Hall with 'Thrushcross Grange', and there is also Brontë waterfall.

Three large quarries on Penistone Hill have now been tidied up. The stone is a tough gritstone of the Millstone Grit series, the building material used throughout the area. The thin covering of acid soil is clothed in heather, whereas the lower slopes (on shales and sandstones) are covered by moorland grasses. West Yorkshire Met CC, who lease the land from the Craven Water Authority, hope later to provide additional interpretative services. There is scope for a footpath link to Wycoller Country Park in Lancashire.

3 OAKWELL HALL

Kirklees Met DC 60 acres (25 hectares)
On the S side of M62 and NW of Birstall. The country park is not yet open to the public, but access will be from A652 via Nutter Lane at SE 211268. Oakwell Hall Museum (separately administered) is open 1 April–31 October, except on Mondays, weekdays 10.00–18.00, Sundays 13.00–17.00. Closed Sunday and Monday during rest of year, but otherwise open 10.00–17.00.

When completed this country park will have open S-facing hillslopes, set among newly planted trees. So far the former Gomersall Colliery site has been reclaimed, and the old railway line will become a riding trail round the N edge of the park. It is hoped to convert farm buildings into an information and craft centre.

Oakwell Hall is a fine stone Elizabethan mansion, built by John Batt in 1583. It appears as 'Fieldhead' in *Shirley*. Inside one can see evidence of an earlier wooden building. The particular glory of Oakwell is the great hall, with the added interest of its association with Charlotte Brontë. There are other historical associations with the area. In Birstall (and indicated by signs) is the birthplace of Joseph Priestley, who discovered oxygen. The lane running N from Oakwell has been known as Bloody Lane in memory of Parliamentarians retiring from the battle of Marston Moor.

4 NEWMILLERDAM

Wakefield Met DC 239 acres (97 hectares)
On A61 in Newmillerdam village, 1½ miles (2½km) S of central Wakefield. Main car park at W end of dam SE 331157. Freely open at all times. Accessible by bus.

Newmillerdam is a very accessible and justly popular country park on the S edge of Wakefield. It owes its present appearance to developments in the 18th and 19th centuries. The Pilkington family, who owned Chevet Hall nearby from the mid-18th century, turned the lake into an ornamental addition to parkland surrounding their estate. The two lodges and boathouse were added in the 19th century. Newmillerdam village was also largely owned by the Pilkingtons, and much of the village is now a conservation area.

Following the establishment of the country park, a first priority was to acquire the timber rights, in order to preserve the mixed woodland surrounding the lake. Parts of the lake shore and footpaths have now been repaired, mainly by volunteer groups. Picnic facilities and viewpoints are being developed, and an arboretum has been

Fishing at Newmillerdam near Wakefield in West Yorkshire. Water from this lake powered a succession of ancient water mills below the dam. *City of Wakefield Met District Council*

planted. It is hoped to open East Lodge as an information centre, and later to repair the boathouse. Fishing is controlled by Wakefield Angling Club, which has open membership (tel Horsforth 584624). Two public bridleways cross the park, but riding is not otherwise permitted. It is hoped to establish a wildlife refuge in part of the area. Wakefield Council also own Seckar Wood, W of A61 and linked to Newmillerdam by paths and a disused railway line. There are facilities for scout camps here.

Much work at Newmillerdam has been done by voluntary groups, both local and international. There are some 50 honorary wardens, as well as junior wardens and a local Wildlife Youth Service. Local schools have been involved, and there are open days and organised walks.

5 BRETTON PARK
City of Wakefield Met DC 94 acres (38 hectares)
On A637 (Barnsley to Huddersfield road) just N of Junction 38 with M1 and S of West Bretton village. Entrance at SE 295124. Freely open at all times. Dogs not allowed because of grazing animals. Accessible by bus.

Bretton Deer Park was acquired by Wakefield Met DC in 1978 to protect an area of high landscape value which has historical and ecological interest, and to allow public access for informal recreation. So far the car park and an interest trail have been laid out and a permanent information and display centre will follow.

The Bretton Hall estate belonged to the Beaumont and Wentworth families in the 18th and 19th centuries. In its heyday, the 18th-century mansion and outbuildings were the centre of an integrated community. Now the mansion complex is Bretton Hall College of Higher Education, with the Yorkshire Sculpture Park in its grounds and accessible (following signs) from West Bretton Park Lane. Lakes within the former deer park are a nature reserve and designated an SSSI. Public access is restricted to permit holders or parties with special permission.

The remaining parkland sloping S to the Dearne Valley, and including the Lower Lake, is to be developed as a country park. (The Dearne is heavily polluted and bypasses the lakes.) A programme of treeplanting should restore the deer park to something of its original appearance (Capability Brown is believed to have been involved in the design) and a fine collection of mature trees remains. Farm animals now graze where the deer used to roam. There is

Worsbrough Mill Museum near Barnsley, South Yorkshire. The oldest parts of this working water mill date from around 1625. *A. Booth, South Yorkshire CC*

also evidence of iron-working in the remains of bell pits, and the clinker and ash from smelting. Bretton Park is directly linked to Cannon Hall Country Park by minor roads through High Hoyland, and there is also Litherop Picnic Site near the SW corner of the Bretton estate.

6 CANNON HALL PARK
Barnsley Met BC 98 acres
(39½ hectares)

4½ miles (7km) W of Barnsley and beside Cawthorne village. Approach on A635, turning N on the minor road towards High Hoyland. Park entrance at SE 273079. Park freely open at all times. Cannon Hall Museum open free weekdays 10.30–17.00, Sundays 14.30–17.00. (Closed Good Friday, Christmas and Boxing Days.) Accessible by bus.

This country park consists of the lawns, ornamental lakes and landscaped parkland round the mansion itself. It is a popular open area for picnics, fishing and informal games and is also the venue for local shows and events. The landscaping of the park and the creation of the ornamental lakes and bridges dates back to the 1760s, and there are many fine specimen trees. A ha-ha (sunk wall) separates the inner gardens and terrace round the house from the main park. The gardens and shrubberies are attractively planted and well maintained; they contain architectural fragments taken from Cawthorne and Silkstone churches at the time of their restoration.

The hall is now a museum administered by the education department and therefore technically not part of the country park; effectively it is an additional amenity and includes a good collection of furniture, family paintings and glass.

Footpaths lead from Cannon Hall park into Cawthorne village. This is now a conservation area, with few signs of its former association with iron-making or coal-mining. A leaflet available locally on the Cawthorne Village Walk provides background information on this attractive group of buildings. The minor road leading N from the park entrance, through the stone-built village of High Hoyland, leads directly towards West Bretton and the entrance to Bretton Deer Park, now another country park.

7 WORSBOROUGH MILL
South Yorks Met CC 95 acres
(38½ hectares)

On A61 1½ miles (2½km) S of Barnsley at Worsbrough Bridge, SE 352033. Approach from M1 Junction 36 along A61. Country park freely open at all times. Mill museum open free, Wednesday to Sunday inclusive, 10.00–18.00 (or dusk if earlier). Accessible by bus.

This small country park is in attractive open land beside Worsbrough Reservoir and the river Dove. It includes woodland and marsh at the upper end of the reservoir, and open hillside with stands of recently planted trees. The reservoir was originally constructed to provide water for a canal and is now available for fishing. It is hoped later to extend the country park; there are already footpaths round the reservoir and into surrounding farmland, and there is a programme of guided walks.

The great attraction here is the working water mill (strictly a separate organisation and not part of the country park). An interpretative centre contains a display on the history of Worsbrough Mill, and the mill museum has a small shop. There has been a

73

mill on this site for 900 years, and the present building dates from about 1625. All the processes can be watched, as water from the millpond above drives a complex of cogs and gear wheels. The old Worsbrough village centre on the hill above includes attractive stone buildings, the church and ruined hall. This should be visited on foot; there is no suitable car-parking space.

8 CUSWORTH PARK
Doncaster Met BC 60 acres (22 hectares)

3 miles (5km) NW of Doncaster. From Doncaster follow A1, turning left into Cusworth Lane just before the Sun Inn. From A1(M) follow A635 towards Doncaster, turn right at sign to Cusworth and next left. Entrance at SE 545041. Park freely open daylight hours. Museum open free daily, 1 March to 31 October 11.00–17.00, 1 November to 28 February 11.00–16.00. Accessible by bus.

Cusworth Park is a fine Georgian mansion set four square on a hilltop in the midst of its landscaped parkland. Its history resembles that of so many other stately homes; death duties led to the sale of all the furnishings in 1952, leaving the building forlorn and empty. Fortunately it was bought by the local council in 1961 and has now been restored to form the background to an interesting museum collection. A Norman castle mound beyond the W limit of the country park was probably the forerunner of Cusworth Hall.

The grounds, lakes and cascade are essentially as they were laid out by Richard Woods around 1763, but the herd of deer escaped in the 1950s. The view from the S front is as extensive as ever, but now includes industrial Doncaster. There is a

café, picnic facilities and a cricket field, and day permits are available for fishing.

The museum collection features particularly aspects of local mining, transport and agriculture, and has a children's room with a collection of dolls. It is widely used by schools and a teacher is based at Cusworth. A newsletter records changes in the displays and there are special arrangements for organised parties.

9 BURTON CONSTABLE
Mr Chichester-Constable 200 acres (81 hectares)

8 miles (13km) NE of Hull. Approach camping site and car access to country park following camp-site signs through Sproatley village to lodge at TA 187355. Open 1 March to 1 November. Admission charge. Separate entrance to the hall (signed) from minor road between Sproatley and New Ellerby at TA 193368. House and associated entertainments open daily (except Mondays and Fridays, but open Bank Holidays) Spring Bank Holiday to late September and weekends from Easter to Spring Bank Holiday, 12.00–17.00. Admission charge. This is a privately developed country park. Tel Skirlaugh 62400.

There are three aspects to the Burton Constable estate: the house with its associated entertainments, the holiday homes, caravan and camping site, and the country park. The camping site is on part of the country park land, and the open parkland and lakes lie beyond and are accessible by car through the camp-site entrance. The country park is essentially this landscaped parkland and lakes, with opportunities for boating and picnicking, and is an added amenity both for campers and visitors to the house. It is possible to walk from house to camp site in about 10 minutes.

The hall (not part of the country park) is a fine Elizabethan mansion. The outbuildings have been converted to a variety of new uses, including a cafeteria, a shop, and exhibitions of vintage motor cycles and agricultural machinery.

10 NORMANBY HALL
Scunthorpe BC 168 acres (68 hectares)

4 miles (6½km) N of Scunthorpe. Approach via B1430. The entrance at SE 887168 is immediately E of Normanby village. Park freely open daylight hours. Hall open April to October, weekdays except Tuesdays, 10.00–12.30 and 14.00–17.30, Sundays 14.00–17.30. Rest of year, same days, hall closes at 17.00 instead of 17.30.

Normanby Hall and its surrounding park form a remarkable oasis in an area suffering from intrusive industry. Once among the fine trees of the deer park or watching peacocks on the lawns in front of the Regency mansion, the visitor can forget that Flixborough chemical plant and Scunthorpe iron and steel works are near neighbours. The estate is still owned by the Sheffield family. In 1963, the Regency section of the hall was leased by Scunthorpe Corporation, who have redecorated and refurnished the main rooms (from Scunthorpe Museum and Art Gallery collections) in the manner of the 1830s, with the aim of creating a 'lived in' appearance.

Outside there are ornamental gardens, a lily pond and fine mature trees. A lido has been constructed in the old walled garden. Other facilities include a cafeteria and workshops with a working potter and a blacksmith. There is a putting course, an aviary and a nature trail. The caravan and camping site is reserved for organised groups. There are three varieties of deer in the park beyond the gardens, and fishing is available in the lake.

OTHER SCHEMES
A STUDLEY ROYAL PARK
North Yorks CC

2 miles (3km) W of Ripon. From B6265 turn S at sign to Studley Roger village and the entrance to Studley Park at SE 291700. Freely open daylight hours. Fountains Abbey open all year, weekdays from 9.30, Sundays from 14.00. (The abbey closes at 21.00 on weekdays in July and August, 19.00 in May and September, earlier in the rest of the year, and at 16.00 on Sundays.) Admission charge.

Studley Royal is advertised as a country park but is not so recognised by the Countryside Commission. The park is real enough, but most visitors may regard it as no more than a prelude to visiting Fountains Abbey. (The most direct entrance to Fountains Hall and Abbey avoids the Studley Royal entrance and is by minor roads, well signed, from B6265 W of Studley park or from B6165 NW of Ripley.)

The visitor enters Studley Royal Park along a magnificent avenue leading towards a church (unsafe and not open to the public). To the right are the ruins of the great house, destroyed by fire. The drive continues across the deer park, with its 3 herds of deer, towards the lake and cascade at the entrance to Fountains Abbey grounds. There is a restaurant here. Many visitors will wish to enter the grounds (administered by the DOE), passing the 18th-century water gardens before reaching the magnificent ruins of the Cistercian abbey itself.

B FILEY NORTH CLIFF
Scarborough BC 114 acres (46 hectares)
At the N edge of Filey at TA 115813, and signed from the town centre. Freely open at all times. Accessible on foot from Filey.

Filey North Cliff (or Filey Brigg) is known locally as a country park but is not so recognised at present by the Countryside Commission. It consists of an extensive area of grass-covered cliff top with picnic sites and an excellent view towards Flamborough Head. There is a very large car park and a caravan site. In addition there is a shop, cafeteria and information office, and an 18-hole miniature golf course. The beach below is directly accessible, and a nature trail and bird hide have been provided. A range of recreation is possible, from swimming and kite-flying to hang-gliding. The park is also at the S end of the Cleveland Way long-distance footpath.

C DANE'S DYKE, Flamborough Head
Humberside CC
Immediately W of Flamborough village and crossed by B1229 and B1255.

There are plans to develop a country park on Flamborough Head, centring on Dane's Dyke, and probably including Sewerby Hall (where there is already a small zoo and museum). The fine chalk cliffs of Flamborough Head are accessible at North Landing, South Landing and at the lighthouse. Dane's Dyke is a huge ditch and embankment, believed to date from the Bronze Age.

North-west England

1 BEACON FELL
Lancs CC 269 acres (109 hectares)

An isolated hilltop 8 miles (13km) N of Preston. Approach, following signs, from Longridge or Broughton on A6 3½ miles (5½km) N of Preston, or Brock Bridge on A6 14 miles (22km) S of Lancaster. A single-way road encircles the fell. The toilets and main car park are at SD 564427. The information centre, refreshments and emergency telephone are at Carwags, SE of the fell at SD 578422. Freely open at all times.

Beacon Fell is an isolated summit rising to 873ft (266m) on the edge of the Forest of Bowland, and in an area now designated an AONB. While the fell dominates much of the Lancashire plain (and was therefore a beacon site for many centuries), visitors must penetrate a maze of minor roads in order to reach the summit, but fortunately there are good road signs.

Beacon Fell was farmed until 1936 from Fell House Farm (now the main car park where the ranger has a hut). Years earlier it had been bought as a water-gathering ground for Barnsfold Reservoir, and large coniferous plantations were established. In 1959 it was decided that water could be more economically supplied by larger reservoirs, and the fell was acquired by Lancashire CC to create one of the earliest country parks. The older plantations (mainly Sitka spruce but including larch and pine) have been thinned, and footpaths have been opened up. This is a very exposed site and the thin acid soils developed on the Millstone Grit make commercial growing of timber impossible. New tree plantings include more native trees such as rowan, birch, oak and alder. Wet hollows on the fell are colonised by interesting bog plants. Elsewhere heather and ling, bilberries and moor grasses cover the ground.

The aim of the present management is to increase opportunities for informal recreation. There are car parks beside the road encircling the fell, and the more energetic visitors can easily reach the summit direction indicator, which helps to interpret the magnificent view. The park display centre is to the SE and outside the park proper. Refreshments are normally available here at weekends and during the summer. This is a very popular park and visited by over 300,000 people a year. It is also rough Pennine moorland; hence the emergency telephone and the large number of volunteer and part-time rangers who serve the park and conduct guided walks. From the N side of Beacon Fell one looks across at the remoter and unspoilt parts of the Forest of Bowland. Lancashire CC have negotiated access agreements to parts of this land, and their leaflet incorporates a map showing the footpaths and areas accessible to the public.

NORTH-WEST ENGLAND

COUNTRY PARKS
1 BEACON FELL
2 WYCOLLER
3 WITTON PARK
4 HAIGH HALL
5 PENNINGTON FLASH
6 JUMBLES RESERVOIR
7 HOLLINGWORTH LAKE
8 TANDLE HILL PARK
9 DAISY NOOK
10 WERNETH LOW
11 ETHEROW
12 CHADKIRK
13 LYME PARK
14 TEGG'S NOSE
15 STYAL
16 TATTON PARK
17 MARBURY PARK
18 LITTLE BUDWORTH COMMON
19 EASTHAM WOODS
20 THE WIRRAL
21 CROXTETH PARK

OTHER SCHEMES

A BEACON PARK

LANCASTER

Forest of
Bowland
AONB

Pennine Way

BLACKPOOL   LANCASHIRE

PRESTON

BURNLEY

3   BLACKBURN

SOUTHPORT

6

7

BOLTON

8

OLDHAM

4

WIGAN

GREATER
MANCHESTER

MERSEYSIDE

A

5

9

ST HELENS

MANCHESTER

21

10

11

BIRKENHEAD

LIVERPOOL

12

20   19

16   15

13

17

MACCLESFIELD

CHESTER

CHESHIRE

14

18

CREWE

Peak District
National Park

0   10   20   30   40km
0   10   20   25miles

2 WYCOLLER
Lancs CC 363 acres (147 hectares)

3 miles E of Colne. From Colne follow A6068 towards Keighley for ¾ mile (1km), turn right towards Trawden (B6250) and shortly left through Winewall, following signs. From the car park at SD 926395 a 5-minute walk leads to the hamlet. Freely open at all times. Bus access to Trawden.

Wycoller covers an extensive area of hill farm and moorland, rising up from the Wycoller Beck and hamlet to viewpoints at 1,000ft (305m). On much of this higher land access is limited to established footpaths (there is a useful map in the park leaflet). This is a landscape where rock predominates; Millstone Grit outcrops on the moors provide the building stone, the roofing material and the field boundaries. In medieval times cattle-breeding farms (vaccaries) were established in this part of the Forest of Trawden, and the extraordinary jagged stone teeth which bounded the fields are an immediate surprise to the visitor.

Wycoller hamlet is another surprise. It is a fine collection of stone buildings whose preservation was due initially to the efforts of the Friends of Wycoller. Lancashire CC bought the estate and much of the hamlet in 1973, establishing both the country park and a conservation area. With the help of job creation schemes, Wycoller is coming back to life.

There are three stone bridges of particular interest. A clam bridge (a single stone slab), a clapper bridge (with several slabs) and a packhorse bridge all cross the beck close to the hall ruins. The aisled barn, once the coach house of Wycoller Hall, is being restored to become the park visitor centre. A picnic site is being developed beside the

pond beyond this. The ruined hall is believed to have been the model for Ferndean Manor in Charlotte Brontë's novel *Jane Eyre*. Several of the houses are now occupied; the distinctly incongruous sight of solar panels and a burglar alarm should remind the visitor that this is a private house beside a working farm. A new entrance to this country park may be developed from the N, to a car park nearer the hamlet, but at present only disabled drivers should attempt to drive into the hamlet itself.

3 WITTON PARK
Blackburn BC 472 acres (191 hectares)

Immediately W of Blackburn. From M6 take Junction 28 or 31; from M61 Junction 8. Main S entrance off A674 beside bridge over river Darwen at SD 663270. Main N entrance in Billinge End Road, just off A677 at SD 663284. Also accessible from Buncer Lane, B6447. Freely open at all times. Accessible by bus.

Witton Park was the ancestral home of the Feilden family, Lords of the Manor of Blackburn, and the park and farmland of the estate were bought by the council in 1946. Witton House was later demolished, but the woods and parkland became a country park in 1973. The park occupies a rectangular area rising up from the river Darwen to Billinge Hill, at over 800ft (244m), and includes fine trees, a lily pond and beautiful rhododendrons and azaleas. The lower meadowland has been developed for sporting activities, with an arena for athletics and a horse-riding trail.

Billinge Wood is the focus of interest at the N end of the park. There are excellent views from the summit, and strategically placed picnic areas. A tree trail takes visitors

An ancient clapper bridge and a medieval packhorse bridge at Wycoller Country Park in Lancashire. The hamlet is now a conservation area, and it is interesting to compare this nineteenth-century photograph with the present scene. *Colne Library*

up one of several routes to the top, and emphasises the competition between heather and woodland, and the new plantings made necessary after fire damage to some of the rhododendrons. The main nature trail starts from Buncer Lane, opposite St Mark's church.

A visitor centre is now being developed in renovated farm buildings. The first phase of this, due to open in 1980, includes both an information room and natural history display (and adds to the range of inter-pretative material already available for school use). Later a local history exhibition will be added, and other features which tell the story of the change from privately owned country estate to public recreation area. A wayfaring course is also planned.

4 HAIGH
Wigan Met BC 371 acres (150 hectares)
NE of Wigan town centre. Car access N of Haigh Hall at SD 596087. Approach through Haigh village or by signed minor roads from B5238 (Wigan to Aspull road) or B5239 (Standish to Aspull road). Pedestrian access in Wigan Lane (A49) opposite Wigan Royal Infirmary (a leisure train runs between this gate and the hall during the main season). Freely open daylight hours. Accessible by bus.

Haigh Hall and park were acquired by Wigan Corporation in the 1940s, and have long provided a popular area for recreation on the city's doorstep. The woods and gardens are particularly beautiful in May. There are essentially two sections to this country park. The upper part round the hall and car park is the centre of most recreation facilities, and has views across the city and over the municipal golf course on the hillside. The Plantations, the lower wooded section in the deep Douglas valley, provides the most convenient entry point from Wigan and, beside its springtime beauty, has other less obvious features.

The estate once belonged to the Bradshaigh family, who came here from Bolton in the late 13th century. Today Haigh Hall is used for various functions, but is not otherwise open to the public.

Beside the car park and hall are the golf course, club house and shop. A large acreage of glasshouses holds outstandingly fine plant collections. There is a children's play area, miniature golf and a small zoo and aquarium in the walled rose and cactus gardens. A nature trail has been developed which starts at the hall and descends to the Douglas Valley and the Wigan Lane gates.

Concealed within The Plantations beside the river Douglas is the evidence of early developments in mining and industry, of great importance to anyone interested in industrial archaeology. Some survivals are clearly visible; others have long been forgotten. To understand the significance of what remains, one needs the booklet on the mining and geology trail (recently published by Wigan Department of Leisure). The trail starts from the entrance gates in Wigan Lane, a product and flamboyant advertisement of the Haigh Foundry within. It passes evidence of different methods of coalmining and the re-erected Gauntley Pit Headgear. Detective work is needed to establish forgotten waterways, lost railways, 17th-century glass works and illicit coal mines dating from the General Strike of 1926. The geological interest of the trail is linked to exhibits in Wigan Museum and Wigan College of Technology Museum.

The trail ends at the Great Haigh Sough, one of the greatest engineering feats of its period which drained water from mine workings and was begun by Sir Roger Bradshaigh in 1652.

5 PENNINGTON FLASH
Greater Manchester C and Wigan Met BC 650 acres (263 hectares)
Beside A572 SW of Leigh. The entrance (sign to golf course) is at a bridge 1 mile (1½km) W of Pennington at SD 646985, on the N side of A572. Freely open at all times. Bus access on A572.

The waters of Pennington Flash cover two-thirds of the extensive area of this country park, and are already used by local anglers and 3 sailing clubs. The country park is still incomplete, but already there is a 9-hole golf course (which will later be extended to 18 holes). The park centre provides changing facilities, and there is a dispenser for snacks. A café and information centre will be added, and a nature trail and riding trails will be developed. The flash is frequented by a variety of birds, and a small nature reserve is being established on the waterside.

6 JUMBLES RESERVOIR
NW Water Authority and joint committee 255 acres (103 hectares)
Between Turton and Bradshaw NE of Bolton. Approach from A676 1 mile (1½km) N of

*Bradshaw. Turn down approach road beside
Harmer's Hatchery at SD 740140 (no sign).
Freely open at all times.*

Jumbles is a compensation water reservoir
covering some 51 acres (21 hectares) and this
and the surrounding wood and meadowland
were first recognised as a country park in
1973. Now managed by a joint committee of
local authorities with the water authority, it
is defined as a low-key recreation area. This
means in practice that there are no signs to
help potential visitors, and no published
information on the park. Pedestrian entry is
possible at points on the W and S sides.

The facilities include car-parking overlooking the reservoir (special places for the
disabled), toilets and a warden's post and
information centre. Walks have been laid out
in this pleasant setting, but one cannot walk
round the reservoir. Day tickets are available
for fishing. A club has an exclusive lease on
sailing facilities, and canoeing is available for
organised groups only.

7 HOLLINGWORTH LAKE
**Rochdale Met BC 208 acres
(84 hectares)**
*2 miles (3km) NE of Rochdale. Approaches
(signed) from B6225 between Milnrow and
Littleborough. Park centre at SD 939153.
Freely open at all times. Accessible by bus and
train (Littleborough).*

Hollingworth Lake lies in open country
below Blackstone Edge and the Pennine
summits. It is a reservoir, completed in
1805, to provide water for the Rochdale
Canal. The rural setting and opportunities
for sailing, fishing, swimming and skating
have attracted large numbers of visitors ever
since the Manchester and Leeds Railway

reached Littleborough in 1839, making it
readily accessible to the Lancashire cotton
towns. The decision to create a country park
was taken because of the need to control
traffic and to reconcile the competing
demands for recreation, if its attractive
character was to be maintained. The park is
now managed by a committee representing
the councils of Rochdale and Greater
Manchester with the North West Water
Authority.

The park's attractions are focused on three
areas. Two of these, Lakebank on the NW,
and the promontory on the SE side of the
lake, were very popular a century ago. A
third centre, near the Fishermen's Inn in the
Easlees Valley, is new and directly accessible
from Littleborough by footpath. Here is the
new visitor centre, picnic site and main car
park. The centre provides a cafeteria and
displays and sells material about the local
area. A circular trail around the 2½ mile
(4km) perimeter of the lake starts from this
point. More ambitious walks can be
developed up tracks and minor roads
radiating out beyond the park boundary,
towards Blackstone Edge or an impressive
section of M62. (The Pennine Way runs
along Blackstone Edge and the Calderdale
Way crosses both this and the Littleborough
Valley near Todmorden.)

The lakeside trail leads over retaining
dams towards a nature reserve frequented by
a great variety of water birds. Traffic is no
longer allowed on the toll road, and paths
lead round to the promontory on the SE
lakeside. There is a pavilion here, set in
woodland and rhododendrons, which
provides shelter and refreshments during the
main season. There is also a children's
playground and picnic site and a popular
area for paddling and swimming.

The toll road continues round to the

Beach Hotel and Lakebank car park. Here visitors may launch their own sailing boats or small motor boats from the public slipway, or may hire rowing boats. In the season a motor launch ferries visitors to the promontory or tours the lake, and there is a regular programme of regattas. Permits for coarse fishing are available. Lakebank is also the setting for the great Easter Fair, which has drawn large numbers of visitors for more than a century.

8 TANDLE HILL PARK
Oldham Met BC 109 acres (44 hectares)
3 miles (5km) NW of Oldham. Approach on A627, turning W (at sign) from the hilltop between Oldham and Rochdale to park entrance at SD 907087. Freely open daylight hours. Accessible by bus.

Tandle Hill Park was given to the people of Royton by Mr Norris Bradbury in gratitude for the ending of World War I. It is a valued stretch of open grassy hillside, crowned by beechwood, conifers and heathland. The hill rises almost to 600ft (183m) and provides excellent views over the surrounding district. The main facilities include an aviary and a nature trail; the 9-hole pitch and putt course and the cafeteria are open throughout the summer. In winter the park is popular for tobogganning and skiing, when conditions are suitable. An orienteering course is being developed and South East Lancashire Orienteering Club have organised events for children.

Tandle Hills were still unenclosed and uncultivated in the early 19th century, and it was here that reformers met in secret and men drilled before the Peterloo Massacre of August 1819, and the Luddite breaking of cotton looms which followed.

9 DAISY NOOK
Oldham Met DC and GMC 85 acres (34½ hectares)
In the Medlock valley between Oldham and Ashton-under-Lyne. Main vehicle entrance from S at SD 921004. From A627 turn W in Waterloo along Newmarket Lane to Boodle car park and information point. Pedestrian access from A627 at Bardsley Bridge or from Oldham and Woodhouses via canal towpath to Crime Lake. (Additional car parking planned at E and W ends.) Freely open at all times. Accessible by bus.

Daisy Nook Country Park incorporates land owned by the National Trust and other open countryside in the Medlock Valley, within a densely populated and industrialised region. Parts of the valley have been popular for informal recreation for many years, and it was the need to manage the area more effectively to protect it from deterioration which led to its designation as a country park. Daisy Nook is part of a wider scheme to tackle problems of dereliction in the Medlock Valley through work sponsored by a joint committee (the councils of Greater Manchester, City of Manchester, Oldham and Tameside, with the National Trust and North West Water Authority). The old stable block at Park Bridge (on the Medlock 1 mile NE of Bardsley Bridge) is now being converted to provide an interpretative and information centre for this wider scheme.

At Daisy Nook itself the first 2 phases of the country park have now been completed. The park includes a section of the former Manchester to Ashton-under-Lyne Canal and its Hollinwood Branch, extending S towards Droylsden. The aqueduct carrying this branch canal over the river is the striking centrepiece and symbol of Daisy Nook Park, and is just N of the Boodle car park, picnic site and information point. There is boating on Crime Lake, beside the main canal, and refreshments are available here in the main season, and at Hencote Cottage, Daisy Nook (the National Trust warden's house). Fishing is available from the banks of the canal, and smaller water areas are set aside for sailing model boats. Much of the area is being managed to protect and encourage wildlife. Footpaths and separate bridle paths run through the park and link it to the surrounding minor roads. At a later stage there will be additional car-parking at the E and W ends of the park, and improvements and new facilities at Crime Lake.

10 WERNETH LOW
Hyde War Memorial Trust with Tameside and Greater Manchester Councils 195 acres (79 hectares)

8 miles (13km) E of central Manchester. Approach from A560 in Hyde, turning S along Spring Avenue and Higham Lane. Park centre at Lower Higham Farm, SJ 961936. Freely open at all times.

The townspeople of Hyde bought the Lower Higham estate by public subscription, as a war memorial following World War I, and a large area of hillside and summit has been kept open and maintained for public recreation ever since. Additional land has now been purchased, and the country park covers the N flank of the Werneth Low ridge, with additional car-parking on the summit at Quarry car park (SJ 960929), and Windy Harbour Farm further E. Part of Lower Higham Farm has been converted to provide a visitor centre, and there are exhibitions featuring local wildlife and aspects of former farming, including the old field names. Material related to the war memorial and the Hyde Memorial Trust is also on display.

From the centre, a path and separate bridle track lead up to the memorial, across grass-covered hillsides, and walkers can continue by a path across the golf course to the Windy Harbour Farm site, on the main Werneth Low ridge. The view from this narrow ridge, formed of Millstone Grit and rising to over 800ft (244m) takes in the W edge of the Pennines. In the opposite direction it is possible on a very clear day to see the Welsh hills beyond the Cheshire Plain, and the whole of Greater Manchester. There is a linking route southwards from the summit, which descends into the deep Goyt Valley, and Etherow Country Park. It is hoped later to provide refreshments within the country park.

11 ETHEROW
Stockport Met BC 162 acres (65½ hectares)

At Compstall 1 mile (1½km) NE of Marple. Approach along B6104 between Romiley and Marple Bridge to entrance at SJ 965909. Freely open at all times. Accessible by bus.

The deep and winding valley of the river Etherow brings unspoilt Pennine scenery to the very edge of the built-up area E of Stockport. This country park, designated in 1971, was formed from two separate estates. Following the closure of Compstall cotton mill in 1966, the council acquired the lower part of the valley, with the canal feeder and reservoir beside the mill. The Keg woodlands were acquired in 1971 and provide the more extensive areas of wooded hillside, and the marshes and fish ponds of the less developed valley section. Keg House was built in 1865 as a hunting lodge, and the surrounding woods were stocked with game. (Visitors can see a collection of game birds in cages on the slope below Keg House.) The unusual name may commemorate the storage of gunpowder for engineering works associated with the cotton mill.

The park centre and cafeteria buildings stand at the entrance to the valley, and the reservoir adds greatly to its attractions. Several clubs have facilities here, and the reservoir is used for sailing, rowing, canoeing, fishing and the sailing of model boats. Paths lead from the lakeside, running between the river and the feeder canal back towards the fine woodlands of the Keg estate. The Keg Trail climbs up the W side of the valley, passing the house and descending to the old fish hatchery and fish ponds (no longer used). These woods and the riverside marshes form a haven for wild life, and large numbers of bird and plant species have been recorded here. The Cheshire Conservation Trust manage a local nature reserve E of the river (and not open to the public). Picnic areas have been laid out and there are views up the valley and over surrounding moorland.

Etherow is close to the more recently developed Werneth Low and Chadkirk country parks. It is also within the wider Goyt and Etherow valley area where facilities for recreation and conservation are being jointly planned by the 3 councils directly involved. This should provide many more footpath links through the area.

12 CHADKIRK
Stockport Met BC 59 acres (24 hectares)
Between Marple and Romiley, E of Stockport. Approach on A627 to car park in Vale Road just N of Goyt bridge at SJ 937897. Freely open at all times. Accessible by bus.

The first phase at Chadkirk Country Park was opened in October 1979, and in essence consists of a farm trail round the fields of Chadkirk Farm. This is a working dairy farm, so visitors cannot enter the farm buildings. The farm lies in lowland beside the river Goyt on fertile alluvial soils and sheltered by the surrounding wooded slopes. The farm trail starts from the car park, circles the main fields, and extends into Kirk Wood and Little Wood above the house. Stockport Recreation and Culture Division publish a trail guide, and there are information boards along the trail which explain the various farming activities. There is a picnic area near the river at the N end of the farm, and the chapel adjoining the farm buildings has been restored to form an interpretative centre.

Work is in progress on reclaiming the orchard, where it is hoped later to have old farm machinery and beekeeping on display. Chadkirk is already linked by footpaths to the surrounding area, and lies immediately below the Peak Forest canal and towpath. Now a scheme initiated by the councils of Stockport, Tameside and Greater Manchester will provide more footpath links through the wider area of the Goyt and Etherow valleys.

13 LYME PARK
Stockport Met BC 1289 acres (535 hectares)
5 miles (8km) SE of Stockport. Vehicle entrance from A6 just W of Disley at SJ 965846. (Pedestrian entry at several points on 9-mile park perimeter.) Park and gardens freely open daylight hours throughout the year. House open 1 April to 30 September, Sundays and Bank Holidays 13.00–17.30, Tuesday to Saturday 14.00–17.00. Also in March and

October, Sundays 13.00–16.00, Tuesday to Saturday conducted tours only at 14.00, 15.00 and 16.00. Admission charge. Accessible by bus and train (Disley Station; bus shuttle service from the station to the hall during the high season).

Lyme Hall is within the Peak District National Park, and one of Britain's major stately homes. The estate was given to the National Trust in 1946 by Richard Legh, 3rd Lord Newton, but is now managed by the councils of Stockport and Greater Manchester. The country park includes both the deer park, gardens and hall, but parts of the latter may be temporarily closed due to an extensive programme of repairs. The estate has been the home of the Legh family for more than 600 years, but the oldest parts of the present house are Elizabethan. The state rooms are furnished with pictures, tapestries and period furniture and include carvings attributed to Grinling Gibbons. Terraces, an orangery and formal gardens with very fine displays of flowers surround the hall, and there are many mature specimen trees, both native and exotic. There is a free exhibition illustrating life

Lyme Hall near Stockport, a magnificent house given to the National Trust in 1946, and now the focal point of one of our largest country parks. The deer park retains its herd of red deer. *Countryside Commission*

at Lyme Hall in its 19th-century splendour.

There are obvious parallels between Lyme and neighbouring Tatton Park, but whereas the latter lies in the softer surroundings of the Cheshire Plain, Lyme takes its character from the Pennines. The house stands at 800ft (245m) and the park rises to over 1,000ft (305m). Sandstones in the Lower Coal Measures underlie the estate, and were quarried to provide its building stone. (There were attempts to mine coal within the park, and in 1947 it was suggested that opencast mining should be undertaken.) The last Ice Age left its mark here. Boulder Clay covers parts of the estate, and melt waters cut the deep valley in which the car park is situated. Soils tend to be acid and ill-drained, with heather moorland on higher ground.

The deer park is much older than the present hall, and the splendid red deer are believed to be descended from wild herds which once roamed Macclesfield Forest. Today's visitors have a choice of various activities. There is a cafeteria during the main season, an adventure playground for children, a putting course, a nature trail and an orienteering course. Lyme Park is in excellent walking country. Two suggested walks circle the park (the Inner and Outer Rounds). The shorter of these passes the Cage, built in the 1520s probably as a watch tower, and the Lantern (parts of the Elizabethan house rebuilt as a folly). Both routes visit the Bow Stones, fragments of Anglo-Saxon crosses set up just beyond the park boundary. Other suggested routes include 4 which radiate N to end by a bus stop or station, or a walk to Marple along the Peak Forest Canal. The long-distance Gritstone Trail starts at Lyme Hall and runs southwards to Tegg's Nose Country Park and the Staffordshire border.

14 TEGG'S NOSE
Cheshire CC 133 acres (54 hectares)

2 miles (3km) E of Macclesfield. Approach on A537 Macclesfield to Buxton road, turning S at Walker Barns (the National Park boundary) on to Old Buxton Road and car park at SJ 950733. Freely open at all times. Bus access to Langley village (near S end of park).

Tegg's Nose will particularly appeal to those who enjoy walking, moorland scenery and panoramic views. Tegg's Nose itself is a prominent summit rising to 1,265ft (386m) above the Cheshire Plain and just outside Peak District National Park. Formed of sandstones in the Middle Coal Measures, this hilltop was extensively quarried until 1955. The car park (on the site of Windyway Head Quarry) is separated by privately owned land from the main part of the park on Tegg's Nose. There is an information centre at the car park and picnic facilities with excellent views over Macclesfield Forest. (It is hoped to provide refreshments here in the main season.) The easiest way to reach the main view points on Tegg's Nose is by a level upper route; there are 3 alternative waymarked lower routes of varying length, which descend SE towards the Bollin Valley and woods beside Tegg's Nose Reservoir, before climbing back to the summit. Direction indicators help to interpret the excellent views. The main trails pass a quarry face and exhibition about the methods used by quarrymen in the past. Macclesfield Town Hall is one of the buildings faced with stone from here—and Tegg's Nose quarries were an important source of material for runway construction during World War II.

Moorland birds, bracken, bilberries and gorse are typical here, and the steep slopes and poor soils limit the range of plants, except where springs provide nutrient-rich water. There is a nature trail and a programme of guided walks during the main season. Most walks start from the car park, but some start from Tegg's Nose Reservoir dam near Langley village. The village itself is worth exploring; it was a centre of the silk industry until 1964. There are other attractive areas to be explored in the National Park further E, notably walks in Macclesfield Forest and rock climbing N of Wildboarclough. Finally there is the long-distance Gritstone Trail; Tegg's Nose is at the halfway point on this route from Lyme Park to the Staffordshire border.

15 STYAL
National Trust 63 acres (25½ hectares)
2½ miles (4km) N of Wilmslow. Approach on B5166 Altrincham to Wilmslow road, turning W at sign in Styal village to car park at SJ 835830 above Quarry Bank Mill. Wood and village freely open always, mill museum and shop open Tuesday to Saturday 12.00–17.00 in summer (12.00–16.00 in winter), and Sundays or Bank Holidays 14.00–17.00 in summer (14.00–16.00 in winter). Admission charge.

Styal will particularly interest the industrial archaeologist or social historian, but the buildings and their setting in the deep and

Styal Country Park in the Bollin valley in Cheshire. The oldest part of Quarry Bank Mill was built in 1784 by Samuel Greg, and is particularly interesting to the industrial archaeologist. His own house is just visible beyond.

wooded Bollin Valley will appeal to everyone. As at neighbouring Tatton Park, what can be glimpsed here is a complete way of life. In 1784 Samuel Greg founded a cotton mill, powered by the river Bollin, and one of the earliest in the country. The impressive buildings of Quarry Bank Mill form the central feature of the country park. Inside there are displays illustrating the development of the cotton industry and the life of a mill worker. It is hoped to restore old machinery to provide working displays, and the dam and leets which generated the power are being reinstated.

When the mill opened, Styal was still a hamlet, and Samuel had to provide housing for his workers. In 1790 he built the Apprentice House above the mill, where up to 100 children from the local poorhouse lived, and a small display at this house sets out the conditions. Quarry Bank House (where Samuel lived) was built in 1797 (the house and grounds are private). As the mill expanded, cottages were built to house more workers. Samuel bought an existing farm and built a chapel, school and shop for his community. All can be seen on a special 'village walk', but since this community is still very much alive, visitors are asked to respect the privacy of residents. It is fascinating to reflect that Samuel Greg was developing Styal at exactly the time that the Egertons were building and furnishing Tatton Hall (next entry). Taken together, these two Cheshire country parks provide a unique insight into early 19th-century ways of life. Quarry Bank Mill survived the vicissitudes of the cotton industry and was adapted to use water-driven turbines in 1904.

There is a shop and cafeteria in buildings behind the mill, and opportunities to picnic beside the river. Attractive walks lead through the valley and surrounding woodland, passing a packhorse bridge. A leaflet guide to the Bollin Valley Project is obtainable from the County Offices, Chapel Lane, Remenham, Wilmslow.

16 TATTON PARK
Cheshire CC 988 acres (400 hectares)
Just N of Knutsford. Main entrance (Rostherne Gate) in Ashley Road at SJ 748827 on NW side. Approach is well signed from Knutsford or A556. From M6 Junction 19 or M56 Junction 7 follow A556. Knutsford Gate (for fishing permits) in Knutsford at SJ 752790. For admission times and charges, tel Knutsford 3155 or 52748. Everything closed on Mondays (except Bank Holidays, when times are as Sundays). Park open weekdays 10.30–19.00 summer, 11.00–18.00 spring and autumn, 11.00–dusk winter. Sundays 10.00–19.00 summer, 10.00–18.00 spring and autumn, 11.00–dusk winter. House open weekdays 13.00–17.00 summer, 13.00–16.00 spring and autumn; Sundays 12.00–17.00 summer, 13.00–17.00 spring and autumn, and limited winter opening. Admission charges. Accessible by bus.

Tatton is one of the great country parks; it must also be one of the best known. The short, free audio-visual programme in the pavilion near the house provides the best starting point. The estate is owned by the National Trust but maintained by Cheshire CC, and administered by a joint committee. It was the subject of a study in interpretation techniques, referred to in Chapter 4. In essence its facilities fall into 3 groups: the hall with the gardens, information centre, shop and restaurant; Tatton Mere and the recreation facilities beside it, and Old Hall and Melchett Mere (with associated historical and nature trails). Each has its own car-parking area, and the whole park is linked by walking trails and a horse-drawn carriage drive.

Tatton has belonged to the Egerton family for over 380 years, but the estate is much older. The manor of Tatton is mentioned in the Domesday Book. Old Hall, which dates mainly from the 15th and 16th centuries, lies at the centre of the park, whereas the present hall was built between 1790 and 1815 by the architects Samuel and Lewis Wyatt. What makes Tatton Hall exceptionally interesting is its completeness. The rooms are decorated in the original splendid fashion and furnished exclusively with the Egertons' possessions.

The gardens at Tatton are as celebrated as the hall. The rhododendrons and azaleas are renowned, but there is also a terraced Italian garden, an orangery, a fern house and a beautiful Japanese water garden (built by Japanese workmen). The surrounding deer park was created in the 18th century, and landscaped by Humphrey Repton. There are cattle and rare breeds of sheep as well as deer in the park, and it is also the setting for special events. There is ample opportunity for walking (the park is open free to pedestrians from 9 am). Visitors may launch their own sailing craft in Tatton Mere or swim from its E shore, and there is coarse fishing by permit. Melchett Mere, formed by subsidence following salt extraction, is now important for bird-watching and the focal point of a nature trail.

The most recent developments at Tatton concern the period before the present hall and deer park existed. Old Hall is being progressively opened to the public. Already visitors can enter the Great Hall and get some idea of how life was lived here 500 years ago. Other parts will be opened once

these have been restored according to a contemporary inventory. The best introduction to this aspect is a new audio-visual programme to be seen in the stables. A thatched 17th-century barn, rescued from a site at Frodsham, has been re-erected here to house a collection of old farm equipment. Beside Old Hall stood the houses and fields of the lost village of Tatton (destroyed when the park was made). An unusual historical trail takes visitors round this site with the help of excellent information boards. When Old Hall is fully restored, Tatton Park should provide a unique record of the evolution of a great estate over 5 centuries.

17 MARBURY PARK
Cheshire CC 190 acres (77 hectares)

2 miles (3km) N of Northwich. Approach from Northwich on Runcorn road A533, turning N through Anderton towards Comberbach. The entrance is signed at SJ 649763. From M56 Junction 10 follow A559 to Seven Oaks Service Station, turning right to Comberbach. From M6 Junction 19 follow road to Great Budworth. Freely open at all times. Accessible by bus.

Marbury is a quiet green oasis of parkland beside Budworth Mere, yet close to the industries of Northwich. Its main attractions are opportunities for bird-watching, walking or riding. The area has other claims to fame. Salt-working in Cheshire goes back to Roman times, but it was the discovery of rock salt on the Marbury estate (just E of the park) in 1670 which led to the development of salt-working, and later of the huge chemical complex nearby. The extraction of brine also led to problems of subsidence. Marbury Lane (once the private estate road) shows examples of this. This area was an

A picnic in quiet parkland beside Budworth Mere in Marbury Park in Cheshire. It was the discovery of rock salt on this estate in 1670 which led to salt working and to the chemical industry in nearby Northwich. *Cheshire CC*

important routeway. The river Weaver was made navigable in the 1730s, and 50 years later the Trent and Mersey Canal (which runs along the park boundary) was completed, linking the Staffordshire pottery towns to the sea. At Anderton, just outside the park and sign-posted from it, is the extraordinary lift mechanism which raises boats from the river Weaver some 50ft up to the canal level.

The Marbury estate was bought by the Barry family in 1680, and they and their successors, the Smith-Barrys, lived at Marbury until 1932. The fine trees of the park are a legacy from its heyday as a country estate. Thereafter Marbury became a country club, a prisoner-of-war camp, a refugee camp and a temporary home for ICI employees. Finally the hall was demolished, but strenuous efforts have now been made to reinstate and replant the surrounding park. A small exhibition explains how this has been tackled.

The park is a quiet setting for informal recreation. There is a choice of walks; the path beside Budworth Mere is the most

91

attractive starting point, and the longest route extends to the canal. There are separate riding trails. The Cheshire meres are well known to bird-watchers. At Marbury there is a bird hide by the water, opposite reed beds now designated an SSSI and managed by the Cheshire Conservation Trust. The view of the mere is enlivened by the activities of Budworth Sailing Club and Marbury Angling Club (permits not available to non-members). Swimming in the mere is not recommended, but there is a swimming pool near the car park for which day permits may be available.

18 LITTLE BUDWORTH COMMON
Cheshire CC 82 acres (33 hectares)
4 miles (6½km) W of Winsford and immediately N of Oulton Park racing circuit. Approach from either A54 or A49 along minor roads, following signs to Little Budworth or Oulton Park. Car parking at various points on Coach Road across the common. Toilets at SJ 590655. Freely open at all times. Accessible by bus.

Little Budworth Common remained unenclosed and uncultivated because of the poverty of its soils. In this part of Cheshire the last Ice Age left behind great spreads of sand and gravel, later colonised by heath and birchwood vegetation. Now both Delamere Forest and the heathlands S of it are mainly valued as areas for informal recreation. At Little Budworth there is freedom to picnic, ride or walk to explore the grassy clearings among bracken and woodland. The facilities are essentially those provided at many picnic sites. Indeed Cheshire CC maintain a much smaller but attractive picnic site close by, beside the river and pond at Oulton Mill. This is on the minor road just W of Oulton

Park entrance at SJ 579650, and there are other picnic sites in Delamere Forest and at Whitegate Station. The other tourist attraction nearby is Beeston Castle, and the Sandstone Way Walk which has now been developed along the Peckforton Hills.

19 EASTHAM WOODS
Wirral Met BC 72 acres (29 hectares)
At Eastham Ferry 1 mile (1½km) N of Eastham village. When approaching on A41 turn E into Eastham village (avoiding the bypass), turning E again near the church. Follow Ferry Road to the entrance at SJ 365817. From M53 southbound take exit 5 on to A41. From M531 northbound follow signs to Eastham Locks into Eastham village. Pedestrian access from A41 via Green Lane. Freely open at all times. Accessible by bus.

Eastham Woods Country Park was established in 1970 as a contribution to European Conservation Year, but the site has long been popular for recreation. This is the one unspoilt stretch of foreshore on the Mersey side of Wirral. It is backed by woods and has excellent views across the Mersey from the low clifftop.

Ferries across the Mersey were established by monastic houses before the Reformation, and that at Eastham belonged originally to St Werburgh's Abbey. The ferry routes became very much more important when steamships were developed early in the 19th century. The *Princess Charlotte* was the first steamship on the Eastham to Liverpool service, and this rapidly became a favourite route for holidaymakers. Thousands came from Liverpool to picnic in Eastham Woods. The handsome Ferry Hotel was built in 1846, and pleasure gardens were developed around it which included a small zoo.

Neighbouring Carlett Park was also developed in the 1840s, and many exotic trees were planted in the grounds. When plans were made to build the Manchester Ship Canal entrance at Eastham, many regarded this as desecration of a favourite resort. The ferry continued to operate until 1929. Eastham itself has managed to preserve something of its village character, with its church and green. The immediate impression at Eastham Ferry is of stepping right back into the Victorian era, in spite of the proximity of both motorways and oil terminals.

A roadway has been built along the clifftop linking a series of parking bays. This is an excellent spot to study seabirds or watch shipping navigating the channel at the entrance to Queen Elizabeth Dock and the ship canal (the entrance locks are a half mile upstream). The main car park is further back beside the visitor centre. There is a children's play area and a most attractive tea garden (open for refreshments during the summer). A nature trail follows the waterfront and leads into the woods. Fine stands of beech, oak and other hardwood trees rise from a springtime carpet of bluebells. Rhododendrons and azaleas have been planted in the dell which once housed bears and monkeys.

20 THE WIRRAL
Cheshire CC and Wirral Met BC
106 acres (43 hectares)
The 12 mile (19km) stretch of former railway line between West Kirby and Hooton. Numerous access points; main car parks and access points signed from A540. For park centre at former Thurstaston Station, approach down minor road passing Thurstaston church and Hall to entrance at SJ

238835. Park freely open always; visitor centre open daily from 10.30, closes 20.00 in June, July, August; 17.00 in April, May, September, October, and 15.30 in winter. Accessible by bus and train at West Kirby, Neston and Hooton.

The last train ran between Hooton and West Kirby in 1956, and various proposals to convert the route to a long-distance walkway followed this. Finally in 1969 proposals by Cheshire CC were approved, and the Wirral became (with Elvaston Castle, Derbyshire) one of the earliest country parks in England. This was a single-track railway; the Hooton to Parkgate section opened in 1865, and the connection to West Kirby in 1886. With the exception of 2 short stretches, the whole route has been converted into a walkway and separate riding trail, a task which involved major clearance and draining operations. There are picnic and parking sites at Caldy, Parkgate Baths, Parkgate Station, Lees Lane (just off A540 at SJ 306776) and Hadlow Road Station.

At Thurstaston there is a purpose-built visitor centre, with excellent interpretative displays, a theatre for audio-visual programmes, an information and sales desk and a refreshment kiosk. Permits for riding and fishing are available here. A camp site for tents is in the former station yard (there is a caravan site just beyond the entrance to the centre). A wartime anti-aircraft gunsite has been cleared to provide a picnic site and informal games area on the clifftop overlooking the Dee estuary and Welsh coast. There is a nature trail here, and ponds stocked for coarse fishing (shore fishing is also available). The park rangers lead guided walks throughout the summer and a newsletter sets out the park's activities. The emphasis is on interpreting the landscape,

Hadlow Road Station at Willaston in Wirral Country Park. This typical country station has been preserved and refurnished as it was about 1950. Wirral Way follows the old single track railway line, which opened here in 1865 and closed in 1956. *Cheshire CC*

and there are special educational facilities (tel 051 648 4371 for bookings).

To enjoy this park to the full means walking or riding the Wirral Way; it also means getting a copy of the invaluable walkers' guide. This divides the route into 4 manageable sections, provides a map and detailed information on each, and suggests a variety of side excursions and alternatives which turn the linear park into a series of circular trips. The N section follows the coast of the Dee estuary, through settlements whose names recall 10th-century Viking raids. There are views across to the coast and hills of Wales. Side excursions can be made

to rocky hilltops among gorse and heather on National Trust land at Caldy Hill and Thurstaston Common. Alternatively one can walk along the foreshore below cliffs cut in Boulder Clay. Beyond Heswall, saltmarsh replaces tidal sands. Neston and Parkgate, successively outports of Chester when shipping could no longer reach that city, have lost not merely their role as ports but virtually all contact with the sea. Parkgate retains echoes of its importance as a packet station. Here Handel stayed at the George Inn awaiting a passage to Ireland, and seaside holidays with shrimp- and cockle-fishing continued into the 1930s, before the inexorable advance of silt and marsh grass altered everything.

At Neston the railway turned inland, climbing through a deep cutting in sandstone. A nature trail has been developed in this sheltered and wooded section, readily accessible from the Lees Lane picnic site. The final section runs through pleasant farmland towards Hooton Station. The focus here is Hadlow Road Station. The buildings have been restored and refurnished as they were about 1950, with a display explaining how such country stations operated. A side excursion to Willaston, with its green and fine old buildings, is a further alternative.

21 CROXTETH PARK
Merseyside Met CC 514 acres
(208 hectares)

5 miles (8km) NE of central Liverpool, at centre of area bounded by A580, A5058, A57 and M57. The vehicle entrance is from A5049 Muirhead Avenue East, at its junction with Oak Lane, at SJ 399943. Freely open daylight hours. Hall and exhibition open daily 10.00– 12.30 and 13.00–16.30 in winter, 9.30–17.00 in summer. Admission charge. Walled garden also open, admission charge.

Croxteth Park was given to Merseyside CC following the death of the 7th Earl of Sefton in 1972, and its conversion into a country park is still incomplete. It is already a major facility within the Liverpool city boundary. Many of the traditional activities on the estate continue, so that visitors can see farming, forestry and game management in action. At the same time new displays are being developed to show the history of the estate and the way of life of those who lived here.

Viewed from its surrounding gardens, the finest part of the hall is in Queen Anne style, but the building was begun in 1575 and dates from several periods. (An architectural trail is to be developed to take advantage of this variety of building styles.) Inside there are more than 200 rooms, but less grandeur than might have been expected. A visually exciting display on the history of Croxteth has now been opened, and in the principal rooms a display of costumes, backed up with paintings and furniture, may be further extended to illustrate life above and below stairs on a great estate. Sport was a major interest of the Earls of Sefton (the Grand National is run on part of the estate) and these interests will feature in displays.

Lawns, gardens and a lily pond surround the hall, and have been developed to provide sites for picnics, putting and croquet. Horse-drawn carriages are on display in the courtyard. The early 19th-century walled garden is outstandingly interesting. In its heyday, when up to 30 gardeners worked here, it provided flowers, fruit and vegetables for the hall. The equipment remains intact; there are hollow walls heated by flues, various types of greenhouse, beehives and old fruit trees pruned to a startling variety of shapes. A countryside trail takes visitors into the surrounding woodland. Once this was a royal hunting forest, but now the woodland needs reinstating after neglect. There are problems with lack of drainage and pollution of surface waters, but this is a wildlife reservoir within the city boundary.

There is already an educational service based on Croxteth, and special facilities for schools. It is hoped to develop the Home Farm to show both present and past farming methods. There is also a programme of guided walks and special events based at Croxteth.

OTHER SCHEMES

Joint committees representing local authorities, the National Trust, water authorities and amenity groups are developing a number of schemes for environmental improvement and public recreation, linked to existing country parks. The best known is a 20 mile (32km) stretch of the Bollin Valley which includes Styal Country Park. (An excellent explanatory guide is obtainable from County Offices, Chapel Lane, Wilmslow.) A similar scheme in the Medlock Valley includes a visitor centre at Park Bridge, close to Daisy Nook Country Park, and there are other developments in the Mersey, Tame, Croal and Irwell Valleys of Greater Manchester. Merseyside CC with other authorities is developing a linear park in the Sankey Valley at St Helens, improving a stretch of the Leeds and Liverpool Canal, and providing new facilities at Formby Point, linked to coastal protection. Recreation areas on Anglezarke and Rivington Moors near Horwich are managed by the NW Water Authority, and resemble other country parks.

A BEACON PARK
West Lancashire DC 297 acres (120 hectares)
Immediately NE of Skelmersdale on the slopes of Ashurst Beacon, SD 502077. Still at the planning stage.

It is hoped to develop a country park on the upper slopes of Ashurst Beacon, a ridge rising to 552ft (168m) between Skelmersdale and Wigan, and a municipal golf course is already being constructed at the N end of this.

Wales

1 PADARN
Gwynedd CC 320 acres (129½ hectares)
At the SE end of Llyn Padarn SN 587603. Approach from A4086 in Llanberis via a road opposite the Snowdon Railway station, passing the tourist information office. (The park entrance adjoins what is at present the huge construction site of the Dinorwic hydro-electric station.) Freely open daylight hours.

This extensive country park would be an interesting place to visit even if it were not within Snowdonia National Park and in full view of Yr Wyddfa (Snowdon) itself. It has many features, but the great Dinorwic slate quarries (the largest in the world) form the core. One part of Dinorwic, the Vivian Quarry, where work stopped in 1963, is now open to the public. A quarry trail has been laid out which enables visitors to understand how slate was quarried, split, dressed and transported down the mountainside. It also provides insights into the hard and dangerous life of slate workers; the quarry hospital is now the visitor centre and includes, in addition to displays of the local natural history, three small hospital wards set out with the original medical equipment. The quarry trail, a nature trail and other waymarked walks take one through the beautiful surviving sessile oak woodland which formerly covered all the valley sides.

Adjoining the main car park are the impressive buildings which used to be the maintenance workshops for the Dinorwic quarries. Built of granite and slate in 1870, they were bought by Caernarvon CC shortly after closure in 1969, and have now been developed by the National Museum of Wales into a museum illustrating the quarrying industry.

Also adjoining the car park are the separate facilities of the Llanberis Lake Railway, with a shop and café adjoining the station (Gilfach Ddu). This railway has 5 old steam locomotives which pull carriages the length of Lake Padarn, a round trip of 4 miles. Trains run daily from mid-April to the end of September (tel Llanberis 549 for timetable details). Visitors cannot be dropped or picked up at Penllyn (where the engine turns round) but can leave the train at Cei Llydan on the return journey if they wish. Here there are attractive lakeside picnic facilities, with a commanding view of the Snowdon massif.

2 MOEL FAMAU
Clwyd CC 2,375 acres (961 hectares)
4 miles (6km) W of Mold; picnic site, toilets and main car park at SJ 171611. Approach from A494 Mold to Ruthin Road. At Tafarn-y-Gelyn, ½ mile (1km) W of Loggerheads Inn (and Country Park) fork right at sign. The picnic site is 1 mile (1½km) further up this minor road. There is additional space for parking ½ mile (1km) further, on the road

(above) The Clwyd Hills from the West. Moel Famau Country Park includes a five mile stretch of heather-covered summits along the line of Offa's Dyke Path. Moel Fenlli, on the right of the picture, is crowned by an Iron Age hill fort, and trails through Forestry Commission woodland on the slopes beyond lead up to the skyline. *Clwyd CC*

(left) The view towards Snowdon (Yr Wyddfa) across Llyn Padarn from Penllyn at the western end of the country park. On the left the Llanberis Lake Railway runs along the lakeside towards the slate quarries and museum. *Countryside Commission*

summit overlooking the Vale of Clwyd. (This minor road continues down the W side of the Clwyd Hills to rejoin A494 on a hairpin E of Ruthin, but it is steep and narrow and not recommended.) Freely open at all times.

Moel Famau is arguably the finest of our country parks for hill walkers. It includes the most impressive 5 mile (8km) section of the Clwyd Hills and a particularly fine stretch of Offa's Dyke long-distance footpath (although the dyke itself is missing here). To the E is Clwyd Forest, owned by the Forestry Commission, but effectively part of the same amenity land; indeed the picnic site, toilets and nature trail are on Forestry Commission land. The country park proper is open moorland on the crest of the Clwyd Hills and formerly the ancient lands of the Manor of Ruthin. It includes several summits above 1,500ft (500m) and commands magnificent views.

Shales and sandstones of Silurian age form the hard backbone of the Clwyd Hills. To the E these rocks dip below younger rocks on the edge of the Cheshire Plain. To the W the contrast is even more dramatic. A fault line marks the steep W side of the hills. Below in the Vale of Clwyd is a landscape of small fields, scattered farms and fortified market towns. A wide stretch of high moorland limits the W horizon; beyond are the peaks of Snowdonia.

The Clwyd range forms a natural frontier. Iron Age hill forts crown a number of the summits. The finest (Moel Fenlli) is at the S edge of the park; the most extensive (Pen-y-cloddiau) is just beyond the N limit, but is accessible via the marked trail on the edge of Llangwyfan Forest. A conspicuous feature on the summit of Moel Famau itself is the ruin of George III's Jubilee Tower.

All visitors will enjoy the picnic site by a

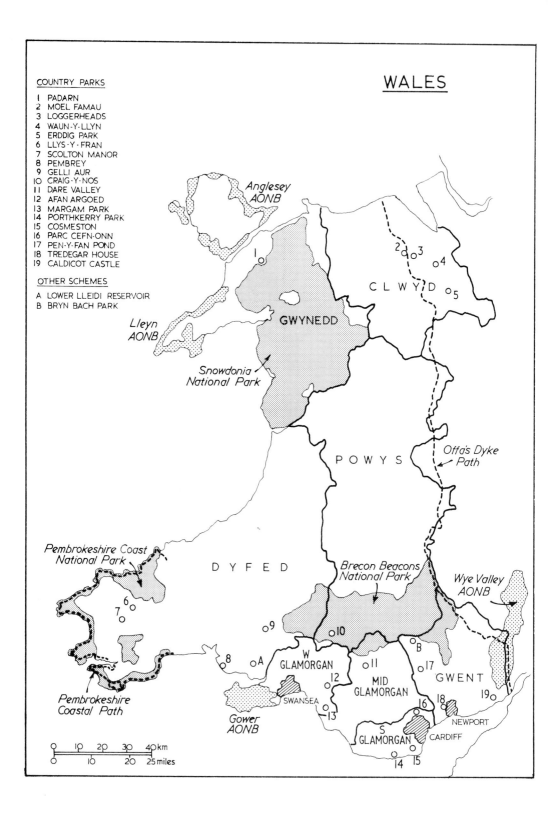

WALES

COUNTRY PARKS

1 PADARN
2 MOEL FAMAU
3 LOGGERHEADS
4 WAUN·Y·LLYN
5 ERDDIG PARK
6 LLYS·Y·FRAN
7 SCOLTON MANOR
8 PEMBREY
9 GELLI AUR
10 CRAIG·Y·NOS
11 DARE VALLEY
12 AFAN ARGOED
13 MARGAM PARK
14 PORTHKERRY PARK
15 COSMESTON
16 PARC CEFN·ONN
17 PEN·Y·FAN POND
18 TREDEGAR HOUSE
19 CALDICOT CASTLE

OTHER SCHEMES

A LOWER LLEIDI RESERVOIR
B BRYN BACH PARK

Anglesey
AONB

Lleyn
AONB

GWYNEDD

CLWYD

Snowdonia
National Park

POWYS

Offa's Dyke
Path

Pembrokeshire Coast
National Park

DYFED

Brecon Beacons
National Park

Wye Valley
AONB

Pembrokeshire
Coastal Path

W
GLAMORGAN

SWANSEA

Gower
AONB

MID
GLAMORGAN

GWENT

NEWPORT

S
GLAMORGAN

CARDIFF

0   10   20   30   40 km
0   10   20   25 miles

stream, planted with American red oak trees. The panoramic view from parking space available at SJ 162606 beside the road summit is also justly popular. For the more energetic there is an extensive choice of hill-walking. A forest trail starts from the picnic site and climbs up wooded slopes and across heather moorland to the summit of Moel Famau. An alternative route up is to take Llwbr Clawdd Offa (the Offa's Dyke path).

A separate country park below Moel Arthur was originally intended, and there is very limited car-parking space on a minor road crossed by the Offa's Dyke path at SJ 138668. The easiest approach is from the W, following signs to Llangwyfan Hospital and continuing past the hospital to the crest of the hill. The descent E to A541, via either of 2 minor roads, is very narrow.

Clwyd County planning department has now published good short guides to the hill forts of Moel Famau and the N section of Offa's Dyke Path, and the Forestry Commission has published a guide to the forest trail.

3 LOGGERHEADS
Clwyd CC 74 acres (30 hectares)
3 miles (5km) west of Mold on N side of A494 opposite Loggerheads Inn. No official car park or toilets but both available by the bridge at SJ 198626 and parking space behind houses a little further W. Freely open at all times. Accessible by bus.

This is a small but interesting country park in an area popular for walking and picnics for many years. The river Alyn has cut a deep gorge at the foot of a bold escarpment of Carboniferous Limestone. In places much of its water disappears down swallow holes. The flora and fauna of the rock face,

limestone pavement above, and wooded valley below are particularly rich, and the whole area is designated an SSSI. There are riverside and woodland walks, and the café and Loggerheads Inn nearby provide additional facilities. The signed turning off A494 to Moel Famau Country Park is ½ mile (1km) to the SW.

4 WAUN-Y-LLYN
Clwyd CC 74 acres (30 hectares)
Entrance, car park and toilets are at SJ 284577. The approach either from Caergwrle (A54) or from Coed Talon (A5104) is steep, narrow and difficult to find. Clwyd CC intend to put up road signs. Ask for the summit of Hope Mountain rather than for Waun-y-llyn. Freely open at all times.

It is worth visiting this small country park, poised on the N crest of Hope Mountain, for the views over the Wirral, the Cheshire Plain and mountains on the Welsh border. It is an exposed moorland habitat, developed on the Millstone Grit rocks which here rise above the Coal Measures of the surrounding lowlands. There is a small lake and old quarries where the sandstone rocks break through the heather and peat-bog surface.

There are several possible routes up from A54 either in Caergwrle itself, or just to the N of it, at an electricity sub-station. Later keep right. From the A5104 turn E at the Railway Inn, Coed Talon; keep right in about ½ mile (1km) and left further on.

5 ERDDIG PARK
National Trust 208 acres (84 hectares)
1 mile (1½km) SW of Wrexham. Approach from Wrexham to Rhostyllen road (avoid the new bypass) and turn S at Felin Puleston

beside river bridge. Country park entrance immediately to the left at SJ 324493; continue forward following signs to main house. Parkland freely open at all times and accessible on foot from Wrexham. Agricultural museum and main house open Easter to 31 October, daily except Mondays (but open Bank Holidays), noon to 17.30. Admission charges to agricultural museum and main house, outbuildings and gardens.

The fine house and estate at Erddig offer several separate opportunities. The park and meadowland along the valley of the Clywedog River between Felin Puleston and Kingsmill are accessible by footpaths at all times. This attractive parkland includes earthworks beside the line of Wat's Dyke, an early fortification which runs parallel to Offa's Dyke on this part of the Welsh border. The centrepiece of the country park is an agricultural museum, housed in a barn which has been rescued from another local site.

The house, outbuildings and gardens, which include a restaurant and National Trust shop, are separately managed by the trust. Restoration work here was judged joint winner of the National Heritage Award. The fine furnishings of the 17th-century house, the reconstruction of life in the servants' hall, bakehouse and smithy, and the restoration of the formal gardens are particularly interesting features.

6 LLYS-Y-FRAN RESERVOIR
Dyfed CC 308 acres (124½ hectares)
8 miles (12km) NE of Haverfordwest. Best approached either from A40 (turn N 1½ miles W of Canaston Bridge to Clarbeston Road) or from Maenclochog on B4313. These routes are well signposted. Park entrance on E side of reservoir at SN 040244 close to Llys-y-fran village. Freely open daylight hours.

This reservoir was completed in 1971 to regulate the flow of water down the Afon Syfynwy. Water is then taken from the river further downstream to supply the oil industry and domestic users in the Milford Haven area. The reservoir holds 2,000 million gallons when full. The dam rests on hard Ordovician slates.

The West Wales Water Authority and the local authorities have jointly developed this very attractive country park, set in pleasant countryside on the S flank of the Presely Mountains. Car-parking and picnic facilities have been developed above the reservoir on both sides of the dam, with impressive views of both natural and man-made features. A temporary building houses a small café and display area. A new footpath and nature trail have been provided round the perimeter of the lake. Nesting boxes have been set up and there are many varieties of moorland and water birds. The name Llys-y-fran means 'Court of Crows' and the crow has been taken as the park symbol.

The West Wales Water Authority control boating and fishing which are very popular here. Day and season permits are available (tel Haverfordwest 3881). The reservoir is stocked with brown and rainbow trout and both bank and boat fishing are allowed. There is a boat park and slipway, and facilities for boating, sailing and canoeing. The reservoir is also used by sub aqua clubs.

There is one problem. It has still to be decided whether to increase the height of the dam. This would alter but would not destroy the park's facilities, and the public would not have access during construction work. Plans to build a permanent visitor centre are held up until a decision is made.

7 SCOLTON MANOR
Dyfed CC 40 acres (16 hectares)
On the W side of B4329, 5 miles (8km) N of Haverfordwest, at SM 991218. Country park freely open daylight hours. Museum (not yet open) likely to be open daily except Mondays, Easter to 30 September.

Scolton Manor was built in the 1840s in a pleasant rural setting. With its surrounding parkland, walled gardens and outbuildings it is a typical country house of its period. The car park and picnic area are in open grassland, and there are scattered clumps of trees, including specimens of various exotic species and fine banks of rhododendrons. There is a nature trail to take the visitor round these grounds and also into the neighbouring Forestry Commission plantation, and it is intended to develop a waterside walk.

When restoration is completed the manor house will be open, and is intended to house a museum collection, including period rooms and equipment related to the former slate and agricultural industries.

8 PEMBREY
Llanelli BC 519 acres (210 hectares)
From A484 in Pembrey village turn S near a railway bridge (sign to park). Cross another railway bridge and immediately beyond on the right is Burrows picnic site and a forest walk through Corsican pine plantations, managed by the Forestry Commission. For the country park continue forward along a newly made-up road, leaving the industrial estate on the left. The approach road continues between afforested sandhills and stretches of new grassland to reach large car parks and the signed route to the beach at SN 415007. Freely open at all times.

Pembrey is one of the most recently designated of our country parks. It has that rarest of facilities, an accessible but undeveloped coastline with superb sands and fine views. Ironically its survival as open coast is due in the first place to the presence of a Royal Ordnance factory which started operations here in the 1880s, and was eventually closed in 1964. A second reason for lack of development is the nature of the land itself. Modern heavy industry could not be built on this peninsula, which is composed of blown sand some 200ft thick. So after various controversial schemes and several public inquiries, the land was eventually acquired by Llanelli BC in 1977. Only the first stage of this park has been completed so far.

At present the sandy beach known as Cefn Sidan, with its opportunities for swimming, kite-flying and shell-collecting, and the view of the N Gower coast, is the great attraction. It is intended to build a visitor centre beside the main route to the beach and to create several lakes and play areas, as well as an exhibition site and camping sites in the grassy hollows behind the coastal sand dunes. Most of the derelict ordnance factory buildings have been cleared (with help through Job Creation schemes), though some may be kept as the focus for an industrial trail. There are plans for both a pony-trekking centre and a boating jetty. These facilities, together with the paths and bridleways which will serve them, should eventually link up the country park, centred near the beach, and the very extensive Pembrey Forest with facilities already provided by the Forestry Commission. Further woodland planting will be needed because it is essential to protect the sand dunes from wind erosion.

9 GELLI AUR (Golden Grove)
Dyfed CC 99 acres (40 hectares)

3½ miles (5km) SW of Llandeilo. Approach either along A476 or B4300. There are road signs to both Gelli Aur and Golden Grove; the drive entrance is from a link road between A476 and B4300 on the W side of the park at SN 590198. Freely open in college vacations only.

Gelli Aur mansion is leased to Dyfed CC as an agricultural college and the public are now able to enjoy the surrounding grounds when the students are out of residence. Parts of the buildings may later be available for interpretative displays, but initially visitors will have access to the gardens, arboretum and former deer park.

The present Gelli Aur mansion is an imposing building in grey limestone, erected between 1826 and 1832 and standing high above the Towy Valley on a steep N-facing slope. There is a fine view across the valley and over Dynevor Castle from the formal garden in front of the mansion, and from terraced lawns behind. Higher still, and rising above rhododendrons and azaleas, is an arboretum planted in the 1870s and held to be one of the finest collections of specimen trees in Wales.

Parts of the surrounding hillsides have been afforested but much is covered with bracken and foxgloves. Formerly the deer park, this area is still visited by deer which are naturalised in parts of the Towy Valley. Several public footpaths lead out from Gelli Aur grounds on to these hill slopes.

10 CRAIG-Y-NOS, Powys
Brecon Beacons National Park Authority 44 acres (18 hectares)

In the upper Tawe Valley and ½ mile (1km) S of Dan-yr-Ogof caves (follow signs to the latter) at SN 840154. On A4067 4 miles (6km) N of Ystradgynlais. Freely open at all times.

Craig-y-nos Country Park is a small but beautiful portion of the upper Tawe Valley and within Brecon Beacons National Park. It surrounds and takes much of its interest from Craig-y-nos Castle, although these buildings are not open to the public. The singer Madame Patti came to live at Craig-y-nos and added a small theatre and other buildings. She also extended and beautified the surrounding grounds and it is this area which has now become a country park.

The car park and information office are in what used to be the kitchen garden. To the N, in woods, is the fish pond. A new bridge over the river leads into wooded pleasure grounds with fine specimen trees. After years of neglect this has now been partially cleared and replanted. Paths run through rhododendrons along the river bank. That to the N leads, via stepping stones, to the Dan-yr-Ogof caves. Downstream another bridge leads back into gardens below the castle and to the tennis and croquet lawns. Here stands the pavilion (now restored) where Mme Patti entertained royalty.

There is now a programme of summer events, demonstrations and guided walks organised by the rangers from Brecon Beacons National Park.

(opposite page) Part of Dare Valley in South Wales before and after the creation of the country park. Two views north towards the Brecon Beacons taken in 1947 and 1973, which show Cwmdare village and the Bwllfa No 2 pit. The new lake is one of three in the country park. *By permission of Glyn Davies and Cynon Valley DC*

11 DARE VALLEY
Cynon Valley DC 477 acres
(193 hectares)

Immediately SW of the centre of Aberdare. Accessible for pedestrians from Aberdare beside the church of St John (an interesting building, basically 12th century). Access by car either from A4059 via Cwmdare village, or from B4277 via Highland Place (signs). Note that visitors may not drive through the park from one entrance to the other. The park centre at SN 962027 is accessible by car from both main entrances; there is also vehicle access, via Cwmdare, to the lakes and W end of the park. Freely open at all times.

Dare Valley Country Park was the first in Wales to be recommended for approval by the Countryside Commission, the first to be established by a district council, and the first to be created largely on reclaimed derelict land, an achievement recognised by a Prince of Wales Award in 1972. It is sited on land scarred by the Industrial Revolution; there were 6 collieries and a score of coaltips in the area. The National Coal Board gave much of the derelict land; other land was bought from private owners and disused railway tracks from British Rail. It is therefore appropriate that an industrial trail has been established largely along the line of the former Dare Valley Railway, which helps the visitor to understand the development of industry and mining in the valley.

Dare Valley offers its visitors much more than industrial archaeology, however. Surrounded by impressive highland rising to over 1,500ft (500m), it offers scope for a wide range of countryside activities. Pony-trekking and walking are the most obvious. There are 3 quite different trails which feature moorland ecology and wildlife, as well as walks which can be extended beyond the park boundaries. The lowest lake and cascade are accessible by a surfaced path from Aberdare centre even to those in wheelchairs, whereas parts of the upper trails are steep and for the energetic. Camping and caravanning are permitted and visitors may bring their own boats to the top lake, stocked with brown and rainbow trout (day fishing permits available). There is already an adventure play area and a barbecue site beside the park visitor centre, and it is hoped to add a more ambitious adventure centre.

One of the proudest achievements of Dare Valley Country Park is the re-establishment of trees on these despoiled valley sides. As its major gift in Wales to mark Tree Planting Year 1973, the Forestry Commission planted 20,000 trees. These are still small and need to be protected, but already their presence is encouraging the return of wildlife. In due time this part of Dare Valley will be green again.

12 AFAN ARGOED
West Glamorgan CC 140 acres
(56½ hectares)

5 miles (8km) NE of Port Talbot on A4107 (signs to the entrance) at SS 821951. Accessible by bus. The park is freely open all daylight hours. Countryside Centre and Miners' Museum normally open April to 31 October, 10.30–18.00, and at winter weekends, 12.00–17.00. Refreshments normally available during the summer, 11.00–18.30.

The Afan Valley will surprise those who retain the conventional view of collieries, tip heaps and industrial squalor as typical of South Wales. This is a landscape of streams and steep wooded hillsides rising to high moorland. The country park is jointly managed by West Glamorgan CC and the

A scene in the Miners' Museum at Afan Argoed Country Park in West Glamorgan. *West Glamorgan CC*

Forestry Commission and is almost entirely on Forestry Commission land; this merges into the much more extensive Margam Forest, covering most of the high ground east of Port Talbot. There is already an Afan Valley Scenic Drive leading over to the Rhondda, and a long-distance footpath (Coed Morgannwg Way).

The park facilities include two free car parks, the Countryside Centre (with displays on geology, archaeology, forestry and natural history), a sales and information desk and a refreshment kiosk. There are picnic facilities at the centre and at several other points in the park.

The Welsh Miners' Museum is a very special feature. It was set up by the South Wales Miners Museum Committee and has won the Prince of Wales Museum of the Year Award. Built by men who know the realities of life at the coal face, and incorporating authentic mining equipment, this gives visitors the nearest experience most will ever have of what coal-mining involves.

Afan Argoed has an important educational role. West Glamorgan maintain a school centre and resident teacher and local schools have small conservation plots.

There is a choice of 5 short forest walks, taking in local viewpoints and other interesting features. There are 2 longer forest trails, an orienteering wayfaring course and the hill trek over to Margam

Country Park. The Afan Valley Angling Club control fishing. A diary of events includes guides walks, film shows, temporary exhibitions and a local 'Farm Day'.

13 MARGAM PARK
West Glamorgan CC 794 acres (321½ hectares)

E of Port Talbot on A48 and 2 miles (3km) E of M4, Junction 38. Entrance (signed) at SS 812849. Accessible by bus. The park is open 1 April to 30 September, Tuesday to Sunday (inclusive), 10.30–18.30, and during the rest of the year Wednesday to Sunday, 10.30 until an hour before dusk. Car-parking charge covers internal bus service.

Margam is a large and outstandingly fine country park. The interesting buildings and landscaped grounds are at the W end, about 1 mile from the entrance and car park. The visitor leaves his car (by toilets and a refreshment kiosk) at the SE corner of the park and takes the free bus to the park centre at the castle, or goes on to the orangery (where there is a souvenir shop, refreshments and toilets). Alternatively he can walk along the new spine footpath across the park, with its 500 fallow deer, passing a nature reserve and heronry at Furzehill Pond.

Margam Abbey was founded in 1147 by Robert, Earl of Gloucester, and given to Cistercian monks, who cleared and farmed the surrounding area. What remains of the abbey church is outside the park, but the impressive ruins of the chapter house can be seen. There is also a small ruined medieval chapel on the hillside above. The Mansel family built a fine 16th-century mansion at Margam, of which a fragment survives (the facade of a banqueting house). The real treasure at Margam is the orangery, built between 1786 and 1790 and now restored to its former splendour. Part still contains orange trees, but one section has been converted to provide a setting for receptions and concerts. The castle, a mansion in Tudor Gothic style, was completed in 1840 by Thomas Hopper (who also worked at Carlton House and Windsor Castle). After years of neglect this is now a shell. Restoration demands more money than is currently available, but the interior is being cleared and surveyed.

The deer park and landscaped gardens are as impressive as the buildings. Between the orangery and the castle is a rhododendron avenue, many fine specimen trees, a fish pond and a newly reconstructed cascade. The kitchen garden covers the site of Margam village, now revealed by excavation. Outbuildings here are being converted to provide refreshment facilities. There is boating on the lake, donkey rides and an adventure playground. The deer park provides a whole range of walks: up to the Pulpit viewpoint, to the Iron Age hill fort on Mynydd-y-Castell or beyond the park boundary by long-distance footpath to Afan Argoed Country Park.

14 PORTHKERRY PARK
Vale of Glamorgan BC 225 acres (91 hectares)

Immediately W of the built-up area of Barry. When approaching from N, via A4050 or B4266, turn right at church (sign to park). The road enters the park at ST 099673. The car park, toilets and picnic site are at the W end below the railway viaduct. Accessible for pedestrians from Barry or Porthkerry village. Freely open at all times.

Porthkerry Country Park lies in a most attractive grass-floored valley between steep wooded hillsides. At the W end 2 streams join and flow into the Bristol Channel, through a fine pebble beach, and there are extensive views across the sea to the Quantock Hills and Steep Holme. Cliffs of fossiliferous Jurassic limestone back the beach and provide nesting sites for a variety of birds. This coast is being actively eroded by the sea and the site of Porthkerry Castle is now marked only by offshore rocks. The cliffs and foreshore are designated an SSSI.

The picnic and informal games area adjoin the car park; there is also a pitch-and-putt course. Fishing is available for club members and there is swimming, but from a pebbly beach. Footpaths lead through the woods and up to the cliff top. To the E Cliff Wood is now a Local Nature Reserve. It is an example of natural woodland developed on limestones and beyond the W limit of beechwoods. It is dominated by maple, ash, pendunculate oak and yew trees, and the ground flora includes Lithospernum pur-purocaeruleum. An Iron Age hill fort called the Bulwarks is just outside the W end of the park.

15 COSMESTON
South Glamorgan CC and Vale of Glamorgan BC 220 acres (89 hectares)
Adjoining B4267 on the S outskirts of Penarth. Entrance at ST 180693. Accessible by bus. Freely open at all times.

Cosmeston Castle once stood where this country park is being developed; the first phase was officially opened in September 1978. Although much of the site has been a limestone quarry, with its associated spoil heaps and a refuse tip, it is the natural woodland, aquatic plants and birds which immediately strike the visitor. The main features so far are 2 lakes beside the car park, picnic area and temporary park centre buildings. The E lake has been allocated for active water sports (angling, sailing, rowing, sub aqua, and model boats) but for organised groups. The water is deep and too dangerous for swimming or casual boating. The W lake is primarily for nature conservation; there are 2 bird hides, and day permits are available for coarse fishing.

Newly built pathways thread between and around the lakes. In places these are raised walkways over the rushes, reed mace and wild iris which have colonised the lake borders. Five cygnets and their parents were the main attraction when I arrived. Further reclamation and landscaping is being carried out and a larger area will be open to the public as soon as newly planted trees and grass have been established. A nature trail and bridle paths will be added and it is intended to build a park centre during 1980.

16 PARC CEFN ONN
Cardiff City C 158 acres (64 hectares)
2½ miles (4km) N of Cardiff on the line of the M4. Easiest approach from A469 Cardiff to Caerphilly road. Turn E (sign to park) at the city limits. The M4 is being built across the park entrance and approach roads are being altered. The car park is on the S side of M4 at ST 178837 and the entrance to Parc Cefn Onn will be under the motorway. Open daily 8.30 till sunset. Accessible by train.

The striking ridge of Devonian Sandstones, running E–W behind Cardiff, is the result of an upfold in the rocks which separates the coastal plain from Coal Measures around Caerphilly. Cardiff City owns a large area on the S-facing slopes of this ridge and about ¼ of this has now been designated a country

park. It is a most beautiful wooded valley filled with azaleas, rhododendrons, camellias, magnolias and other shrubs. At its very best in late May and early June, it is an established favourite with Cardiff people (who can reach it by train). The upper section was developed by the former owner, manager of the Taff Vale Railway. The lower section has been planted since 1944 when Cardiff bought the whole property, including the adjoining golf course.

Between the upper section of the park and the golf course is a field for informal games and picnics, with a fine view over Cardiff and the Bristol Channel. Cardiff City Parks Department prepared guides to Cefn Onn and a local nature trail as part of European Conservation Year, 1970. The nature trail starts beside Cefn Onn station, keeping outside the park, and climbs up to the summit of Craig Llanishen (from which there are footpath links to A469). This provides excellent views and is particularly interesting because of the rapid transition from one rock type and associated vegetation to another.

The Forestry Commission maintain a car park and forest walk some 2 miles to the NE at Ebbw Llwyncelyn on the minor road from Lisvane towards Machen.

17 PEN-Y-FAN POND
Gwent CC and Islwyn BC
33 acres (13½ hectares)
N of B4251, the Blackwood to Crumlin road, via the new industrial estate at SO 197006. The park is signed from the centre of Crumlin, and is freely open all daylight hours.

(opposite page) The beautiful gardens at Parc Cefn Onn, above Cardiff and beside the motorway. *Cardiff City Council*

This small pond, surrounded by an area of open heathland, was originally constructed in the 1800s to store water to compensate for that lost from locks on the Crumlin section of the Monmouth canal. The feeder channel from the pond to Crumlin can still be traced for much of the way. The pond itself, on a plateau between the valleys of the Sirhowy and Ebbw Fawr rivers, with extensive views southwards, is the main attraction for visitors. Although it is too small for casual use by dinghy sailors or canoeists, rowing boats can be hired at weekends from May to September (13.00–18.00) and daily in August. Model-boat sailing takes place on weekend mornings (9.00–12.00) throughout the year. Fishing (for permit holders) is allowed from banks around the W section of the pond. Also on the W side of the pond is an area interesting for its ecology. Part is dry heathland with bracken, gorse and heather, and on wet land nearer the pond are rushes, sedges, cotton grass and mosses. There are opportunities to see some of the rarer plants and birds of a moorland habitat. The whole area is good walking terrain and crossed by public footpaths.

The car park and surrounding picnic area are well sited to make the most of the view S across the pond. Refreshments are available at summer weekends (12.00–18.00) and daily in August.

18 TREDEGAR HOUSE
Newport BC 99 acres (40 hectares)
Immediately W of Newport at ST 290852. From A48 and Junction 28 of M4 turn towards Newport to the next roundabout, taking the third exit from this. Follow the signs past a new school and houses to the large free car park at the entrance. The country park is freely open daily 7.00 to dusk. Tours of

Tredegar House, Wednesday to Sunday, every hour 14.15–17.30. Admission charge. Amenity Farm, Wednesday to Sunday 10.30–19.15 and Bank Holidays. Admission charge. Accessible by bus or on foot from Newport.

Newport BC bought Tredegar House and 40 hectares of parkland in 1974 and are developing a whole series of activities on this site.

Tredegar House itself is the major attraction here. The oldest surviving part of the house dates from around 1500, but it is the magnificent baroque NE and NW fronts, built between 1664 and 1674, which so impress the visitor. The Historic Buildings Council have repaired the house and it is now being refurnished to illustrate changes in taste, and the way a country house functioned in past centuries. A natural spring runs through the cellars, brew house and game larder in the oldest part of the building.

Outside is a magnificent stable block, an orangery and fine wrought-iron gates. The Morgan Bar and Café occupy one range of buildings and other outbuildings are being converted to new uses. It is hoped to have displays of certain craft skills here. There is already a collection of farm animals, including old and rare breeds of cattle, sheep, pigs and poultry, an insect house, bird garden and aquarium, an adventure playground and donkey rides for the children.

The surrounding gardens and park are no more than a small part of the original estate. Fine trees and shrubs have survived and there is an oak avenue, the only one remaining from several avenues which formerly radiated from the main house. It is hoped to restore the gardens to show some of

Caldicot Castle in Gwent, showing the motte and twelfth-century keep. *Wales Tourist Board*

the styles of earlier periods. The parkland includes a large lake backed by woods, with a play area and a picnic site. Boats may be hired daily from noon onwards. Fishing is allowed from 7.00 till half an hour after sunset (day and season tickets available) and there is now a caravan site.

19 CALDICOT CASTLE
Gwent CC and Monmouth DC
49 acres (20 hectares)

On the E edge of Caldicot at ST 487885. The approach is signposted from A48 and B4245. From the Severn Bridge (M4) take Exit 22 (for Chepstow) and later turn left on B4245 into Caldicot. Accessible by bus. The car park and picnic area are freely open, daylight hours. The castle and museum are open 1 March to 30 September, Monday to Friday 13.30–17.00; weekends and Bank Holidays 14.30–19.00. Admission charge.

Caldicot Castle stands on a narrow bank of Keuper Sandstones rising above the coastal levels of the Severn Estuary. It has the typical motte and bailey features. The castle (partly 12th century) was given to the public by the Cobb family. The museum in the castle houses a collection of costume, furniture, guns and other items (mainly from the Cobb family). The picnic and informal games areas are in open grassland among fine trees below the castle. Medieval banquets are frequently held in the evenings at the castle (tel Caldicot Park 425 for details).

OTHER SCHEMES
A LOWER LLEIDI RESERVOIR
Welsh National Water Authority

2 miles (3km) N of Llanelli on A476. Car park entrance at SS 031521 on W side of road beside last house on hill up from Felin-foel. Freely open at all times.

The facilities beside 2 reservoirs in this deep wooded valley are not yet complete, but the scheme may be recognised as a country park. The picnic area is beside the car park above the valley, and walks lead down to the waterside. The lower reservoir is popular for canoeing, and fishing is also available. The upper reservoir is stocked with trout and has special facilities for disabled anglers.

B BRYN BACH PARK
Mid Glamorgan and Gwent CCs and other authorities 509 acres (206 hectares)

Between Tredegar and Rhymney, near the A465 Head of the Valleys road. Not yet open to the public and not likely to be fully complete for some years.

A joint committee of 4 local authorities is developing a recreation area on land which has been restored, following opencast coalmining. When completed the scheme will include a large lake, and probably a camp site, golf course, riding trail and facilities for motor sports.

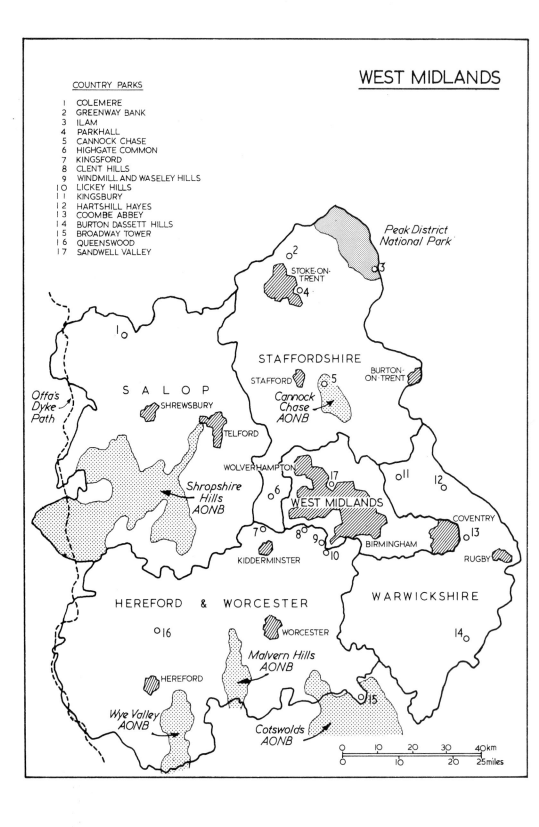

WEST MIDLANDS

COUNTRY PARKS

1 COLEMERE
2 GREENWAY BANK
3 ILAM
4 PARKHALL
5 CANNOCK CHASE
6 HIGHGATE COMMON
7 KINGSFORD
8 CLENT HILLS
9 WINDMILL AND WASELEY HILLS
10 LICKEY HILLS
11 KINGSBURY
12 HARTSHILL HAYES
13 COOMBE ABBEY
14 BURTON DASSETT HILLS
15 BROADWAY TOWER
16 QUEENSWOOD
17 SANDWELL VALLEY

Peak District
National Park

STOKE-ON-TRENT

STAFFORDSHIRE

STAFFORD
BURTON-ON-TRENT

Cannock
Chase
AONB

Offa's
Dyke
Path

SALOP

SHREWSBURY

TELFORD

Shropshire
Hills
AONB

WOLVERHAMPTON

WEST MIDLANDS

COVENTRY

BIRMINGHAM

KIDDERMINSTER

RUGBY

HEREFORD & WORCESTER

WARWICKSHIRE

WORCESTER

HEREFORD

Malvern Hills
AONB

Wye Valley
AONB

Cotswolds
AONB

0   10   20   30   40km
0   10   20   25miles

West Midlands

1 COLEMERE
Salop CC 124 acres (50 hectares)
3 miles (5km) SE of Ellesmere and N of Colemere village. Easiest approach from A528 Ellesmere to Shrewsbury road via minor roads, following signs to Colemere. Bear right at N end of village to car park at SJ 436328. Freely open at all times. No toilets.

Colemere is a quiet spot, approached by minor roads, in the heart of the Shropshire countryside. The mere, which occupies much of the park, is the great attraction. Day permits are available for sailing and fishing, but bathing and camping are not allowed. The picnic site is in an attractive setting beside the lake. There is a nature trail round the mere, and opportunities for extended walks along the Shropshire Union Canal at the N end of the park, or via the footpaths and minor roads which thread the surrounding countryside.

The other aspect of Colemere is its scientific interest. The last glacial period drastically altered the drainage pattern of this part of England. Ice occupied the lowlands of Cheshire and Shropshire, diverting the Severn from its former course N, turning it S to cut the gorge at Ironbridge. When at last this ice melted away it left behind an uneven blanket of glacial drift, in parts clay, but round Ellesmere mainly sands and gravel. The result today is a landscape diversified by small hills and ridges, and pockmarked by hollows containing meres and peat bogs. It is a landscape both visually attractive and scientifically interesting. Ellesmere stands beside the largest mere. At Colemere the water is fringed by trees, and marsh plants have colonised the shoreline. Because of the importance of this bogland vegetation and its associated birdlife, Colemere has been designated an SSSI. It is a fragile environment which needs protection from over-use, and partly because of this the country park is unlikely to be developed further.

2 GREENWAY BANK
Staffs CC 118 acres (49 hectares)
4 miles (6½km) N of Stoke-on-Trent. Approach along A527 turning E on minor road (Bemersley Road), 2 miles (3km) S of Biddulph. Turn left (sign to picnic site) to car park at SJ 890552. Park freely open 10.00–21.00 in summer, 10.00 till dusk October to March. Another pedestrian entrance from Judgefield Lane, E of Knypersley Reservoir at SJ 897548.

Greenway Bank includes part of the valley of the infant Trent on the slopes of Biddulph Moor. (I found it with difficulty, and from the wrong direction, but it is worth discovering.) It is a sheltered oasis on the very edge of Staffordshire industry. There

115

are coal mines immediately to the W; Pennine moorland, where narrow lanes link isolated farms, rises further to the N and E. The car park is in the kitchen garden of the former Greenway Bank House. The shrubbery and lawns have been restored since Staffordshire acquired the site in 1973. A path passes the former croquet lawn and tennis court, now the picnic site, and descends abruptly down steps into a hidden valley. Mature woodland and rhododendrons clothe the valley sides and to the left is the Jubilee Arboretum, a collection of young specimen trees, native or long-established British species. Much of the necessary clearance and replanting has been done by volunteers or through the job-creation scheme.

The path descends to the Serpentine Lake and Knypersley Pool E of this. Knypersley Pool is owned by British Waterways Board and not part of the country park, but a path along its N shore leads into a further section of the park. The Warder's Tower, an estate cottage built in 1828 to enhance the view, may become an information centre. Already there is a nature trail and nesting boxes have been set up; the park is a natural refuge for wildlife. The Head of Trent Valley is a gorge where Millstone Grit outcrops to form cliffs and viewpoints. (The unexpectedly deep valleys here and at Rudyard Lake further E were cut by glacial meltwaters.)

Both the Serpentine Lake and Knypersley Pool are reservoirs, built to supply water to the Trent and Mersey Canal.

3 ILAM

National Trust 140 acres (56½ hectares)
6 miles (9½km) NW of Ashbourne. Easiest approach from A515 N of Ashbourne. Turn W following signs to Thorpe Cloud and continue to park entrance in Ilam village at SK 134508. Alternative route from A52, turn N near Carltonmoor House (SK 117487) towards Blore and later turn left to Ilam. Park freely open always; information room and shop open daily Easter to 31 October, 10.00–18.00, and weekends in winter.

Ilam stands close to the junction of the Dove and Manifold valleys at the S limit of Peak District National Park, and has long been recognised for its beauty. The Ilam estate was given to the National Trust in 1934 by Sir Robert McDougall, and is only a small part of the total acreage in the Dove and Manifold valleys acquired through voluntary effort and administered by the trust. The National Trust also own Bunster Hill, extending NE from Ilam village to the river Dove.

Ilam is an ancient settlement; the church font and crosses in the churchyard probably date from the 11th century, and a stone within the country park is believed to commemorate a battle between the Danes and Saxons. The present Ilam Hall was built in 1821, and though part of the building had to be demolished in the 1930s, what remains has been a youth hostel since 1934. The National Trust information room, shop and café occupy part of the buildings and there is a magnificent view towards Thorpe Cloud from terraces outside.

Both the Dove and Manifold rivers have cut deep winding valleys. The meadows and wooded valley sides are in sharp contrast to the harsher upland landscape, with its outcrops of grey and white limestone. The water of the Manifold disappears through fissures in the limestone and flows underground for 5 miles (8km), to reappear in the celebrated Boil Holes within the country park. The Paradise Walk nature trail takes in these features, with parts of the former landscaped gardens, and crosses the ridge and furrow of one of Ilam's medieval open fields. Part of this area is now a caravan site (tel Thorpe Cloud 310 for bookings). There is also a camping site for tents available during the summer.

4 PARKHALL
Stoke City C and Staffs CC
368 acres (149 hectares)
At Weston Coyney E of Stoke. Not yet fully open to the public. Entrances will be at Weston Coyney from A520 Leek to Stone road and from B5040 near SJ 932440. Part of the park is expected to open in 1980.

Parkhall is an ambitious scheme of land reclamation and country park construction, being undertaken jointly by the county and Stoke City councils. This higher land on the edge of Stoke was heathland similar to Cannock Chase, and used as a deer park before the 17th century. It then passed into agricultural use, until in the 19th century coal-mining and sandstone-quarrying were developed. However it was the gravel-working and rubbish-tipping after 1939 which effectively despoiled the site. Mineral extraction ceased in 1970 and 2 years later the decision was taken to purchase the necessary land and start work.

Earth-moving, draining and reseeding has now been completed and part of the park will be opened as soon as the new vegetation is sufficiently established. There are picnic sites and separate walking and riding routes leading to hilltop view points. The longer term aim of the councils is to develop a golf course along the W side of the park, and to provide a restaurant and permanent visitor centre.

5 CANNOCK CHASE
Staffs CC 2,688 acres (1,088 hectares)
Between Stafford, Rugeley and Cannock. Accessible at many points. Popular centres at N end off A513: Milford Common at SJ 973212, and Seven Springs at SK 004206. Various centres at S end accessible from Penkridge Bank (Rugeley to Penkridge Road) or from Rugeley to Cannock road (now A460, formerly B5013). Also accessible from A34 and A51. Freely open at all times. Accessible by bus.

In terms of the area of the country park, this is the second largest in Britain, but in terms of what is generally understood as Cannock Chase (and now designated an AONB) this is very much the largest publicly accessible recreation area of its kind. The main part of the country park is a triangular area at the NW of the Chase, bounded by Milford, Seven Springs and the Military Cemetery, Broadhurst Green. In addition there are 2 small areas on the Penkridge Bank road, and an extensive area on Brindley Heath, near Hednesford. E of this are the extensive Forestry Commission plantations, and to the N is the National Trust property at Shugborough Hall.

Within a 20-mile radius live 3½ million people, for whom Cannock Chase represents a vital recreation area. Because of its popularity and accessibility, parts of the Chase have become damaged by over-use, a situation made more serious by the fact that some parts are of great scientific importance and designated SSSI. In an attempt to minimise environmental damage, Staffordshire CC created a motorless zone. Because Cannock Chase represents a classic case of the need to reconcile the competing demands of recreation and conservation, the Countryside Commission and the council have been undertaking extensive research and a plan for the future development of the country park has now been agreed.

The appeal of Cannock Chase is its varied and hilly scenery, its approximation to a wilderness. There is heathland, ancient oakwood, boggy hollows and grassland grazed by deer. Much has a gravelly subsoil underlain by Bunter Pebble Beds, but Coal Measures underlie the SE sector. This was once part of a great royal hunting forest. When Edward I sold his rights to the Bishop of Lichfield in 1290, the area was freed from Forest Law and so became a chase. Much of the original forest was later cut to make charcoal, and deer and other grazing animals prevented its regeneration. Very large areas

were enclosed 100 years ago, and the great Forestry Commission plantations were mainly established between 1920 and 1950.

The new country park plan calls for zoned development. To the N, around the popular sites at Milford Common and Seven Springs, recreational needs will predominate. The landscape will be improved by repairing erosion damage. The use of some car parks and tracks will be rotated to reduce wear. A new area in Milford Quarry will be added to what is already accessible. There will also be improvements and additional facilities at the S end (Anson's Bank, the Military Cemetery and Penkridge Bank areas). At Brindley Heath new facilities and additional land will be provided. It is hoped

Cannock Chase in Staffordshire, looking down on the very popular parking and picnic site at Milford Common. Two problems are illustrated here: soil and vegetation have been worn away below the conifer in the foreground, preventing the natural regeneration of the vegetation, and a car just visible to the left of the tree has somehow escaped into the motorless zone.

to develop an information centre, refreshment facilities, nature trails, a camping site and space for events off Marquis Drive at SK 004155.

Between these 2 zones the emphasis will be on conservation. Visitors will still be able to enter this zone, but the opportunities for car-parking will be reduced, and a number of tracks will be closed to vehicles. Anyone who wants to enjoy Cannock Chase to the full should get the map (scale 1:25,000) which is published by the County Planning Department.

The separate Forestry Commission facilities are available at the Forest Centre (just off Penkridge Bank SW of Rugeley at SK 017169). There are deer and forestry museums, much used by schools, and waymarked trails. Permits are available for fishing in Beaudesert Pool or to use the observation tower to study wildlife (tel Rugeley 2035 for bookings). The Forest Centre is open Monday to Friday, 8.00–16.00.

The Shugborough estate is owned by the National Trust but managed by the county council. From the main entrance (off A513 E of Milford) visitors drive through the fine park, past unusual classical monuments, towards the hall and gardens beside the Trent. This was the ancestral home of the Earls of Lichfield and is now the county museum. The hall contains a collection of 18th-century paintings, furniture, silver and porcelain. The outbuildings house a National Trust shop and café, and collections of coaches and farm equipment. The home farm is being developed as an agricultural museum. Shugborough is closed on Mondays but otherwise open in the main season, weekends 14.00–18.00, other days 10.30–17.30, and for more limited hours in winter.

6 HIGHGATE COMMON
Staffs CC 283 acres (114½ hectares)

N of Kidderminster and 2 miles (3km) W of Kingswinford. Crossed by minor roads between Swindon, Enville and Halfpenny Green. From Swindon cross river Stour and later fork right towards Halfpenny Green Airfield. The first parking area is at SO 842900. Freely open at all times.

Highgate Common is an extensive area of open countryside ideal for walking, riding, kite-flying or picnics. There are stretches of heather and bracken, grassy glades, scattered woodland and a small conifer plantation. The views are mainly S towards similar, but much better known heathlands on Kinver Edge. At Highgate Common the appeal is quiet countryside. Signs indicate a number of separate parking areas on the common; the warden's hut and toilet block are near the SW corner. The land has remained unenclosed largely because of the poverty of its acid soils. Bunter Sandstones underlie the area, but are here covered by patches of sands and gravels, a legacy from the last Ice Age.

7 KINGSFORD
Hereford and Worcs CC, Staffs CC
215 acres (87 hectares)

Immediately S of Kinver Edge and 1½ miles (2km) NW of Wolverley. S approach from B4189 following signs to the country park. N approach via Kinver village along either Blakeshall Lane or Kingsford Lane, SW of village. Freely open at all times. Bus access to Kinver.

Kingsford Country Park has been open since 1972, and lies immediately S of the larger area of National Trust land on Kinver Edge in Staffordshire. Plans are now being made for unified management of the whole area (about 495 acres, or 200 hectares), and pending this, no published material is available on facilities. Kinver Edge is a W-facing escarpment; just to the W a major fault brings older rocks (Coal Measures, Devonian and Silurian rocks) to the surface, but the cliffs of Kinver and Kingsford are formed of Bunter Sandstones. In the past these sandstones were excavated to form rock-hewn homes. Heathland, developed on poor acid soils, covers the higher parts, and much of this has been designated an SSSI because of its botanical, ornithological and geological interest. It is also a very popular recreation area.

Most of Kingsford Country Park is wooded—birch and aspen on the sandy parts, and larch, pine and other hardwoods elsewhere. There is a picnic area and camping site near a stream beside Kingsford Lane at SO 823820. A nature trail for the disabled has been set up here. Information boards indicate other woodland walks and a riding trail. In Blakeshall Lane, on the E side of the country park, there are more facilities and car-parking. The National Trust warden's house is also in Blakeshall Lane at SO 838828.

8 CLENT HILLS
Hereford and Worcs CC
371 acres (150 hectares)

3½ miles (5½km) SW of Halesowen. Adam's Hill car park SO 927798 (on W side) is off A491 or can be approached from A456 by turning S at Hagley. Walton Hill car park SO 943803 (on E side), best approached from A456 by turning S at Hayley Green on edge of Halesowen. Freely open at all times. Accessible by bus.

Considering the popularity of Clent Hills with West Midlands residents, it is surprising how well the rural character of these pronounced summits has been preserved. The hills rise to around 1,000ft (305m) and owe their prominence to the resistant rocks, the Clent Breccias, of which they are composed. This formation consists of angular rock fragments in a marly matrix and coated with haematite (from which the soil derives its red colour). This was apparently a scree deposit formed in desert conditions and dating from late Carboniferous times, but the rock fragments are often from very ancient formations. The open hillsides and commons are almost entirely owned by the National Trust. Grassland, bracken and gorse cover most slopes, with scattered trees and some natural regeneration of oak. There is also some woodland.

About 500,000 visitors come to the hills each year, and the main paths and tracks have become eroded in places. Efforts are now being made to restore this damage, and to limit potential conflict between horse riders and walkers. The development of a car park, picnic area and toilets N of Walton Hill should help to reduce pressure on the Adam's Hill site. Another car park is planned at Nimmings Plantation, and it is intended to provide a refreshment kiosk and picnic facilities here.

The appeal of Clent Hills remains what it has been for many years: most attractive open hillsides suitable for walking and riding, and with excellent views extending both W to the Welsh border and E over the Midlands. The W summit has a topographical indicator, and there are also 4 standing stones. These were set up in the 18th century by George Lyttleton, owner of Hagley Hall below.

9 WINDMILL AND WASELEY HILLS
Hereford and Worcs CC
141 acres (57 hectares)

NW of Rubery and 8 miles (13km) SW of Birmingham. S entrance, approach from A38 (from Birmingham fork left and turn right over A38) to park entrance at SO 979768. N entrance near Gannow Green Farm at SO 972783. Best approached from A459 turning E at Dayhouse Farm and crossing over M5. Freely open at all times. Accessible by bus.

These 2 hills lie between the better-known summits of the Clent and Lickey Hills, and are in many ways similar. The hills rise to over 900ft (274m) and a third of the land here is leased from the National Trust. The main difference between them is that the Waseley Hills have remained in agricultural use and are still grazed by cattle. The hillsides are predominantly grass-covered, with some gorse and newly planted trees to provide shelter. Segbourne Coppice, on the W side, has greater ecological interest, and bluebells are a particular attraction here in spring.

The N section of the park was developed first. Here, close to M5, is a picnic site, information board and toilets. Footpaths lead up to the summit, and here there is a topographical indicator which helps to interpret the extensive view. The E slope has been set aside for snow sports. The river Rea, which flows through Birmingham, rises in a spring close to the motorway. Facilities situated beside the southern car park should now be similar to those at the N end and are to include a camping area. There are also paths and bridleways. It is possible to drive from one end of the park to the other, but the route is a complicated one through Rubery housing estates.

10 LICKEY HILLS
City of Birmingham BC 526 acres
(213 hectares)

8 miles (13km) SW of Birmingham. Crossed by B4120 SW of Longbridge. For Beacon Hill, turn N from B4120 at war memorial to main car park at SO 986758 in Monument Lane. Freely open at all times. Accessible by bus.

The Lickey Hills became a country park in 1971, but they have been Birmingham's most readily accessible countryside since the first section was opened to the public in 1887. The hills are probably less visited now than when the trams ran. Over 40 per cent of this extensive area was given to the city by the Cadbury family; the rest was purchased from the Earl of Plymouth. The obelisk in Monument Lane (now a scheduled Ancient Monument), a survival from the former estate, was erected in 1834 to the memory of the 6th Earl by his fellow officers.

As at Clent and Waseley Hills, the main attraction is the space to walk and ride, and the views. There is a topographical indicator on Beacon Hill, and apart from a panorama of the Birmingham area, the view extends westward to the Welsh border. Beacon Hill rises to 987ft (300m) and is formed from the same breccia (angular rock fragments cemented together) as the Clent Hills. However much older rocks form the steep slopes on the E side. At Rednal Hill the rock is mainly a grey-white quartzite of Cambrian age, while at Barnt Green there are even older volcanic rocks comparable to those of Charnwood Forest.

The 2 main centres of the country park are Beacon Hill and the Rose and Crown, on Old Birmingham Road (B4120). The Rose and Crown, now a municipally owned licensed restaurant, was formerly a coaching inn; extra horses were kept here to pull heavy loads up the steep climb. The 18-hole public golf course lies behind, and a refreshment kiosk. A children's nature trail descends from Beacon Hill through woodland and past pools in the small valley of the Arrow River. This has been planted with bulbs and flowering shrubs. Boating is available on a small pond, and any snowfall brings out the winter sports enthusiasts.

11 KINGSBURY
Warwicks CC 447 acres (181 hectares) at present

Between Coleshill and Tamworth, W of A51 and Kingsbury village. Approach along A4097 (the Marston bypass), turning N at roundabout through Marston and along Bodymoor Heath Lane to main entrance at SP 203958. Freely open daylight hours. Accessible by bus.

By repute, Kingsbury was the site of the palace of the Kings of Mercia, but the interest of the country park is entirely contemporary. This was farmland beside the river Tame until gravel extraction began some 40 years ago. Gravel is still being worked on the site, but as operations cease, more land will be restored and added to the park. One uncertainty concerns the construction of M42, which is likely to form the NW boundary of the park.

The first phase of the park was opened in 1975 and is centred on a range of water-based activities. A good starting point is the display centre beside the main entrance. This shows the layout of the park, explains something of the processes of gravel extraction and problems of pollution, and indicates the range of wildlife already established here. The large number of lakes

Kingsbury Water Park, near Tamworth, an excellent example of what can be created on the site of former gravel pits. *Warwickshire CC*

and pools have been adapted for different uses. The largest is used on alternate days by Tamworth Sailing Club and Midlands Hydroplane Club. Public fishing is available here and in nearby Willows Pool. (Day tickets are available by automatic machine near the park entrance.) Other pools are reserved for model-boat sailing, public launching of canoes and inflatable craft, or for private fishing. Part of the area is now a nature reserve and wildlife refuge, with hides for bird-watching. Extensive grassland areas are available for picnics and informal games, or for spectators interested in watersports. There is an adventure playground for children and a pitch-and-putt course. An area is set aside for special events. There are waymarked walks within the park, and public paths lead beyond its boundaries to Kingsbury Church and 15th-century hall, or the 18th-century Hemlingford Bridge.

12 HARTSHILL HAYES
Warwicks CC 22 acres (9 hectares)
4 miles (6½km) NW of Nuneaton. From A47 Birmingham to Nuneaton road turn N into Hartshill, and left (at sign) into Oldbury Road, opposite the school. Park entrance at SP 317943. Freely open daylight hours. Accessible by bus.

At Hartshill the country park proper is a small area, but visitors have access along waymarked footpaths into the Forestry Commission woodland adjoining (a further 114 acres, or 46 hectares). The picnic site is in open grassland on a ridge, with fine views extending into Derbyshire and Charnwood Forest.

The pronounced Hartshill Ridge, which rises to 555ft (170m) is interesting on several counts. A sharp upfold has brought ancient rocks to the surface here. A narrow belt of Coal Measures is responsible for the mining to the SW. The country park, the plantation and the newer sections of the village lie on top of rocks of Cambrian age, the Stockingford Shales, into which igneous rocks have been intruded. Hartshill Green lies on Hartshill Quartzite, a pinkish-grey rock of Cambrian age, and this (like the igneous rocks) is extensively quarried for roadstone. Beyond a major fault (roughly along the line of the Coventry Canal) the Anker Valley is developed on Keuper Marls. The strategic importance of this ridge can be judged from the siting of an Iron Age hill fort here. (Oldbury Camp lies on private land close to the country park.) The Roman settlement here was close to Watling Street, and the site of the Roman pottery kilns E of the village, near Home Farm. In Saxon times a nunnery was built on the ridge, and now water is stored for Nuneaton in a covered reservoir.

On the slopes of the ridge has been preserved what is believed to be a remnant of the ancient Forest of Arden, now within the Forestry Commission plantations. Much of this woodland was replanted in the 18th century. In the past the trees were regularly coppiced, cut to ground level to stimulate new growth. The lime trees provided wood to make hat-blocks for the Atherstone hat-makers. Visitors will enjoy the many birds, and the bluebells and honeysuckle of the more open parts of the woods.

13 COOMBE ABBEY
City of Coventry C 289 acres (117 hectares)
4 miles (6½km) E of Coventry on A4114 Coventry to Lutterworth road. Main entrance at SP 404791. Freely open daily 7.30 till 30 minutes after sunset. Accessible by bus.

Coombe Abbey is a fine estate and an important recreation complex. The abbey was founded by Cistercian monks in 1150, and some parts of the monastic fabric have been incorporated in later buildings. The essential character of the house and grounds dates from the 3 centuries when this was the home of the Craven family. Coventry City Council bought the abbey and its lands over a period, and it was finally opened to the public in 1966. It became a country park in 1971, and has now been restored to something of its former magnificence.

The fine avenue leading towards the abbey is a fitting prelude to the deer park and grounds landscaped by Capability Brown. The large lake is now restored and contributes to the beauty of gardens beside the abbey buildings. Visitors can hire rowing boats or take a motor-launch trip, and tickets are available for fishing. There are many fine trees, including magnificent sequoias, and extensive grassland areas for picnics and informal games. There is a collection of birds and animals (for which a separate charge is made), a woodland walk, and well-signed footpaths and bridleways. The courtyards and outbuildings have been adapted to provide a children's playground, paddling pool and model-boating pool, and there is a café and gift shop. The abbey itself is not yet open to visitors, apart from the 'medieval banquets' held there (tel Coventry 452406 for details). Coombe Court can be hired for special events or is available as shelter in poor weather. It is hoped later to add camping facilities and a golf course.

14 BURTON DASSETT HILLS
Warwicks CC 91 acres (37 hectares)
8 miles (13km) SE of Warwick among minor roads between A41 Warwick to Banbury and A423 Coventry to Banbury roads. Easiest approach from A41, turn E towards Burton Dassett village and follow signs to the park. Main centre at SP 397519. Open always (a public road runs through).

Burton Dassett Hills stand out prominently from the relatively flat Warwickshire farmland which surrounds them, and in consequence provide much wider views than their mere height might suggest. A band of resistant Marlstone is responsible, and has led in turn to quarrying for iron ore at various times over the last 100 years. This spur of highland with its three grass-covered knolls was for centuries the site of a beacon, and this must surely have been used when the first battle of the Civil War was fought in 1642 at Edge Hill, a short distance further S. The Beacon Tower is a scheduled Ancient Monument, erected in the late 14th century, but may have supported a windmill rather than a beacon. Several windmills have stood on these hills; the last was blown down in 1946.

The name Burton Dassett is Saxon (Dercetone meant the abode of wild beasts) and in 1908 a Saxon burial place containing 35 skeletons was found on Pleasant Hill. The hills are grazed by sheep and cattle and may well have been so ever since Sir Edward Belknap gained permission from Henry VII to evict 60 tenants and enclose 600 acres for sheep. Because this is a good example of unimproved hill pasture and has also the botanically rich disused quarries, it was designated an SSSI in 1973. A nature trail illustrates the main features.

Burton Dassett Hills have been a popular area with the public for many years, both for the view and as a place to picnic, and the old quarries provide a natural adventure playground.

15 BROADWAY TOWER
Batsford Estate Co 35 acres (14 hectares)

Off A44 Evesham to Moreton-in-the-Marsh road on the Cotswold crest above Broadway. The signed approach road turns off almost opposite Fish Hill picnic site. Accessible by footpath direct from Broadway. Park entrance at SP 114360 is open daily 10.00–18.00 from 31 March to 1 October. Admission charge. This is a private park (tel Broadway 2390).

The great feature here is the beautiful setting on the crest of the Cotswolds. There is a magnificent view extending into Wales. The park centre and café is an attractive Cotswold stone building. Tower Barn (rescued and rebuilt from a site further down the escarpment) is being developed as a natural history centre. With neighbouring enclosures, this will feature animals and birds native to the Cotswolds and bred on site. It is intended to have fallow, roe and red deer and a collection of machinery formerly used on local farms.

The tower itself is an 18th-century folly, worth climbing for the views and with furnished period rooms. There is an attractively landscaped picnic and children's play area. Waymarked walks and a nature trail lead into woodland on the Cotswold summit. There is also a programme of guided walks, and Broadway Tower is on the Cotswold Way long-distance footpath.

16 QUEENSWOOD
Hereford and Worcester CC 170 acres (69 hectares)

On A49 between Hereford and Leominster. Car park beside the café at the summit of Dinmore Hill, just S of Hope under Dinmore, on W side of A49 at SO 507515. Freely open at all times.

Dinmore Hill is a striking wooded ridge, rising above attractive Herefordshire countryside, and the deep valley of the river Lugg. The woodland here was bought by public subscription in 1935, to commemorate the Jubilee of King George V. Half the area is natural woodland, mainly oak and birch, and carpeted by wild flowers. The remainder has been managed as an arboretum since 1945, and now contains more than 400 tree species. These woodlands are especially attractive in spring and autumn. Woodland walks have now been established, and these lead through to a viewpoint and toposcope on the further edge of the woods.

17 SANDWELL VALLEY
Sandwell Met BC 94 acres (38 hectares)
E of West Bromwich adjoining M5. Approach Swan Pool car park at SP 027923 from Newton Road (A4041) via Forge Lane. Freely open always; also accessible from W and S and by bus.

There are facilities for watersports, riding and refreshments, and a nature trail among woods and lakes where a priory once stood. This is part of a wider scheme to provide for a complete range of sports on farmland and reclaimed sites.

OTHER SCHEMES
Warwicks CC had intended to develop a country park at Draycote Water (adjoining A426, 4 miles or 6½km SW of Rugby). The reservoir itself is still not open to the public, but the picnic site on Hensborough Hill provides an ideal vantage point for watching sailing races on Draycote Water.

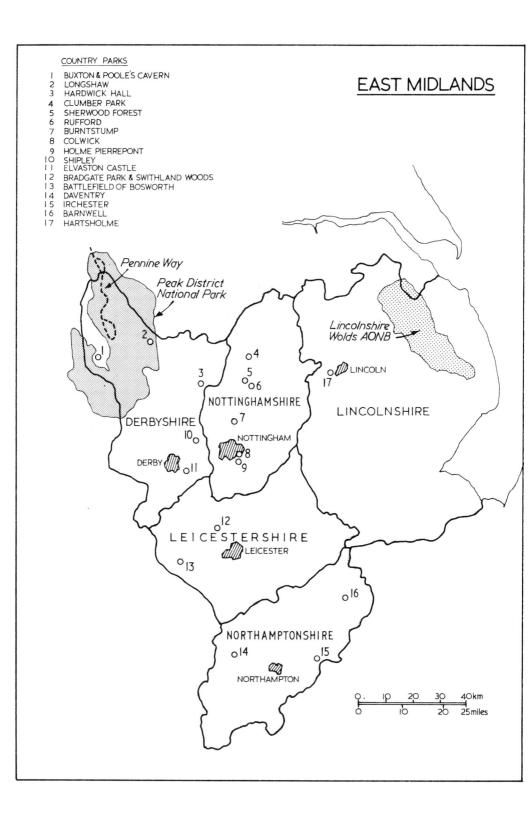

COUNTRY PARKS

1 BUXTON & POOLE'S CAVERN
2 LONGSHAW
3 HARDWICK HALL
4 CLUMBER PARK
5 SHERWOOD FOREST
6 RUFFORD
7 BURNTSTUMP
8 COLWICK
9 HOLME PIERREPONT
10 SHIPLEY
11 ELVASTON CASTLE
12 BRADGATE PARK & SWITHLAND WOODS
13 BATTLEFIELD OF BOSWORTH
14 DAVENTRY
15 IRCHESTER
16 BARNWELL
17 HARTSHOLME

EAST MIDLANDS

Pennine Way

Peak District
National Park

Lincolnshire
Wolds AONB

LINCOLN

LINCOLNSHIRE

NOTTINGHAMSHIRE

DERBYSHIRE

NOTTINGHAM

DERBY

LEICESTERSHIRE

LEICESTER

NORTHAMPTONSHIRE

NORTHAMPTON

0 10 20 30 40km
0 10 20 25miles

East Midlands

1 BUXTON COUNTRY PARK AND POOLE'S CAVERN
Buxton and District Civic Association
99 acres (40 hectares)

On the SW edge of Buxton and well signed from all main roads. Entrance in Green Lane at SK 050727. Country park freely open at all times. Poole's Cavern open Easter to late autumn, daily except Wednesday, 10.00–17.00. Admission charge (tel Buxton 6978). Accessible by bus and on foot from Buxton.

Buxton Country Park is unique on two counts: it centres on a show cave and it is managed by an amenity society. In this project the Buxton and District Civic Association were helped by the Countryside Commission, the Carnegie Trust and the county and borough councils, while the Duke of Devonshire gave Grin Low Wood. As a result of this initiative Poole's Cavern was reopened to the public in 1976. It is a very good example of a cave formed by the action of water on Carboniferous Limestone. The Wye flows through part of the cave and there are particularly fine stalactites and stalagmites, often coloured by the presence of minerals. Prehistoric man lived in the cave and it was visited by Roman soldiers. Mary Queen of Scots named one of the pillars on her visit in 1582 and, among many others, Dr Johnson wrote about it. At the cave entrance is a café and shop, and an interpretative centre with displays and an audio-visual programme about the cave and its surroundings. Special arrangements can be made for school visits, and the caverns are accessible to those in wheelchairs.

The wooded hillside above and around the cave is well worth exploring, and the whole area is designated an SSSI. The woods were originally planted on Grin Low to disguise the scars of quarrying and lime-burning. Now this mixed woodland has a rich ground flora and includes a number of rare species, orchids, hellebore, globeflower and mountain pansy among others. A nature trail and footpaths lead up from the car park and picnic site through the wood on to the open ridge beside Grin Low Tower. From this folly there is a panoramic view over the whole district.

2 LONGSHAW
National Trust 1,360 acres
(550½ hectares)

9 miles (14km) SW of Sheffield and bounded by A625, B6055 and B6054; it is crossed by A6011. The park centre at Longshaw Lodge is best approached by turning S along B6055 from Fox House Inn (on A625). The Woodcroft car park is on the right at SK 267800. Paths suitable for wheelchairs lead down to the centre. Additional car parks on A625 at Hollow Gate (SK 253802), and on B6054 at Sheffield Plantation (SK 267789) and near Grouse Inn (SK 257776). Also

accessible from Upper and Nether Padley and Froggatt. Freely open at all times. Accessible by bus and train (Grindleford Station).

Longshaw is an established favourite with walkers and climbers. This extensive area of open moorland, woodland and valley farms in Peak District National Park was once the Duke of Rutland's grouse-shooting estate. Following the sale of the land in 1927, far-sighted benefactors gave much of the estate to the National Trust to protect it from development and provide public access to open countryside. Further land has recently been bought. The provision of suitably landscaped car parks at key points makes this not only an admirable base for a whole series of hill walks, with rock climbing on Froggatt Edge, but also a place to picnic in full view of some of the best Peak District scenery.

In this landscape rock predominates: the gritstones and Rough Rock of the Millstone Grit Series. Solid-stone buildings, stone walls, old quarries and rough-hewn millstones scatter the higher moorland. The lower valley sides are green and soft by comparison.

The National Trust information centre and shop, a café and toilets are in Longshaw Lodge. A nature trail has been laid out and there are opportunities for riding.

(opposite page) A disabled fisherman in Hardwick Hall Country Park in Derbyshire. In this case there are no special facilities for the disabled, but many parks do make special provision, including platforms to make fishing easier from a wheelchair. Bess of Hardwick's great house crowns the escarpment behind the country park, and is separately open to the public.

3 HARDWICK HALL, Derbyshire
National Trust 250 acres
(101 hectares)

5 miles (8km) NW of Mansfield, beside M1. From M1 Junction 29 take A617 towards Chesterfield and follow signs, turning left on to B6040 into Heath village and left again on minor road to park entrance at SK 453640, just beyond motorway underpass. Park freely open daylight hours throughout the year. Hardwick Hall (separate signed entrance) open 1 April to 31 October, 13.00–17.30 Wednesday, Thursday, Saturday, Sunday and Bank Holiday Mondays. Admission charge. Gardens open 1 April to 31 October daily. Admission charge.

The celebrated hall, built by Bess of Hardwick between 1591 and 1597, crowns the summit of an escarpment. The country park consists of the W-facing slopes below, and does not include the hall and gardens. It is worth exploring in its own right, but most first-time visitors will wish to see the hall and gardens as well. A small information centre at the country-park entrance directs visitors to the main points of interest. The outcrop of Magnesium Limestone which forms the escarpment above has been quarried to provide building stone for the hall. A nature trail passes the 400-year-old Hardwick Oak and the Miller's Pond, and climbs up through fields and parkland. There are herds of an ancient breed of sheep and Longhorn cattle. An ice house and group of fishponds are reminders of former methods of providing a regular food supply. Part of the lower ground is a wildlife refuge, and there are waterside picnic areas. Day permits are available for coarse fishing and visitors may launch their own canoes and boats (with permission). Despite the ever-present hum of the motorway, this is an extensive area of open countryside. Refreshments are available nearby at the Hardwick Inn. The ruins of the Old Hall stand on the hilltop beside the splendid Elizabethan house.

4 CLUMBER PARK
National Trust 3,147 acres (1,273½ hectares)

5 miles (8km) SE of Worksop. Main entrance (Apleyhead Lodge) at SK 645773, signed from A614 immediately S of the junction with A1. Other entrances on W side of park, and from A614 at Normanton Inn, SK 649746. Freely open daylight hours. Chapel open 1 April to 30 September, weekends and Bank Holidays, 12.00–19.00, Monday to Friday, 14.00–19.00.

Clumber Park is the largest and most northerly of those in Sherwood Forest. Its walls enclose a great rectangle of park, meadow, heath and woodland, with Clumber Lake at its heart. To get the full flavour, drive through the classical screen at Apleyhead Lodge and along the famous Duke's Drive, a double avenue of lime trees 2 miles long. Turn left towards the chapel and lake, passing the National Trust information centre and shop. It is an anticlimax to find no great house (it was dismantled in 1938) but the fine stable block and outbuildings provide refreshment facilities and a cycle-hire scheme.

Clumber House was built in 1770 as the new home of the Dukes of Newcastle. The opulence of the house in its heyday can be judged from pictures. Today's visitors can picnic where the balustraded terraces and marble fountain once stood, and can enjoy the view across the lake. The chapel, built in the 1880s, is a fine example of Victorian Gothic, and looks best across the lake from the classical bridge at the W end.

The magnificence of Clumber Park is entirely man-made. Until well after 1700 the area was a wild heathland (it is underlain by the Bunter Pebble Beds), crossed by an insignificant river. Capability Brown undertook the landscaping of the park, a scheme which involved damming the river to create a lake and planting millions of trees. (The lime trees of Duke's Avenue were planted 50 years after the main layout was complete.)

The variety of scenery within Clumber Park and its size encourage exploration, and hiring a cycle adds to the possibilities: this can be done from Easter to mid-September, 13.00–18.00 on weekdays, 11.00–18.00 Sundays and Bank Holidays. At peak times there is also a ferry across the lake, where the large numbers of water birds emphasise Clumber's role as a wildlife sanctuary. There are 2 nature trails: the longer starts from the National Trust information centre, the second on South Lawns passes a classical temple above the lake.

5 SHERWOOD FOREST
Notts CC 500 acres (202½ hectares)

On B6034 immediately N of Edwinstowe. The visitor centre entrance is at SK 627677. Park freely open daylight hours. Facilities at the visitor centre open during the main season, daily from 11.00–17.30 (19.00 on Sundays). Spring and autumn daily except Mondays, 11.00–17.00, and limited times at winter weekends (tel Mansfield 823202 for details). Accessible by bus.

The name alone is enough to make Sherwood Forest one of our most popular country parks. Some 300,000 visitors come each year and the problems this can create are discussed elsewhere. Whatever may be

The famous oak tree in Sherwood Forest Country Park, and a reminder of the need to protect it. *Nottinghamshire CC*

the truth about Robin Hood (and tradition claims his marriage to Maid Marian took place in neighbouring Edwinstowe church), this surviving fragment of Sherwood Forest is authentic enough. A number of ancient oak trees remain of both the usual British varieties, the pedunculate or English oak and the sessile or durmast oak. The most celebrated, the Major Oak, has a girth of 32ft 10in (over 10m) and may be 500 years old. Another famous tree (but outside the country park) is the Parliament Oak, where both King John and Edward I are said to have held councils while hunting in the forest. Individual oak and birch trees grow in a tangle of bracken and undergrowth indicative of the wilderness this area has remained for so long. It is now designated an SSSI because it provides an exceptionally rich wildlife habitat. Sherwood Forest Country Park is on land leased from the Thoresby Estate and was considerably extended in 1978 to include Birklands, W of the Major Oak. Visitors more interested in natural history than in possible associations with Robin Hood can explore these less-frequented paths.

The visitor centre will interest everyone. A series of octagonal structures house display areas, an auditorium, a bookshop with an excellent selection of material, and refreshment facilities. A free audio-visual programme on Sherwood Forest is normally shown at weekends (at 15.00 and 16.30) and some other times. There is an exhibition and a regular programme of talks, films, guided walks and other special events, including those organised by the Robin Hood Society (tel Mansfield 823202 for details or to arrange for organised groups).

131

6 RUFFORD

Notts CC 182 acres (73½ hectares)

15 miles (24km) N of Nottingham, near Ollerton and Sherwood Forest Country Park. Main entrance from A614 just S of the junction with B6034 at SK 642648; N entrance (for lake and mill) on minor road running E from A614 towards Wellow at SK 647656. Freely open daylight hours. Accessible by bus.

Rufford is one of a trio of country parks, all interesting and each showing a different facet of the development of that part of Nottinghamshire known for 2 centuries as the Dukeries. As at Clumber, the mansion has suffered more than its outbuildings and park from 20th century social changes, but it is neighbouring Sherwood which provides the best introduction to Rufford Abbey. Enough ancient wood and heathland survives in Sherwood Forest to give some idea how poor and difficult this land once was. Infertile sands cover large areas (the Bunter Pebble Beds of Triassic age), creating an environment improved only with difficulty. At Rufford it was Cistercian monks from Rievaulx in Yorkshire who developed an estate here in the 12th century. Only the shell remains of part of the huge mansion, a composite building from many periods, including parts of the monastic structure.

Since Rufford became a country park in 1969 the surrounding ornamental gardens, parkland and lake have been largely reinstated, following a period of neglect. The lake had been created to supply power to the mill. The attractive mill buildings have now been converted to provide offices and a shop. The lake itself required elaborate restoration following silting and damage due to mining subsidence. Much of the mature timber was sold in World War II and there has been much replanting. Successive generations of the Savile family had landscaped the grounds to meet contemporary tastes and fragments remain from several of these designs. A wildlife sanctuary and new paths have been created. A craft centre with exhibitions, demonstrations, a craft shop and a cafeteria is in the converted stables.

7 BURNTSTUMP

Gedling BC 61 acres (24½ hectares)

7 miles (11km) N of Nottingham between A60 and A614. From A60 turn E along a minor road opposite Seven Mile House. The park entrance (signed) is on the right at SK 573507. Freely open at all times.

This is a small country park almost at the S limit of ancient Sherwood Forest. The name commemorates one ancient tree. From the park entrance a drive leads up to extensive car-parking on the hillside. There is a walk through rhododendrons and woods to the top of Burntstump Hill, beside a sports field, with views W. In the grass-covered valley below is a cricket pitch and space for informal games and picnics.

Immediately NW of this country park are Newstead Abbey (approached from A60) and Papplewick Pumping Station (1 mile W along B6011) with its 2 Boulton & Watt beam engines.

8 COLWICK

Nottingham City C 259 acres (105 hectares)

Immediately E of Nottingham, beside the race course. Approach along B686 following signs to the race course; the entrance is at SK 600391. (The entry for water sports facilities is from Mile End Road, Colwick.) Freely open daylight hours. Accessible by bus.

Colwick Park is a major development by Nottingham with the water authority, the Sports Council and several other organisations but is still incomplete.

The present Colwick Hall dates from 1776 and there has been a manor house on this site since Saxon times. The hall has now been restored as a public house and restaurant beside the main car park and the ruins of St John the Baptist church. Beyond is a wooded slope leading down to Colwick Hall Pool and a nature reserve. Two new lakes have been constructed for fishing and water sports. Colwick Lake has been stocked with trout, and day and season tickets are available for both trout and coarse fishing.

Dinghy parks, car parks and slipways are being constructed. Sailing, boating and bathing are available on West Lake. A new marina with berths for 200 craft has now been opened.

A riding trail and a network of new footpaths thread the area, and there are picnic sites well placed for viewing both the water sports and the wildlife attracted to these new lakes.

The race course (outside and immediately N of the park) has a programme of major events throughout the year. In addition there is a newly constructed greyhound stadium and a transit caravan site (tel Nottingham 53814 for details).

Colwick Hall in the country park opened by Princess Margaret in 1979, within the Nottingham City boundaries. The hall, built in 1776, has been restored, and overlooks lakes, woodland and a new marina. *Nottingham City Planning Department*

9 HOLME PIERREPONT
Notts CC 300 acres (121½ hectares)

Immediately SE of Nottingham on S side of river Trent. From Trent Bridge turn E along A52, following good signs to entrance at SK 606386. Freely open except during major competitive events (when an admission charge is made). Accessible by bus.

Holme Pierrepont is the National Water Sports Centre and was opened by Edward Heath in 1973. The country park is on land surrounding the 2,000m rowing course and is designed to provide not only a grandstand view for water-sports events, but also facilities for a range of other activities. The Water Sports Centre is run jointly by Notts CC and the Sports Council and has a gymnasium, conference rooms, residential accommodation, etc, in addition to the main rowing course (built to Olympic standards) and a smaller water-ski training area. These facilities are used for practice and training during the week, and there is a programme of spectator events most weekends between early May and late September (tel Nottingham 866301 for details).

The whole complex has been developed on land left derelict by gravel extraction. Over 1 million cubic metres of rock and silt had to be moved when reclamation began in 1970. Material excavated to provide the rowing course was used to landscape the country park, and the result is an attractive series of low hills and grass-covered banks, now partly planted with trees. Two smaller lakes have been left. There is a shop at the park centre, a pets' corner and adventure playground for children, and a trim trail to encourage adults to try something athletic. Horse-riding is allowed on the towpath beside the Trent. Fishing is well catered for; there are day fishing permits and pike-fishing championships take place on the 2,000m lake during the autumn. The nature reserve and lake at the N end attract a variety of waterbirds and there is a hide for bird-watchers. It is hoped to add further facilities and it may later be possible to cross over the river to the country park being developed at Colwick by Nottingham City Council.

10 SHIPLEY
Derbys CC 815 acres (330 hectares)

Between Heanor and Ilkeston. Country park main entrance signed from A608 in Heanor to car park at SK 426458. Another entrance at Woodside SK 447446, direct from A6007 (later to be the main Britannia Park entrance). For Mapperley Reservoir turn off A609 at sign to Mapperley village and continue downhill to entrance at SK 435433. Visitors may not drive across the park but there are special arrangements for the disabled. Freely open at all times. Accessible by bus.

Shipley Country Park is an ambitious scheme and unlikely to be complete for some years. Derbyshire CC is hoping to create a regional leisure centre to serve both local and regional needs throughout the year. The country park is part of this wider project. The total area to be developed is almost 1,000 acres (400 hectares). The W, rural side is already open as a country park; the E section nearest to Ilkeston is intended as an entertainment complex, to be developed jointly by the council and private enterprise, and called Britannia Park. Facilities for active recreation, such as golf, riding, sailing and water-skiing will be between the two. The E section remains largely undeveloped, although there is already some sailing on Shipley Lake and a riding centre at Lodge Farm.

134

The country park is on the former Shipley Hall estate and includes the prominent Shipley Hill, now tree-covered but formerly the site of the hall and its magnificent gardens. There has been coal-mining here for at least 200 years, and since 1970 the National Coal Board has worked 500 acres (200 hectares) by opencast methods, extracting 1½ million tons of coal in 3 years. The land has been restored; Shipley Lake has been re-created, and reseeding and tree-planting have been extensively carried out. The Heanor entrance leads into recently reclaimed land, crossed by walking and riding trails. There is a picnic site near Osborne's Pond, and a trim trail.

The Mapperley entrance leads to mature woodland near the reservoir and on Shipley Hill. A nature trail (with bird hide) has been laid out round the reservoir, and day fishing permits are available. (A nature reserve managed by Derbyshire Naturalists' Trust, and not open to the public, is further E.) It is intended to develop farmland and Home Farm itself as a farm-interpretation centre. A marked trail features the limited remains of Shipley Hall.

11 ELVASTON CASTLE
Derbys CC 200 acres (81 hectares)

6 miles (9½km) SE of Derby. Main entrance off B5010 Burrowash to Thurlston road, N of Elvaston village at SK 413332. Pedestrian access from Borrowash, Alvaston or the A6 via Golden Gates. Parkland freely open all year. Park centre open daily, Easter to October 12.00–16.00 (10.00–18.00 at summer weekends). Disabled drivers may park at the castle. Accessible by bus.

Elvaston Castle was one of the first country parks to be opened and it remains one of the best. This is an estate in the grand manner.

Elvaston was for centuries the home of the Stanhope family, the Earls of Harrington (another branch of the same family owned Chevening in Kent). Although the estate suffered a period of neglect before the county acquired it in 1969, it is being carefully restored and managed to allow large numbers of visitors to follow different interests. In essence this country park consists of the castle and its associated buildings (which now include an interpretative centre, a café and shop, and a countryside museum), the particularly interesting gardens and the wilder surrounding parkland.

Throughout the summer the public have access to the information centre, café and shop on the ground floor. (There is also a field-studies centre for schools.) A countryside museum, intended to form an introduction to farming practices on the estate, is being assembled in the outbuildings, and it is intended to develop craft workshops here.

The gardens at Elvaston have long been famous. Capability Brown declined to submit a design, but presented the Cedars of Lebanon which stand E of the castle. It was William Barron from the Edinburgh Botanic Gardens who laid out the grounds. At one time 90 gardeners worked on the estate, and elaborate topiary was a major feature. Visitors today will appreciate the formal garden layout, the Old English, rose and herb gardens, the rhododendron dell and the many fine trees.

Elvaston has its own riding centre where lessons are given (tel Derby 751927). There is a bridle path through the park and a programme of riding events. The county show and other events are also staged here. A site for touring caravanners and campers is open from Easter to October (tel Derby 73735 for details).

12 BRADGATE PARK AND SWITHLAND WOODS

Bradgate Park Trust 1,238 acres (501 hectares)

Bradgate Park main entrance and visitor centre off B5327 in Newtown Lindford village at SK 522098. From M1 Junction 22 follow A50 towards Leicester and then B5327 to Newtown Lindford. Other entrances and car parks at the NW corner (SK 523117) and NE corner from B5330 (SK 543114). Special access for disabled drivers by permit, Thursdays 14.30–19.30, 1 April to 30 September. House ruins open 1 April to 30 September on Wednesday, Thursday and Saturday, 14.30–17.00 and on Sunday, 11.00–12.30. Visitor centre (Marion Cottage) open 1 April to 30 September on Wednesday, Thursday and Saturday, 14.00–18.00. Accessible by bus.

Swithland Woods, immediately N of Bradgate Park on B5330 with car parks at SK537117 and SK 537130. Freely open all times. Accessible by bus.

In Charwood Forest north of Leicester and crossed by M1, ancient rocks protrude like ribs through the soft flesh of younger sands and marls covering the Midland plain. They are of great geological interest and considerable economic importance. Mountsorrel Granite, Swithland Slate and Markfieldite and other pre-Cambrian rocks which underlie Bradgate Park have been extensively quarried and used in local buildings or for road stone. These rocky outcrops provide excellent recreational areas. The largest, Bradgate Park, was presented to the people of Leicester by Charles Bennion in 1928 and is managed by

The deer at Bradgate Park in Leicestershire, and the ruins of the great house built around 1500, which was once the home of Lady Jane Grey. *East Midlands Tourist Board*

the Bradgate Park Trustees (who act for the City and County of Leicester). The country park has now been extended to include Swithland Woods (given to the trustees by Leicester Rotary Club). There are other smaller picnic sites on Beacon Hill and the Outwoods further N.

The displays at the visitor centre and a series of illustrated booklets are invaluable for those who wish to understand the history, geology and natural history of the park. The rocks at Bradgate were formed by volcanic action at least 700 million years ago. The thin soils of the park have never been ploughed and 700 years ago the forest was cleared to make a deer park. Bradgate Park still retains its deer herds, its ancient trees and bracken-covered hillsides. There are many inviting footpaths, a nature trail and a riding trail.

Only the ruins of the great house at Bradgate, built between 1490 and 1510 for the Grey family, remain; it was here that Lady Jane Grey, Queen of England for 9 days, spent most of her life. Old John Tower, on the ridge at the NW corner of the park, commemorates the accidental death of a retainer of the Grey family. The view from this point is particularly fine across the park and Cropston Reservoir.

Swithland Wood is a mature oakwood rich in wildlife. Swithland slate was quarried here. There are attractive walks from car parks at the N and S ends. Further NW in Woodhouse Eaves is Broombriggs Farm, where there is a farm trail (car park at SK 523144) and another excellent viewpoint, Beacon Hill (car park at SK 510147).

13 BATTLEFIELD OF BOSWORTH
Leics CC 3½ miles (5½ km) of footpaths
3 miles (5km) S of Market Bosworth and between A447 Hinkley to Coalville and A444

Nuneaton to Burton-on-Trent roads. Well signed from surrounding main roads. The entrance road turns S from the minor road between Shenton village and Sutton Cheney at SK 404005. Footpaths, Battle Trail and car parks open all daylight hours. Battlefield visitor centre open late March to late October, Monday to Saturday inclusive, 14.00–17.30. Sundays and Bank Holidays, 13.00–18.00. Shenton Station information centre open Sundays and Bank Holidays, 13.00–18.00. Admission charge to Battlefield Centre (tel Market Bosworth 290429 to check details or to make bookings).

This unique country park brings to life the great battle fought here on 22 August 1485, when Richard III, the last Plantagenet king, was defeated and killed, and Henry Tudor became King Henry VII. This was the last time an English king led his troops into battle, and the last occasion that knights in full armour went into action. It brought to an end the Wars of the Roses.

The project of portraying the battlefield began in 1973 through the enterprise and cooperation of the local authorities, Leicester Museum Service, Leicester University, local landowners and farmers, and the Council for the Protection of Rural England. The completed scheme won major awards in 1975. The battlefield visitor centre is the best starting point. Here in converted farm buildings on Ambion Hill there are film and slide shows, models of the battlefield and replicas of the armour and weapons used. There is also a bookstall and a café (normally closed on Mondays). From the hilltop outside the centre the layout of the battlefield is immediately apparent. The standards of the opposing armies mark where their command positions stood. A carefully signed battle trail leads to all the important places associated with the struggle, including the spring where King Richard drank and the place where he fell. Another information centre (with refreshments) is halfway round the trail in Shenton Station buildings. Those who prefer not to walk the whole trail can see the main places of interest by judicious use of the various car parks. Visitors are asked particularly to respect the privately owned and intensively farmed land which surrounds the trail.

Open areas for picnics and informal games are on Ambion Hill and at Shenton Station; similar facilities can be found at Market Bosworth Park and Arboretum on B585, just to the E of the centre of the interesting small town of Market Bosworth.

14 DAVENTRY
Northants CC and Daventry DC
208 acres (84 hectares)
1 mile (1½km) NE of Daventry on B4036 (Daventry to Market Harborough road). Signed entrance at SP 576642. Freely open daylight hours. Accessible to pedestrians from Daventry.

Daventry Country Park is recently opened and not yet fully developed. It is centred on the old Daventry Reservoir, built between 1796 and 1804 to provide water for the Grand Union Canal (which runs just N of the park and enters a tunnel W of B4036). The great attraction here is coarse fishing, particularly for bream. At present this is allowed from the N and W banks but there may later be fishing from boats. Day tickets are available and anglers must have a rod licence from the Welland and Nene Division of the Anglian Water Authority.

The S half of the park is managed as a nature reserve; a nature trail is being developed on the edge of this area. The marshy S end of the reservoir is particularly important for water birds; the fen-type vegetation is attractive to butterflies and dragonflies. There is a temporary display centre to provide information to visitors, and a programme of organised walks. Meadowland by the car park provides space for picnics and informal games.

15 IRCHESTER
Northants CC 200 acres (81 hectares)
2 miles (3km) SE of Wellingborough. Entrance (signed) on N side of minor road between A509 and Irchester village at SP 912657. Pedestrian entrance from A45. Freely open, daylight hours. Accessible by bus.

Irchester is on rising ground and immediately S of the site of a Roman town. This was an opencast ironstone quarry which was subsequently afforested, and it is a good example of how such land can be reclaimed for informal recreation. The park centre and picnic site are in a grassy glade which was once the marshalling yard for the mineral railway serving the quarry. Much of the park is wooded, and still has the hill and dale formation left by ironstone excavation in the 1940s. The variety of trees and hedgerow plants have now become the haunt of squirrels and birds, including less common species such as longtailed tit and goldcrest. A nature trail leads through the woodland and there is also a senior citizens' walk. There is provision for organised camping and it is hoped later to build a visitor centre. Irchester is one of the country parks which have been able to benefit from the job-creation scheme and from work done by a volunteer conservation group. There is a regular programme of events and guided walks.

16 BARNWELL
Northants CC 30 acres (12 hectares)
½ mile (1km) S of Oundle on A605. Entrance (signed) at TL 037874, opposite the Marina. Freely open at all times. Accessible by bus.

This small country park lies beside the river Nene and close to the attractive small town of Oundle. Sand and gravel had been excavated here for a dozen years before the council bought the site in 1970. The area has now been attractively landscaped. A variety of shrubs and trees have been planted in addition to the willows and marsh plants which have colonised the site. Much of the area is open water and attracts a variety of birds including tufted duck, coot, mallard, moorhen and crested grebe. Coarse fishing is popular and day tickets are available. Special facilities are provided for disabled anglers. The park provides pleasant picnic sites and opportunities to study wildlife by willow-fringed lagoons.

OTHER SCHEMES
Several sites in the East Midlands provide facilities comparable to those in country parks. The best known is managed by the Anglian Water Authority at Rutland Water (between Oakham, Manton and Empingham). The Iron Age hill fort at Burrough Hill (6 miles or 9½km south of Melton Mowbray) and several sites in Charnwood Forest have been provided by Leicester CC. The county councils of Derbyshire and Nottingham are jointly responsible for the visitor centre and nature trail at Cresswell Crags (4 miles or 6½km SW of Worksop). Because of its limited extent this is officially listed as a picnic site, but it is an SSSI and includes caves inhabited by Stone Age Man during a cold phase of the last Ice Age.

17 HARTSHOLME
Lincoln City C 59 acres (24 hectares)
3½ miles (5½km) SW of Lincoln centre. Approach from A46 through Boultham and along Skellingthorpe Road. Entrance (signed) at SK 948697. Freely open at all times. Accessible by bus.

A small country park near Lincoln, the land-scaped parkland of Hartsholme Hall. The hall itself has been demolished, but the out-buildings have been converted to provide a visitor centre (with displays on the hall and its grounds) and a café. Fishing is available in an attractive lake fringed by woodland and meadow. A camping and caravan site open to touring campers is very popular.

EASTERN ENGLAND

COUNTRY PARKS

1   HOLT
2   SANDRINGHAM
3   FERRY MEADOWS
4   BRANDON PARK
5   WEST STOW
6   KNETTISHALL HEATH
7   FRITTON LAKE
8   SUFFOLK WILD LIFE PARK
9   LONELY FARM LEISURE PARK
10 EASTON FARM PARK
11 CLARE CASTLE
12 HATFIELD FOREST
13 KNEBWORTH
14 STOCKGROVE PARK
15 ALDENHAM RESERVOIR
16 GREAT WOOD
17 WEALD PARK
18 THORNDON PARK
19 WESTLEY HEIGHTS
20 ONE TREE HILL
21 NORSEY WOOD
22 HADLEIGH CASTLE
23 MARSH FARM
24 DANBURY PARK
25 CUDMORE GROVE

OTHER SCHEMES

A   LEE VALLEY REGIONAL PARK
B   GRANGEWATERS

Norfolk Coast AONB

NORFOLK

NORWICH

CAMBRIDGESHIRE

SUFFOLK

CAMBRIDGE

IPSWICH

Suffolk Coast AONB

BEDFORD

BEDFORDSHIRE

COLCHESTER

LUTON

HERTFORDSHIRE

ESSEX

CHELMSFORD

ST ALBANS

Chilterns AONB

0   10   20   30   40km
0   10   20   25miles

Eastern England

1 HOLT
North Norfolk DC 96 acres
(39 hectares)

Immediately S of Holt village and bypass, on E side of B1149, the Holt to Norwich road. Car park entrance at TG 083375; pedestrian entrance direct from Holt. Freely open at all times. Accessible by bus.

Holt Country Park was opened before it was fully developed, and its completion is planned for 1982. The park consists of 2 contrasted areas. The SE sector is composed of heath and commonland, with views over the Glaven Valley. This has been under the control of the Holt Lowes trustees and publicly accessible for many years. It is an important example of lowland heath and is an SSSI, so that careful maintenance is necessary. The NW sector is the Holt Lodge Woodlands, plantations mainly composed of Scots and Corsican Pine. Some of these trees are as much as 20 years old. The car park is in a cleared area within this woodland, and the picnic area is situated beside a pond on the edge of the woods. There are waymarked walks through the area, and a nature trail, information boards and leaflets will later be available and will explain the significant wildlife habitats. Further picnic sites and a touring camp site may be added eventually.

2 SANDRINGHAM, Norfolk
The Sandringham Estate
524 acres (212 hectares)

W of Sandringham House. Approach at signs from A149 or by following signs to Sandringham House. Main car park at TF 689287. The country park is freely open to pedestrians throughout the year but the car parks, information board and other facilities are available only between mid-April and late September. Opening times for Sandringham House, its grounds and the church are too complex to be set out fully. The house and church are always closed on Friday and Saturday or when a member of the royal family is in residence, but are otherwise generally open from 1 May to 30 September, 11.00–16.45. Accessible by bus.

Sandringham Country Park covers a large area to the W of the main house and grounds, and is in 2 sections linked by pathways. A narrow belt of hills (formed where Lower Greensand rocks outcrop) runs in a crescent S from Dersingham, and the whole district is now designated an AONB. The N park section is wooded and includes a popular scenic drive through rhododendrons on the crest of the ridge. This single-track road starts from the S end near Folly Lodge at TF 678281, passes a series of picnic sites and ends at the main car park and park centre. The cafeteria, souvenir shop and flower stall at the centre are open when the house is open and are not part of the country park. Regular guided walks start from the park centre, where there is a useful information panel. The waymarked woodland walks and 2 nature trails also have information posts. Fallow deer, squirrels and woodland birds are numerous; less common visitors include nightingales and nightjars.

A separate quieter section of the country park lies further S. The entrance and car park are off the minor road between A149 and B1439 opposite Lynn Lodges at TF 682274. Two areas here are open heathland. Further S still is a camping site managed by the Caravan Club (to whom all inquiries should be addressed).

3 FERRY MEADOWS
Peterborough Development Corp
494 acres (200 hectares)
Between A605 and A47 1½ miles (2½km) E of A1 and W of Peterborough. Main entrance (signed) from A605 along Ham Lane at TL 156967. Freely open at all times. Accessible by bus and Nene Valley Railway. Pedestrian access from A47.

Ferry Meadows, intended eventually to form the centre of a larger Nene Valley Park, has been developed on land worked for gravel until January 1978. Three new lakes have been created and provision for water sports is a major feature. A water-sports centre, with refreshments and changing rooms, has been built on Gunwade Lake, the largest. Sailing dinghies are available for hire, or visitors may sail their own craft. Sailing and wind-surfing tuition is available. A wildlife reserve is being created at the S end. Coarse fishing is available on a day-ticket basis and there are special facilities for the disabled. A

boat-hire service and cruiser moorings are provided at Overton Lake and the smallest lake is reserved for children's boating and model-boat sailing.

The surrounding land has been carefully landscaped and there are some 4 miles of new footpaths and bridges. Much is grassland, fringed by woods, and there has been extensive tree-planting. From the temporary information centre and café a miniature railway takes visitors to picnic facilities and Roman remains, restored and displayed beside Lake Overton. (There is an archaeological field centre near the park entrance.) The Caravan Club of Great Britain provides a site open to touring campers. Outside the park to the S is Lynch Farm, being developed as a riding centre. The Nene Valley Steam Railway, opened in 1977 and operating on summer weekends, runs along the S edge of Ferry Meadows, with a new station to serve the park.

4 BRANDON PARK
Suffolk CC 31 acres (12½ hectares)
1 mile (1½km) S of Brandon on B1106. The entrance is signed at TL 787854. Freely open May to October, 10.00–21.00, and November to April, 11.00 to dusk.

Though Brandon Park is small, it gives free access into the surrounding Brandon Forest, which is in turn part of the Forestry Commission's huge Thetford Forest. The numerous paths and bridleways offer great scope for further exploration. Visitors can get more details for the whole of Thetford Forest from the information centre at Santon Downham, 2 miles (3km) NE of Brandon at TL 816878.

The country park consists of the gardens and parkland surrounding Brandon Park

The Nene Valley International Steam Railway running past Ferry Meadows Country Park near Peterborough. In this case a Swedish locomotive is pulling Danish carriages. *Nene Valley International Steam Railway, photographed by John Titlow*

House. This is a Regency building, but is at present in some disrepair and not open to the public. There is an information room in the outbuildings. From the lawn, framed by fine specimen trees and flowering shrubs, one looks W across a reconstructed lake with goldfish, and down a wide vista through the forest. There are also the ruins of a mausoleum.

5 WEST STOW
St Edmunsbury BC 151 acres
(61 hectares)

6 miles (9½km) NW of Bury St Edmunds and 1½ miles (2km) W of West Stow village. From A1101 Bury St Edmunds to Mildenhall road turn E at Rampart Field (TL 787714) to the park entrance at TL 801715. Country park freely open 9.00 till an hour before sunset. Anglo-Saxon settlement site open Tuesday to Saturday, 14.00–17.00, Sundays and Bank Holidays, 11.00–13.00 and 14.00–17.00. Admission charge.

West Stow is a pleasant country park on a site beside the river Lark, and includes an archaeological site of international importance. Parts of the country park are on land redeveloped from other uses, while the remainder is woodland and heath typical of the Breckland. A new lake has been created and stocked for coarse fishing, and there is a nature trail and extensive grassland beside the river for picnics and informal games. Some day fishing tickets are available for those with an Anglian Water Authority rod licence.

Excavations have shown that a sandy knoll beside the river has a history of intermittent human occupation stretching back to around 2000 BC. Its particular importance is the early Anglo-Saxon village, dating mainly from between 400 and 650 AD. The ground-plans of a series of substantial buildings have been excavated. The site is managed by the Anglo-Saxon Village Trust, which has been reconstructing some of the buildings on their original sites, using the materials and technology available to the Anglo-Saxons.

The Rampart Field picnic site is to the W beside the Icknield Way. To the E is the entrance to the Forestry Commission's King's Forest site at TL 815715, with trails in Thetford Forest.

6 KNETTISHALL HEATH
Suffolk CC 180 acres (73 hectares)
On the S side of Little Ouse valley, 7 miles (11km) E of Thetford. Best approach from A1066, turning S to the main car park and new toilet block at TL 956807. Freely open at all times.

This is one of the few remaining areas of indigenous Breckland Heath, and interesting to naturalists. The land (leased from the Riddlesworth estate) has a frontage on the Little Ouse River and has long been popular for casual recreation. The main hazard on this sandy heath is fire, and visitors should take precautions. It is a quiet country park and no further development is intended. It is at the S end of the Peddar's Way long-distance path, which follows the line of a Roman road E of Thetford and Swaffham, through Castle Acre to the coast at Hunstanton.

7 FRITTON LAKE
Lord Somerleyton 232 acres (94 hectares)
3 miles (5km) SW of Great Yarmouth. Entrance (signed) from A143 at TG 472004. Open daily 1 April to 7 October, 11.00–18.00 and from 7.00 after 16 June. Admission charge. (This is a private park, tel Fritton 208.)

Fritton Lake is part of the Somerleyton estate and was opened as a country park in 1976. The grounds have been beautifully landscaped and a variety of wildlife has survived in this quiet setting. The lake itself, some 2½ miles long, is thought to have been formed by peat cutting in the 12th century. It is set in woodland and gardens and attracts many species of water bird. For centuries, and up to 1960, wild ducks were caught in decoys, but now the lake offers fishing (day tickets available) and rowing boats may be hired. There are walks in the surrounding woodland.

A bronze statue by Kathleen Scott (widow of Captain Scott of the Antarctic), a memorial to 5 young men killed in World War II, is a feature of the gardens. Fritton Lake was requisitioned in 1942 for the development and testing of amphibious tanks, and in 1945 2 USAAF fighter aircraft collided over Fritton and fell into the lake (one has since been recovered). It is appropriate, therefore, that the US Eighth Army Memorial Museum should be housed here.

There is an adventure playground, a putting course and pony rides for children. Refreshments are available in Old Hall (dating in part from the 16th century) and there is an information room, with guides to local wildlife.

Fritton church, close to the country park,

has Saxon features and a thatched roof. Somerleyton Hall 3½ miles (5km) away is also open to the public during summer.

8 SUFFOLK WILDLIFE PARK
Mr L. F. Wright 59 acres (24 hectares)
On B1437 at W end of Kessingland and just off A12, 5 miles (8km) south of Lowestoft. Entrance (signed) at TM 520866. Accessible by bus. Open daily in spring and summer, 10.00–18.00 (or an hour before dusk if earlier). Admission charge. (This is a private park, tel Lowestoft 740291.)

At the N end of the Suffolk Heritage Coast, this country park lies in attractive open countryside (designated AONB), dotted with trees and sloping S to the levels of the Hundred River. The animals and birds, both foreign and British, are the main feature and the park aims both to preserve and breed endangered species. The cat family is represented by lions, tigers, pumas and leopards; there are also smaller carnivores and special enclosures for wolves, monkeys and many other animals. Among those in their natural setting are deer, Shetland ponies, donkeys and several breeds of sheep. The visitor can walk through a special aviary for exotic birds and see a variety of water birds on a lake and beside the river.

Facilities at the park centre include a cafeteria, gift shop, pets' corner and children's play area. Fishing in the river Hundred is free. Special facilities are available for handicapped visitors, including free wheelchairs.

9 LONELY FARM LEISURE PARK
Mr C. Rope 49 acres (20 hectares)
W of Saxmundham. Approach from A12 along B1119 (the Rendham and Framlingham road). The entrance at TM 365649 is signed. Open daily throughout the year (except Christmas). Admission charge. (This is a private park, tel Saxmundham 3344.)

Lonely Farm Leisure Park, which opened in 1977, is pleasantly situated in rural Suffolk and provides for a range of countryside activities. Two man-made lakes form the central attraction. One is stocked for coarse fishing, the other with trout from the neighbouring hatchery. Day and half-day fishing tickets are available. In addition the visitor can hire a rowing or paddle boat, or can sail his own dinghy or canoe. Two camping sites are provided for caravans and tents, one sheltered by woodland and the other in grassland. There are walks in the surrounding open land and a range of entertainments including pony rides, crazy golf and an adventure playground. There is a shop, refreshments and (unique among country parks) a public house. Special facilities are available for the handicapped to drive to a car park beside the lakes.

10 EASTON FARM PARK
Mr J. M. Kerr 32 acres (13 hectares)
3 miles (5km) S of Framlingham. Easiest approach is from A12: take B1116 ½ mile (1km) N of Wickham Market and follow signs to Easton village. The park is then signed; entrance at TM 277586. Open daily, Easter to early October, 10.30–18.00. Admission charge. (This is a private park, tel Wickham Market 746475.)

Easton Farm Park was opened in 1974 as the second farm park in the country, and won first prize in a national competition for Places of Recreation and Leisure in the Countryside in 1975.

Watching the dairy herd being milked at Easton Farm Park in Suffolk, from the special viewing platform in the dairy centre. *Easton Farm Park (Suffolk) Ltd*

The farm buildings were erected by the Duke of Hamilton in about 1870 as a model dairy farm on his large estate in the Deben valley. Like the attractive estate houses in Easton village, these are brick with tiled roofs. For most visitors the great feature is to see the animals at close quarters, and to compare modern and Victorian farm techniques and machinery. Visitors can see some of the ancient and uncommon breeds of farm animal, for example the Old English longhorn cow, the Suffolk Punch horse, Shetland pony and so-called 'Iron Age' pigs. This is also a working farm. Visitors can watch the milking of the dairy herd of some 130 Friesians from a specially designed catwalk. (There is an explanatory commentary.) Milking normally begins about 14.30 and lasts approximately 1½ hours. From the newly built dairy, the visitor can walk across to its decorative Victorian counterpart and see the equipment which was then in use.

There is an extensive collection of farm machinery and tools (and even several old tractors becalmed in the children's play area). Another building houses a collection of vintage motor cycles and delivery vehicles. There is a blacksmith's shop (where a smith is at work on weekend afternoons), a gift shop, a tearoom and a riverside picnic area. Fishing is available in the river Deben and there is a nature trail, mainly on made-up paths. Most of this country park is fully accessible to those in wheelchairs.

11 CLARE CASTLE
Suffolk CC 22 acres (9 hectares)

In Clare at TL 770451. The park is signed from A1092 at the S end of the village. Accessible by bus. Freely open all daylight hours.

Clare is one of a number of extremely attractive villages and small towns in this part of Suffolk, owing their former wealth to the medieval wool industry. The main street runs N to S between ancient earthworks and the Norman castle. Within the country park are the scant remains of the castle keep on its motte (from which there is a view of what survives of an Augustinian priory founded in 1248). Much of the bailey and part of the moat are also within the park. More recently this was Clare Station. The station buildings have been preserved to act as the park centre. There is an information room and a useful display map. The picnic area is in the old station yard, and one can walk E beyond the limits of the park, along the line of the former track. N of the station (and separately accessible from the centre of Clare) is the games area on open grassland, and a bowling green. To the S in woodland beside the old millstream is a pond, with a collection of water birds. It is intended to provide a nature trail.

12 HATFIELD FOREST
National Trust 998 acres (404 hectares)

4 miles (6½km) E of Bishop's Stortford (not to be confused with Hatfield, Herts). Easiest approach via A120 between Bishop's Stortford and Great Dunmow. Turn S in Takeley Street (sign to park) down E side of Hatfield Forest to the entrance at TL 547199. Always accessible to pedestrians but limited off-season access to cars.

Hatfield Forest is justly popular. An attractive and very extensive area of woodland and open parkland, it offers great scope for picnics, walking, fishing, boating and informal games. At its centre is a lake and Shell House, both created in the 18th century by the Houblon family. There is a café and shop; visitors can obtain fishing permits or hire a boat. There is a nature trail and a display on local wildlife.

Hatfield Forest is much more interesting than is immediately apparent, however. This was a royal forest owned by Earl Harold before the Conquest, and seized (as part of Hatfield Manor) by William I. The early Norman kings extended the royal forests to cover a fifth of England. Forest, in this sense, was a legal term. Special Forest Laws applied (whether the land was tree-covered or not), the primary aim being protection of game for the royal hunt.

Through centuries of conflicting ownership, Hatfield Forest preserved more completely than anywhere else in Britain the elements of medieval forest management. At its core is pasture for cattle as well as deer, and the specially created rabbit warren. Pollard oak trees, perhaps 300 years old, survive in isolated splendour. A series of separately emparked coppice woodlands ring the open centre. Because this land has remained unploughed it is unusually rich in wildlife and is designated an SSSI. The red deer have gone, but there are still fallow deer, foxes and badgers. Uncommon plants such as herb Paris and the true oxlip may be found, and a nature reserve has been created on marshland at the N end of the lake. Visitors interested to learn more about the unique features of Hatfield Forest can find details both in the National Trust guide and in Oliver Rackham's *Trees and Woodland in the British Landscape* (1976).

Knebworth House near Stevenage is still the home of the Lytton family, and stands at the centre of a country park which caters for many different interests. *Knebworth Estates*

13 KNEBWORTH
Hon David Lytton-Cobbold
190 acres (77 hectares)

On the SW edge of Stevenage and immediately beside A1(M) Stevenage S exit. Follow road signs to Knebworth House. Entrance at TL 237220. House and park open daily (except Mondays) 1 April to 30 September and on Bank Holidays. Open Sundays only in October. Park 11.00–18.00, house 11.30–17.30. Admission charge both to country park and to house and gardens. Extra charges for special events. (This is a private country park, tel Stevenage 812661.)

Knebworth is very much a stately home and an entertainment complex. Knebworth House is still the private home of the Lytton family, as it has been since 1492. The country park is the extensive deer park surrounding the house and gardens. From North Lodge the visitor drives up through herds of deer and attractive open parkland, past St Mary's church (with Norman chancel arch and fine Lytton family monuments) to car parks near the house. The deer park and its lake are worth exploring, but many visitors will be attracted by the shop and licensed restaurant, or by the adventure playground, skateboard park and narrow-gauge railway with steam locomotives. (Separate entry charges for some of these.)

The house and gardens are well worth visiting. The house is basically a brick Tudor building, but its exterior has been refaced with stucco and mock Tudor ornamentation.

Knebworth caters for special parties, provides camping facilities for organised groups, and also stages a series of special events. Typical activities are jousting, show jumping, autocross, car rallies and an antiques fair. Check the current diary.

14 STOCKGROVE PARK
Beds CC and Bucks CC 59 acres (28 hectares)

On the county boundary 2½ miles (5km) N of Leighton Buzzard. Best approach is along A418 (between Leighton Buzzard and A5). At the N end of Heath and Reach turn W on a minor road towards Great Brickhill. The park entrance (signed) is at SP 920294. Freely open at all times.

Much of the landscaping of the estate of Stockgrove House was carried out in the 1920s. The house itself is now a school and a portion of the estate was bought jointly by the 2 councils to create this country park. It is an area of low hills, developed on an outcrop of Lower Greensand (the sands are worked commercially round Heath and Reach). The park straddles a small valley running SW towards the river Ousel, and including an artificial lake. It is mainly important as an attractive open area for walking, fishing, picnics and informal games, but it also includes woodland designated an SSSI.

A nature trail, which starts from the car park, takes the visitor first on to the open stretches of hillsides to the NW, where there is a rabbit warren. It descends past pine trees and rhododendrons to the lake. The trail then continues into Baker's Wood, an area of primary oak woodland where a number of uncommon plants and birds may be seen (including the greater spotted woodpecker). These woodland areas are now being carefully managed, with selective felling and replanting. Public footpaths link the country park with surrounding heath and woodland.

15 ALDENHAM RESERVOIR
Herts CC 185 acres (75 hectares)

Easiest approach along A411 (between Watford bypass and the centre of Elstree). Turn N (sign to park) along minor road towards Letchmore Heath. The one-way entry to the park is on the left at TQ 168962. From M1 take Exit 4 to Elstree, turning left on to A411. Additional pedestrian access from the S (A411). Freely open, daylight hours. Accessible by bus.

Aldenham Reservoir lies in pleasant open countryside within the Green Belt, and is very accessible by main road or motorway. Though the reservoir and its associated water sports are the main feature, there is plenty of open grassland for informal recreation, and an attractive footpath along the E shore. On the W side is an adventure playground. From the extensive landscaped parking and picnic sites, one looks across the tree-fringed reservoir towards Elstree church on its hilltop, or into Aldenham Park (now Haberdashers Askes School). Unhappily the mature elms have had to be felled but there is much new tree planting.

At the SE end of the park is a cricket field,

the premises of a sailing club and an angling club (with facilities for members only). There is also coarse fishing available to the public (day tickets available) and boats may be hired for fishing.

16 GREAT WOOD
Welwyn and Hatfield DC 247 acres (100 hectares)
Entrance on B157 Brookmans Park to Cuffley road on The Ridgeway, 2 miles (3km) W of Cuffley at TL 283038. Freely open daylight hours.

Properly called Northaw Great Wood, this is the remaining section of ancient woodland preserved in London's Green Belt. The dominant tree species is oak, generally in association with either hornbeam or birch, and it seems likely that this land has been under continuous woodland cover at least since Norman times. One reason is the poor and waterlogged soils developed on London Clay and overlying glacial gravels. The formerly more extensive forest belonged to the Abbots of St Albans and became Crown property at the dissolution of the monasteries. Queen Elizabeth I granted it to Dudley, Earl of Warwick, and it passed through many hands until the London and Hertfordshire councils bought the remaining woodland in 1938.

Because of the interesting fungi and bird species Great Wood was designated an SSSI in 1953. The naturalist will find much of interest and will wish to consult *Northaw Great Wood: its History and Natural History*, edited by B. L. Sage (1966), and the detailed management plan prepared for Hatfield RDC.

For the ordinary visitor the main attraction is the freedom to walk through open woodland. There is a choice of 3 marked trails which lead down from the car park towards glades and streams flowing into the Cuffley Brook. Because of its location this is a popular park, and parking has been restricted to prevent too many visitors. The car park itself is screened by rhododendrons, but elsewhere a careful policy of planting and regeneration by native species is being carried out. The park warden is assisted by volunteer wood wardens.

17 WEALD PARK
Essex CC 429 acres (173½ hectares)
2 miles (3km) NW of Brentwood. Best approach is from the S to South Weald village. (From London along A12 turn on to A1023 towards Brentwood and then first left at Brook Street.) Car parks each side of South Weald church at TQ 574940 and 567941; additional parking on W side of park. Freely open daylight hours. Accessible by bus. Additional pedestrian access at several points.

This fine park was bought by Essex CC in 1953 as part of London's Green Belt. The SE section (still called The Park) is what remains of an ancient deer enclosure established by the abbots of Waltham Cross before the Norman Conquest. The herd of deer survived until fences were destroyed in 1945, and wild fallow deer may still be seen. Some of the oak and hornbeam trees may be 500 years old. The ornamental lakes, the fine chestnut avenues and the rhododendron-covered Belvedere mound remain from 2 18th-century schemes of landscaping (the earlier by the French surveyor Bourginion, as at neighbouring Thorndon Park). Sadly the hall, a Tudor building with later additions, where Mary Tudor is believed to have stayed, had to be demolished in 1950

Part of Weald Park, near Brentwood in Essex, was a deer park before the Norman Conquest, and this attractive parkland also shows the effects of an eighteenth-century landscaping scheme. *Essex CC*

because of wartime neglect and damage.

Day and season permits are available for fishing in the lakes and annual riding permits give the owner access to marked riding trails across the park. Sandy Lane, which forms the E boundary of the park, cuts through an Iron Age defensive site at TQ 578947. Further N are recent plantations which will be progressively and selectively felled to leave mature oak and beechwood.

Thornton Park North can be reached via Brook Street and Mascalls Lane, avoiding Brentwood.

18 THORNDON PARK
Essex CC 353 acres (143 hectares)

S of Brentwood and W of A128; the park is in 2 sections linked only by footpaths. N section entrance at Lion Gate TQ 604915. Turn W off A128 1 mile (2km) S of central Brentwood (signs) along The Avenue. S section entrance at TQ 635899 immediately N of the intersection of A127 and A128 at Halfway House. (The signed turning from A128 is just N of the hilltop church.) Both sections freely open daylight hours. Accessible by bus.

Thorndon Park is part of a much larger estate whose origins go back to Norman times. Essex CC acquired the land in 1939; it is part of London's Green Belt and became a country park in 1971. At the core of the estate here, as at neighbouring Weald Park, is an ancient deer enclosure. The land was emparked in 1414 and herds of red and fallow deer were kept here to within the last 50 years. What survives today in both park sections is a landscape of ancient oak and hornbeam trees, set in grassy glades and providing a variety of natural habitats. Much of this land has remained undisturbed and unpolluted and has been designated an SSSI.

Nothing now remains of Thorndon Old Hall, which stood in the SW of the park. The New Hall, built in the 1760s, stands sadly neglected beside a golf course and outside the park boundary (but visible from a footpath). One can recognise in the outlines of Old Hall Pond and Octagon Plantation part of the elaborate 18th-century landscaping scheme of the French surveyor Bourginion, and later work of Capability Brown. There are considerable areas of recently afforested land where selective felling will eventually leave stands of mature hardwoods. Fishing and riding permits are available and there are many opportunities for walking both within the park and on signed footpaths outside. All Saints church stands isolated and redundant on its hilltop overlooking the Thames Estuary, in a detached fragment of the park.

19 WESTLEY HEIGHTS
Essex CC 131 acres (53 hectares)

Immediately S of Basildon on B1007. Main car park behind the Crown Inn at TQ 681867. Additional parking by the church and at the junction of B1007 and Dry Street, TQ 679865. Freely open at all times. Accessible by bus.

Westley Heights is part of the Langdon Hills and close to One Tree Hill Country Park. The Langdon Hills rise sharply out of the Essex lowlands and command much wider views than their mere height might suggest. The hills have a capping of Plateau Gravels overlying Bagshot and Claygate Beds, and the resulting sandy and pebbly soils support a heath and woodland vegetation. The E section of Westley Heights is grass-covered hilltop with good views; there are convenient seats and footpaths link the area to its surrounding farmland. Hall Wood, Coombe Wood and the Park on both sides of B1007, beside the church and watertower, are extensively wooded. Footpaths and bridle paths offer additional opportunities for informal recreation.

Dry Street is the direct link to One Tree Hill Country Park (turn S at the road sign at TQ 695867).

20 ONE TREE HILL
Essex CC 128 acres (52 hectares)

Between A13 and the SE edge of Basildon. Approach along minor roads from Basildon via Dry Street, or from A13 by turning N at the cross roads where B1420 turns S to Coryton. Car park at TQ 697861. Freely open at all times.

As at the neighbouring Westley Heights Country Park the great attraction is open grassland and woods on small steep-sided hills. There are footpaths and seats strategically placed to make the most of the extensive views. One Tree Hill gives a panoramic view of parts of the Thames Estuary. Above all, this is an attractive oasis above the hectic traffic of the A13.

21 NORSEY WOOD
Basildon DC 165 acres (67 hectares)
Immediately NE of Billericay. The car park entrance is from a minor road on the E side of the wood at TQ 692957. From Billericay approach via Norsey Road, turning right on the further edge of the wood. Pedestrian entrance at TQ 680953 at W end. Freely open at all times. Accessible by bus and train.

Because of the importance of the plants and animals it contains, Norsey Wood is now both an SSSI and a local nature reserve. Though the oldest of the existing oak trees may not be more than 150 years old, there has been woodland here for many centuries. As at the nearby country parks of Thorndon, Weald and Havering, the land may never have been ploughed. This woodland was important to man, however. There is a burial mound dating back to the Bronze Age, and when gravel pits were worked here in the mid-19th century, Iron Age pottery and a Roman pottery kiln and smelting furnace were discovered. At the S edge of the wood is an embankment which was once part of the medieval deer park boundary, and intended to keep the deer inside the wood.

There is a small park centre beside the car park (open at weekends and also available for school use), with displays related to the history and wildlife of the wood. A way-marked woodland trail starts from this point, and leaflets indicate the variety of plants and birds which may be seen, and why coppicing has been reintroduced here. On the drier and higher parts of the wood the main trees are oak and hornbeam, with the more recently introduced sweet chestnut. The wetter parts on clay valley soils include alder, ash, hazel and willow. The coppicing (cutting the trees back to stumps every 18 years or so) rejuvenates the trees and brings sunlight to plants like wood sorrel, violet, speedwell, yellow pimpernel and many more. This in turn attracts many insects and birds.

22 HADLEIGH CASTLE
Essex CC 336 acres (136 hectares)
On the S edge of Hadleigh. Not yet open to the public. The park entrance is likely to be from B1014 Canvey Island to Benfleet Road via Shipwrights Close at TQ 795868.

Hadleigh Castle was the subject of a celebrated painting by Constable. The ruins date mainly from the 13th century and stand on a clifftop with commanding views over marshland, Canvey Island and the Thames estuary. Admission to the ruins (small entrance charge) is controlled by the DOE. The approach from the centre of Hadleigh is signed down Castle Lane. This becomes a narrow lane ending in a gate and with very limited parking space. The projected country park includes extensive areas of grassy slopes and reclaimed marshland, and is crossed by a network of footpaths.

23 MARSH FARM
Essex CC 240 acres (97 hectares)
1 mile (1½km) S of South Woodham Ferrers, at the head of the Crouch estuary. Approach via Hullbridge Road, the minor road leading S past Woodham Ferrers Station, to the farm at TQ 814961. Freely open daily, 8.30 till dusk.

Marsh Farm is being developed over 5 years and should be fully opened during 1982. It is a working farm, stocked with cattle, sheep and pigs, and producing arable crops. The aim is to show the public how a farm enterprise operates, and to have a farm information centre and farm trail. The public will have access over the whole farm, with opportunity to see the seasonal round of activities in the fields, and the handling of stock both outdoors and indoors (there is no dairy herd).

The boatyard on the river Crouch at the end of Hullbridge Road may also be developed to allow boats to be launched (on payment of harbour dues).

24 DANBURY PARK
Essex CC 41 acres (16½ hectares)
SW of Danbury village, 5 miles (8km) E of Chelmsford. Main car park at TL 769048 beside Woodhill Lodge on minor road from Sandon to Danbury Common. (A second car park off the same road a little further E.) Approaches to the park are signed from A414 Chelmsford to Malden Road and from minor roads. Freely open at all times. Accessible by bus.

Though this country park is small, it is one of several attractive open spaces around Danbury village, all interconnected by footpaths and bridleways. N of A414 are National Trust properties at Blakes Wood and Lingwood Common. Danbury Common (also National Trust) is S of the village, with a car park at TL 782043. The low hills on which stands the scattered village of Danbury resemble those further W at Westley Heights and One Tree Hill in being islands of pebbly and sandy soil rising above surrounding lowlands. Here the countryside is more rural, a landscape of woodland and hedgerow, orchard and common. The country park itself is the S and more wooded section of the grounds of Danbury Palace. (The palace buildings and immediate surroundings are now a management-training centre and not open to the public.) The artificial lakes provide opportunities for fishing (day permits are available). There are fine named specimen trees in the park and flowering shrubs and garden beds adjoining the palace. Open grassland is available for picnics and organised camping.

25 CUDMORE GROVE
Essex CC 35 acres (14 hectares)
S of Colchester at E end of Mersea Island at TM 067146. Follow signs to East Mersea and continue until the park is signed to the right. Freely open at all times.

Cudmore Grove is on the low-cliffed shore of Mersea Island, with a good view across to Brightlingsea and sailing in the Colne estuary. The extensive car parks and new toilet block stand beside a pleasant open grass area among patches of gorse. There are picnic tables and space for informal games. Low trees fringe the cliff top and below is a sandy upper beach. The cliffs (cut in London clay) are evidently subject to active erosion but there are ways down to the beach. This is a popular country park for picnics, kite-flying and swimming. There is a nature reserve (not open to the public) beyond the park boundary.

154

OTHER SCHEMES
A LEE VALLEY REGIONAL PARK
Lee Valley Park Authority

A series of leisure facilities along the Lee Valley between Ware and Tower Hamlets in London. Two of these are comparable with other country parks: Clayton Hill Country Park on B194 just E of Broxbourne at TL 384060, and Hayes Hill Farm, just S of this on B194 at TL 383030.

The Lee Valley Regional Park Authority was established by Act of Parliament in 1966, and its facilities are paid for out of the rates of Greater London and neighbouring areas. Clayton Hill is an area for picnics and informal games beside a lake frequented by water birds, and backed by grassy hill slopes. (No toilets.) Hayes Hill Farm is open between Easter and 30 September, on Saturdays 14.00–18.00, and Sundays and Bank Holidays, 11.00–18.00 (admission charge). This is a working farm of 435 acres (176 hectares), with a dairy herd, and sheep, turkeys, geese, ducks and chickens. Also open at other times for organised groups (tel Nazeing 2291 between 9.00 and noon).

B GRANGEWATERS
Thurrock BC 63 acres (25½ hectares)

Immediately E of B186 at South Ockendon. Park signs from A13 and B186. Entrance via Buckles Lane at TQ 605814. Freely open at all times. Bus and train in South Ockendon.

Grangewaters is the first stage in the development of the proposed Mardyke Country Park. Thurrock BC should be congratulated on this reclamation of a despoiled landscape, helped by a grant from the Countryside Commission. The whole area has been exploited for gravel and parts are now being infilled with rubbish. What has so far been achieved is a large car park, an area of new grassland backed by young trees, and 2 lakes, 1 reserved for anglers, the other for noisier water sports. A clubhouse, café and warden's house are the next phase, and more land will be reclaimed later for a riding centre. Public footpaths lead to South Ockendon Hall and North Stifford, where some attractive buildings survive from a rural past.

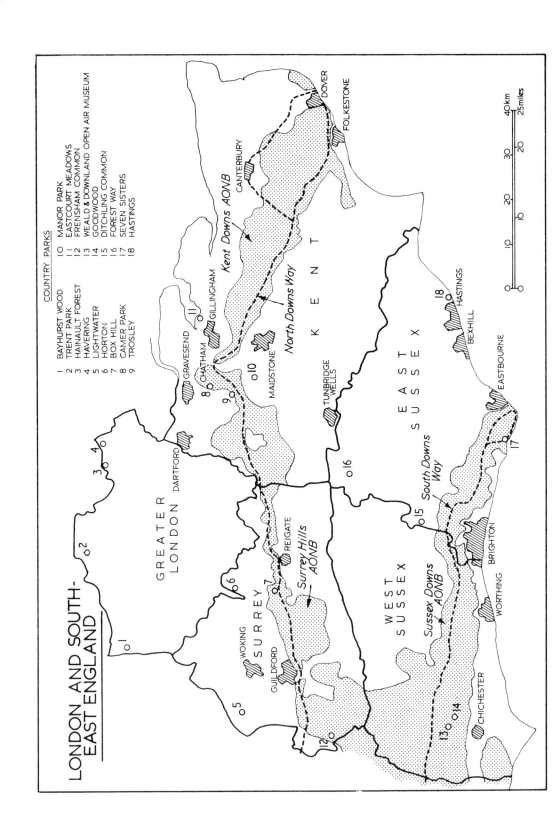

LONDON AND SOUTH-EAST ENGLAND

COUNTRY PARKS

1. BAYHURST WOOD
2. TRENT PARK
3. HAINAULT FOREST
4. HAVERING
5. LIGHTWATER
6. HORTON
7. BOX HILL
8. CAMER PARK
9. TROSLEY
10. MANOR PARK
11. EASTCOURT MEADOWS
12. FRENSHAM COMMON
13. WEALD & DOWNLAND OPEN AIR MUSEUM
14. GOODWOOD
15. DITCHLING COMMON
16. FOREST WAY
17. SEVEN SISTERS
18. HASTINGS

GREATER LONDON

SURREY

WEST SUSSEX

EAST SUSSEX

KENT

Kent Downs AONB

North Downs Way

Surrey Hills AONB

South Downs Way

Sussex Downs AONB

DOVER
FOLKESTONE
CANTERBURY
GILLINGHAM
CHATHAM
GRAVESEND
MAIDSTONE
DARTFORD
TUNBRIDGE WELLS
HASTINGS
BEXHILL
EASTBOURNE
BRIGHTON
WORTHING
CHICHESTER
GUILDFORD
WOKING
REIGATE

40km 25miles

London and South-east England

1 BAYHURST WOOD
Hillingdon BC 96 acres (39 hectares)
2 miles (3km) N of Uxbridge. Approach on minor road between Uxbridge and Harefield (Breakspear Lane) to entrance W of road at TQ 072891. Freely open at all times.

This ancient woodland on a hill E of the Colne Valley is in London's Green Belt, and one of a number of recreational areas collectively known as Colne Valley Regional Park. It is also linked E by paths through Mad Bess Woods to Ruislip Lido and the local nature reserve just N of this. The local council publishes seasonal nature trail guides to this wider area. Bayhurst Wood itself is mainly oak, hornbeam and sweet chestnut trees, many showing signs of former coppicing. This quiet and rather wet woodland is an important wildlife habitat, rich in fungi, and designated an SSSI. It is crossed by waymarked trails; the riding trail is not open to the general public. There are picnic facilities and barbecue grills, with brushwood and piped water available.

2 TRENT PARK
GLC 560 acres (227 hectares)
W of Enfield. Accessible at several points. Main entrance from Cockfosters Road (A111) just N of Cockfosters underground station at TQ 280965. Another vehicle entrance in Hadley Road, between Hadley Wood and Enfield at TQ 293982. Pedestrian entry beside Oakwood underground station and at other points. Freely open at all times but car parks are shut at night. Note vehicles cannot be driven across the park; each vehicle entrance leads to extensive landscaped car park and picnic sites. Free parking available on Sundays in Cockfosters station car park with direct access to the park. Accessible by bus and underground.

This extensive country park on the inner edge of the Green Belt in N London combines good accessibility with remarkably secluded countryside. The land was once part of a royal hunting forest, called Enfield Chase after the king relinquished his hunting rights. A private estate was developed here in the 18th century which was later much extended by the Sassoon family. Middlesex CC bought Trent Park in 1952—the mansion, outbuildings and surrounding gardens are now part of Middlesex Polytechnic, and not open to the public.

The GLC has developed the country park from the woodland, meadows and farmland of the estate. Much of the area is landscaped park on the slopes of 2 small valleys which drain E, and there are 2 attractive lakes and a water garden. In the centre of the park is a nature trail adjacent to the lakes; a woodland trail for the blind has been laid out near the main entrance. Most of the SE sector of the

park is a public golf course, and there are riding stables, a riding school and extensive horse rides in the woodlands.

The Hadley Road entrance is more remote from urban pressures, and there is considerable scope for walking and observing wildlife. In the NW corner of the estate is a working farm which is not part of the country park but is linked to it by a farm trail, with entrances near the 2 main car parks and the central area.

Trent Park may soon be provided with a combined refreshment and information centre, and later with a boating lake in the S part of the park. Annual and day fishing permits are available.

3 HAINAULT FOREST
GLC 954 acres (386 hectares)

On GLC boundary E of Chigwell. Approach along B196 and B174 between Romford and Chigwell Row. Main entrance at TQ 474924 (other entrances at N from Manor Road). Freely open at all times but car parks are shut at night. Accessible by bus.

The LCC bought this extensive area of public open space in 1903, with a further extension in 1934. Like Epping and Hatfield Forests, Hainault is a surviving fragment of the medieval royal forest of Essex. Once called Henholt, it was preserved for hunting deer, but was finally enclosed by Act of

Parliament in 1851. Almost immediately nearly all the forest vanished for ever. The area saved by the LCC purchase was mainly Lambourne Common and this has now been partly reafforested. It is further protected as part of London's Green Belt, and became a country park in 1970.

The park offers a wide choice of recreation. Waymarked paths lead up to local hilltops and through woodland on the N side of the park. The picnic site overlooks a lake. There are 2 golf courses, pitches for football and cricket, facilities for cross-country running, orienteering, fishing and riding. There is a camp site used by organised groups. The park centre provides changing rooms and refreshment facilities. Animals from the GLC children's zoos are wintered in the park.

4 HAVERING
GLC 166 acres (67 hectares)

At Havering-atte-Bower, 2½ miles (4km) N of Romford. First phase completed so far. Main entrance at TQ 500927; approach via Clockhouse Lane by turning N from B174 in Collier Row. There are also pedestrian entrances at TQ 510931 and TQ 509928. Freely open at all times, but car park closed at night. Accessible by bus.

The full facilities at Havering are not yet developed. A multiplicity of linear plots have been bought, rubbish and unsightly buildings and fences have been cleared, toilets and a car park in the SW corner of the park are provided, and access to pleasantly rural Green Belt land has been opened. The park lies on the S and W slopes of the Havering Ridge and has good views towards Epping Forest. Much is woodland, mainly oak, birch and pine, and new planting has

(opposite page) Two views of Trent Park in Greater London which epitomise opportunities in a typical country park: the quiet lakeside or the convivial barbecue. (Here the participants have brought their own equipment, but a number of country parks provide barbecue stoves and fuel.) *Greater London Council*

The riding trail in the woods of Havering Country Park north of Romford. *Greater London Council*

replaced diseased and damaged trees. As at Epping Forest and neighbouring Hainault Country Park, this was once part of a royal hunting forest. A waymarked riding circuit has been laid out. There is an avenue of Wellingtonia trees. Bracken-covered hillsides and a S-facing grassy field are available for picnics.

The village of Havering-atte-Bower is most attractive, surrounding a green on a hilltop site. Immediately to the SE (off B186 opposite the white tower) is Bedfords Park. This beautiful park is managed by Havering BC and is freely open during daylight hours. It includes a deer enclosure, a nature trail and a café, on slopes facing S and E.

5 LIGHTWATER
Surrey Heath DC 126 acres
(51 hectares)

Beside M3 and SW of Lightwater village. From M3 Exit 3, take A322 towards Guildford and immediately turn right into Lightwater village. Turn right (at sign) along The Avenue to entrance at SU 921622. Freely open daylight hours. Accessible by bus.

Lightwater Country Park is a small part of Bagshot Heath, an area of rolling heathland rising to some 400ft (130m), and providing extensive views. Thin acid soils developed on sands and gravels support ling, bell heather and stands of birch and pine, which make the park attractive for walking or riding. At the lower end of the park a picnic site overlooks a pond, with resident waterfowl and opportunities for fishing. The sports complex and games fields, developed before the country park was created, are available to club members only.

6 HORTON
Epsom and Ewell BC 245 acres (99 hectares)

1 mile (1½km) W of West Ewell Station and beside Long Grove Hospital. The entrance at TQ 191618 is in Horton Lane (which links B280 and B284). From Epsom follow signs to Long Grove Hospital and turn left at hospital entrance. Park facilities still incomplete and access limited, but freely open otherwise. Accessible by bus.

This country park lies in an extensive belt of open country, crossed by public footpaths between Epsom and Chessington. Much land remained undeveloped here because it belonged to several large hospitals. In 1972 the council bought half of the Horton estate from the hospital authorities to preserve it as open countryside and to improve public access. Facilities are still incomplete; there is an area for picnics and informal games beside the car park, but access is otherwise limited to footpaths on the edges of fields and to woodland. Because the area is still in farming use visitors have to take care to observe the countryside code and not allow dogs to worry grazing stock. Butcher's Grove, an area of hazel and hornbeam coppice, is open to the public and directly accessible from roads at the N end of the park. An information board at the car park indicates the extensive walks within the park and in open countryside beyond.

7 BOX HILL
National Trust 581 acres (235 hectares)

On North Downs 3½ miles (6km) S of Leatherhead. Approach via A24 to Burford Bridge car park at TQ 172520 for lower slopes, or from A217 turn W along B2032 for car parks at summit near TQ 178513. Freely open at all times. Accessible by bus and train (West Hamble).

The scenery of Box Hill has caught the imagination of its visitors for at least the last 300 years, and for good reason. This is not the highest stretch of the North Downs, but it is the most striking, and provides views extending right across the Weald to Chanctonbury Ring. Many come to enjoy this view, to wander on slopes still clothed with the plants characteristic of chalk downland, or to admire the fine beech trees and bluebell woods on the summit. To the generations of students who came on field excursions or stayed at Juniper Hall, the area will evoke studies of swallow holes in the Mole riverbed or terraces on its banks (outside the park), or the great river cliff above Burford Bridge whose slopes are so steep that only yew and box have succeeded in establishing themselves.

There have been no great changes since Box Hill became a country park in 1971; efforts continue to preserve its essential character, and to repair erosion caused by too many feet on thin topsoil. There is no information centre or nature trail, but everyone interested in natural history will find invaluable the guide book published by the Friends of Box Hill (available from the National Trust). There is a café and National Trust shop at the summit and a picnic site and hotel at Burford Bridge. The whole area is an AONB, and most of it is designated an SSSI. There is a viewpoint indicator situated at TQ 179512.

The most ancient of the interesting features on Box Hill are two trackways, one along the scarp foot and known as the Pilgrim's Way, but dating from long before such pilgrimages, and the other near the crest and now the preferred line of the North Downs Way. Both cross the river Mole, at the stepping stones, and near here also cross the line of Stane Street, the Roman road from London to Chichester. By contrast the fort, buried in woodland on Box Hill summit, is relatively recent, and one of a chain designed to protect London from invasion in the late 19th century.

The National Trust also owns 2 other neighbouring areas outside the country park: Mickleham Down and White Hill, N of Box Hill, and similar downland with views W and N. Headley Heath, E of Box Hill and now connected to it by a footpath, is common land and mainly heath-covered.

8 CAMER PARK
Gravesham BC 44 acres (18 hectares)
4 miles (6½km) S of Gravesend, between Sole Street and Meopham. park entrance from B2009 at TQ 649670 just E of its junction with A227. Pedestrian entrance (Sole Street) at TQ 655674. Freely open at all times. Accessible by bus and train (Sole Street).

Camer Park is a small, attractive area of landscaped parkland which formerly belonged to Camer House. This grassland, with fine specimen trees (each labelled with its botanical name), in an area designated an AONB, is popular with local residents for walking their dogs, and provides opportunities for picnics and informal games, or to sit and admire the quiet countryside almost dangerously close to A2.

Camer Park is also close to the interesting village of Cobham; the church has a magnificent collection of memorial brasses.

9 TROSLEY
Kent CC 116 acres (47 hectares)
2 miles (3½km) NE of Wrotham. Approach along A227 Wrotham to Meopham road. At crest of downs turn E towards Vigo village and follow signs. Park entrance at TQ 636612. (Will be close to M20 and M26 interchange when this is completed.) Freely open at all times. Accessible by bus.

Trosley is a linear park on a fine section of the North Downs, designated an AONB, above the Medway Valley and the village of Trottiscliffe (called Trosley). A display map beside the main car park and toilets at the W end indicates the features of particular interest. The North Downs escarpment faces S here, and the North Downs Way runs just below the crest through woodland in the country park at about 600ft (183m). The ancient Pilgrim's Way follows a parallel route at the foot of the slope. The best views, from patches of open downland, are at E end of the park, just below the North Downs Way. The escarpment itself is steep and covered by typical chalk downland plants, but reverting to scrub in places. Waymarked trails lead through the park, and footpaths and bridle paths lead to 2 bluebell woods belonging to the National Trust (at TQ 623601 and TQ 656606). Holly Hill (at TQ 670633) is another similar woodland. Camer Park is 3½ miles (6km) to the NE.

10 MANOR PARK
Kent CC 52 acres (21 hectares)
5 miles (8km) W of Maidstone and at S end of West Malling. From A20 turn S through West

Malling village on A228 (St Leonards Street) to entrance at TQ 677572. Freely open daylight hours. Accessible by bus and train (West Malling).

Manor Park is the landscaped parkland of Douces Manor, and in the heart of Kent orchard country. Although the park itself is small, there are numerous public footpaths which offer opportunities to explore the surrounding villages and farmland. The manor house and its grounds were created by Thomas Augustus Douce in the 18th century. He excavated the lake and so contrived the park that one is not immediately aware that house and grounds are on opposite sides of St Leonard's Street. The springs which feed the lake rise along faults in the underlying Kentish Ragstone. (This rock is exposed opposite the entrance and there are several boulders by the car park; it was formerly used as a building stone.)

Since the council bought Manor Park in 1973 some 600 trees have been planted to replace those lost through neglect and disease. The lake is a popular haunt of water birds and other wildlife. Limited fishing is available (see the information board at the car park). The open grassland is available for picnics, informal games and walks. St Leonard's Tower stands close to the park entrance. A key to view the interior is available at 115 St Leonard's Street nearby.

11 EASTCOURT MEADOWS
Gillingham BC 299 acres (121 hectares) at present
Off B2004 midway between Gillingham and Rainham. Car park (unsigned) on N side of B2004 at TQ 807683. Freely open at all times. Accessible by bus. No toilets.

Completion of this country park awaits additional finance. The site is a strip of foreshore and the tidal estuary of the river Medway extending E from the edge of Gillingham to Motney Hill. There is already a public footpath along the sea wall, providing interesting views of shipping bound for Rochester or Chatham Dockyard. The Medway estuary is an important wildfowl habitat, and a wide variety of bird species breed here. There is considerable potential for further development at Eastcourt Meadows, especially provision for sailing. Developments so far have included land clearance, fencing, the planting of a large number of trees and shrubs and the provision of a riding trail. Work to combat coastal erosion was made particularly necessary by winter floods in 1978.

12 FRENSHAM COMMON
Waverley DC 768 acres (311 hectares)
3 miles (5km) S of Farnham, crossed by A287. Main car park and toilets off A287 at SU 849406. (Other car parks off minor road NW of Great Pond at SU 844407 and near Little Pond at SU 859418.) Freely open at all times. Accessible by bus.

Frensham Common is a large area of Surrey heathland, owned by the National Trust but now managed by Waverley DC. It became a country park in 1971, and a management plan was drawn up by the local authority (then Hambledon RDC), in consultation with the National Trust and other specialist bodies, which sets out the priorities for action. (The plan, *Signpost 2000*, is obtainable from Waverley DC.) Frensham Common, especially Great Pond, is a 'honeypot': sunny summer days may bring over 5,000 visitors. The attractions are obvious: the whole district is an AONB, and the immediate area is heathland and scattered woodland (mainly Scots pine, birch and oak) on low hills beside the ponds. These ponds are artificial and were created in the 13th century to provide fish for Farnham Abbey. The dry heathland is dominated by ling, bell heather and gorse, but there are also wetter heathland areas and extensive reedbeds near the ponds. The varied wildlife habitats encourage interesting and unusual species and part of the area has therefore been designated an SSSI.

The problems are perhaps less obvious. Frensham Common is developed on sandy rocks in the Lower Greensand series (mainly the Folkestone Beds). Once vegetation is destroyed, the sand is soon exposed. This is evident at the N end of Great Pond and where steep hillside paths have been washed out. Now that the common is no longer grazed, Scots pine and other trees tend to invade the heath, and accidental fires can do serious damage. For these reasons car-parking is limited to the 3 official sites. There are many paths and tracks, some of which may be temporarily closed for repairs; efforts have been made to separate walkers from horse riders. Sailing and fishing on Great Pond are limited to club members, and the water is not regarded as safe or suitable for swimming. At Little Pond, the water and E shore are outside the country park.

A second area of Frensham Common (the Flashes and Stony Jump) lies SE of the main section. It is accessible by tracks but will be left undeveloped.

A medieval house, rescued from the site of a Kent reservoir, and re-erected without its later additions in the Weald and Downland Open Air Museum near Chichester.

13 WEALD AND DOWNLAND OPEN AIR MUSEUM
Weald and Downland Open Air Museum 36 acres (14½ hectares)

5 miles (8km) N of central Chichester and just off A286 (Chichester to Midhurst Road) at Singleton. Follow signs to Singleton and then to the park entrance, on minor road between Singleton and the Trundle at SU 876128. Open 1 April to 30 September daily except Monday (open Bank Holidays), 11.00–18.00. Open in October on Wednesday, Saturday and Sunday 11.00–17.00. 1 November–late March open Sundays only 11.00–16.00. Admission charge. Special car park for disabled (most of the best buildings accessible to visitors in wheelchairs). Accessible by bus (tel Singleton 348.)

This is an unusual and extremely interesting country park. The setting is a beautiful stretch of meadow and woodland on the slopes of the South Downs, and in an area designated an AONB. Since 1969 a collection of historic buildings, rescued from decay and destruction, and ranging in date from the 14th to the 19th century, has been re-erected here. The museum is a private non-profit making organisation, registered as a charity.

The best starting point is the Hambrook Barn on the slope above the entrance. The display here explains the structure of medieval vernacular buildings and something of the problems of their restoration. Scattered along the edge of the wood, or set together by a market hall, are a series of buildings, mostly of timber-frame construction. All have come from sites in the Weald or downland areas of SE England. Shorn of later extensions and improvements, they have been repaired and re-erected as nearly as possible in their original condition.

Typical instances are the modest Winkhurst House (probably late 14th-century) and the fine Bayleaf Farmhouse (probably 15th-century). Both were rescued from destruction when a reservoir was constructed in Kent. Titchfield Market Hall, Crawley Hall and a reconstructed brick building from Lavant (now a shop) form the nucleus round which other buildings will be grouped into a village.

There are a number of other structures: a watermill, court barn, cattle sheds, a granary, a tread wheel, a working smithy, a saw pit and a charcoal burner's camp. Some buildings have been reconstructed by reference to archaeological evidence, in particular a Saxon hut and a primitive cottage, perhaps of 13th-century date.

For most visitors interest will centre on this remarkable and steadily growing collection of vernacular architecture. However there is also a nature trail in woodland above, and ample opportunity to picnic or admire the attractive scenery and waterfowl on the lake by the mill. By turning right at the exit, visitors can reach the Trundle (a hill fort with fine views), and Goodwood racecourse and country park about a mile away.

14 GOODWOOD
Goodwood Estate Co 59 acres (24 hectares)

6 miles (9½km) N of Chichester, and beside the racecourse, on minor road running E from Singleton and the Trundle towards A285. Two car parks and picnic areas; information hut at SU 886110. Freely open at all times. Goodwood Park also open to the public, with free parking W of house. Goodwood House open Sundays and Mondays, Easter and early May to mid-October, and Tuesdays in August,

14.00–17.00. Admission charge. This is a privately developed park (tel Chichester 527107).

The country park at Goodwood, which opened in 1971, is only a small part of the whole estate. It includes 2 picnic sites with toilets, a woodland walk, an information hut and children's play area at the W end, and an observation tower to the E. This is on high ground among fine beechwoods above the house and main park, and has extensive views in an area designated an AONB. The racecourse lies on the opposite side of the road, and also an overnight caravan site open from June to September, except on race days. The main park surrounding the house is celebrated for its magnificent trees: beechwoods sweep down from the higher land, and there are cedars, chestnuts, cork oak and tulip trees below. Special events, including dressage and cricket matches, take place in front of the house. Goodwood House, a Jacobean mansion, is suitable for visits by the disabled, and a nature trail for the blind (which is also used by groups of schoolchildren) has been developed on the E side of the park.

Goodwood is close to several other attractions. To the W is the country park at Singleton and the Trundle, an Iron Age hill fort surrounding a Neolithic causewayed camp. To the E is Selhurst Forest, where the Forestry Commission have developed a picnic site at SU 926119.

15 DITCHLING COMMON
E Sussex CC 188 acres (76 hectares)
E of Burgess Hill at the junction of B2112 and B2113. Car park, toilets and information board on B2113 at TQ 337180. Freely open at all times. Accessible by bus.

This remnant of the parish common has survived (in what is otherwise a landscape of fields and farms) largely because of the intractable nature of the soil. The underlying Weald clay makes it muddy when wet and like concrete when dry. E Sussex bought out the common rights in 1974, but cattle are still grazed here for 5 months each year. Because grazing has been reduced, the heath is tending to revert to scrub and woodland. Visitors are free to walk across the common, and there is a bridle path. There is marshland beside a small stream and pond, and because of the variety of interesting plants and birds this area has been designated an SSSI. A park nature trail explores the contrasted habitats of the common.

The B2112 road and a number of similar N to S roads here were once drove roads, linking pastures in the Weald with those on the South Downs. In the 18th century the B2112 itself became the coaching road from London to Brighton. Horses were changed at the Bull Inn in Ditchling, and highwaymen lay in wait on the common.

16 FOREST WAY
E Sussex CC 56 acres (22½ hectares)
The former railway line between East Grinstead and Groombridge. Accessible at many points where roads cross, and at each end. Main car park at Forest Row TQ 426352 (behind Foresters Arms). From A22 turn E in Forest Row along B2110, the Tunbridge Wells Road, and left at sign. Freely open at all times. Bus and rail access (East Grinstead and Groombridge).

Forest Way is a linear park along a former railway. The branch line here was opened in 1866 by the Brighton and South Coast Railways; it survived for a century before

166

closing under the Beeching cuts. The track and ballast have now been removed and a firm surface provided suitable for walking and cycling. Separate tracks and access points have been provided for horse riders where there is room. At Forest Row the route leaves the old railway temporarily, passing through the village. Everywhere else it runs, sometimes in cuttings, often on low embankments, along the Medway Valley. Seats and picnic tables are being provided. The park guide (available at Forest Row car park or from the county planning department in Lewes) is particularly useful in indicating nearby places of interest open to the public. It is possible to extend or vary the route by using public footpaths to visit historic buildings, attractive villages and farms, or the Springhill Wildfowl Collection at Forest Row.

Probably the most interesting section of Forest Way is the ascent W of Forest Row, starting at the Medway bridge on A22. Here the line was cut through sandstones, and it is worth climbing the steps on the S side of the cutting to seats well placed to view the ruins of Brambletye House (completed in 1631) and Weir Wood Reservoir. Permits for fishing or bird-watching at the reservoir are available from the Recreation Officer, Weir Wood Reservoir, Forest Row. The extensive open areas and picnic sites on Ashdown Forest S of Forest Row are well known.

17 SEVEN SISTERS
Sussex CC 692 acres (280 hectares)
At Exceat, between Seaford and Eastbourne. Approach on A259. Main car park at TV 519995 freely open daylight hours. Additional car park during main season on minor road towards Litlington, immediately N of the park centre at TV 518996. Forestry Commission car park in Friston Forest further up the same road at TQ 518002 (freely open at all times). Park centre open Easter to late October 11.00–17.30, and winter weekends 11.00–16.00. Accessible by bus.

Seven Sisters park lies at the heart of what has now been defined as the Sussex Heritage Coast, the area S of A259 between Seaford and Eastbourne, which is also an AONB, and in part an SSSI. The park includes very varied scenery and natural habitats: chalk downland, cliffs, shingle foreshore, salt marsh and meadow. It is crossed by the S branch of the South Downs Way, and footpaths provide links to surrounding areas which are also open to the public. Seaford Head local nature reserve is immediately to the W, the Forestry Commission's Friston Forest is to the N, and the chalk cliffs to the E include National Trust and local authority land extending to Beachy Head. Footpaths and bridleways throughout the area are being waymarked and an accompanying map is available at the park centre.

This part of E Sussex has attracted visitors for many years. The problem now is how to reconcile public demand with protecting the whole environment. East Sussex Council define the main objectives of their policy for the whole Heritage Coast as to maintain the valued character of the landscape and its rural atmosphere, to safeguard the interests of farming, forestry, water supply, nature conservation and residents, and to provide for recreation activities that are based on the resources of the area and do not damage them. This means that while the park is freely open throughout the year, visitors arriving at the busiest times may be unable to find car-parking space.

Most of the park is being grazed by cattle and sheep to retain the rich variety of

167

The famous view of Cuckmere Haven and the Seven Sisters on the Sussex Coast, as seen from the local nature reserve on Seaford Head. The visitor centre and main area of the country park lie further up the Cuckmere valley to the left. *East Sussex CC*

downland flora, so dogs have to be kept under control. The shingle beach at Cuckmere Haven can be reached after a 30-minute walk or short cycle ride, in part over rough tracks, but is not particularly attractive for swimming. Apart from limited permission for canoeing on the Cuckmere, other sports are not offered.

The park centre and ranger service provide an excellent interpretative service. The centre is an 18th-century barn converted to house a sales area, and both temporary and permanent exhibitions. The park trail provides an insight into the varied scenery and wildlife, and covers the physical development of the Cuckmere Valley and the influence of man on this landscape. A guide to this trail is on sale at the centre. A second forest walk starts from N of the centre. Bird watchers will find many species of land and water birds, especially at migration time. There is a hide, and salt marsh and shingle islands have been created to encourage particular species.

Friston Forest (1987 acres, or 804 hectares managed by the Forestry Commission) covers part of the catchment area of Eastbourne Waterworks, and is crossed by many paths and bridleways. Conifers have been used as a nurse crop to be progressively felled, leaving the slower-growing beech trees to form the main forest. A woodland walk starts from the picnic site and car park at TQ 518001. Seaford Head nature reserve is directly accessible from Seaford, from a car park at TV 504980, or beside the Golden Galleon at Exceat Bridge, TV 513993.

18 HASTINGS
Hastings BC 502 acres (203 hectares)

The coast E of Hastings. Main car park and centre at E end; from Hastings follow A259 to Ore, turning right on minor road to Fairlight and Pett Level. Turn right by Fairlight church to entrance at TQ 860117. W end directly accessible from Hastings at East Hill. Additional main season car park and picnic site (the heliport site) W of Fairlight Lodge Hotel at TQ 847117. Freely open at all times. Accessible by bus.

Hastings Country Park includes cliff top, narrow glens and foreshore extending E from Old Town to Fire Hills, a 4 mile (6½km) stretch of unspoilt coast. The scenery is striking and varied; the coastal path passes from the grass-covered East Hill, through wooded valleys and over bracken-clad slopes, to the gorse and heather of Fire Hills. There are excellent views, and the network of paths and tracks has very good signs. Behind the coast the land rises to around 500ft (150m), and 3 small streams have cut short deep valleys almost to sea level. These glens or ghylls (from W to E, Ecclesbourne, Fairlight and Warren Glens) provide equable, moist conditions in which unusual plant species have survived, often beneath ancient oak and ash trees. The coastal cliffs are impressive but unstable and liable to landslips, due to their structure and attack by the sea. On average the cliffs are receding by over 1m a year. Beds of sands and clay alternate: starting from the summit level the sequence is Wadhurst Clay, and below that Ashdown Sands (the main formation exposed in quarries at Fairlight and in the upper cliffs), with Fairlight Clay on the beach and in the lower cliffs. Parts of the coastal path are steep and may be muddy. The shore is accessible in Covehurst Bay down steps (frequently renewed because of local landslips). The stony beach is perhaps more suitable for fossil hunting than swimming. Because of the rich wildlife and unusual species of the glens and the geological interest of the cliffs, part of the area is an SSSI.

The most popular and accessible parts of the park are either close to Hastings or beside the main car parks at Fairlight. The information centre and toilets are at Fairlight, with a café close by. Limited parking space is reserved for disabled drivers at the top of the main picnic field, with views E over Pett Level and Dungeness. The gorse-covered Fire Hills provide easy walking, and the old coastguard hut has been converted to a viewing platform. There are several nature trails: the one in Warren Glen starts from quarries beside the park centre (the others are more accessible from the heliport site via Barley Lane).

169

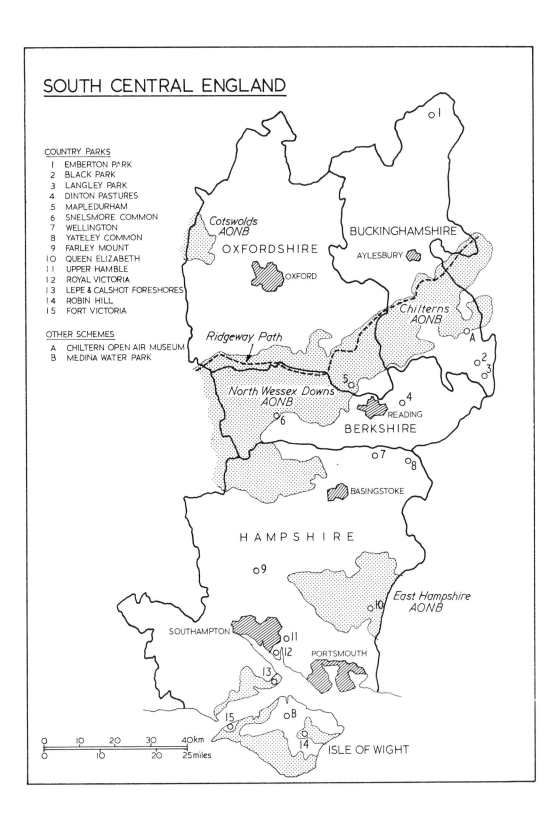

SOUTH CENTRAL ENGLAND

COUNTRY PARKS
1   EMBERTON PARK
2   BLACK PARK
3   LANGLEY PARK
4   DINTON PASTURES
5   MAPLEDURHAM
6   SNELSMORE COMMON
7   WELLINGTON
8   YATELEY COMMON
9   FARLEY MOUNT
10 QUEEN ELIZABETH
11 UPPER HAMBLE
12 ROYAL VICTORIA
13 LEPE & CALSHOT FORESHORES
14 ROBIN HILL
15 FORT VICTORIA

OTHER SCHEMES
A   CHILTERN OPEN AIR MUSEUM
B   MEDINA WATER PARK

Cotswolds
AONB

BUCKINGHAMSHIRE

OXFORDSHIRE

AYLESBURY

OXFORD

Chilterns
AONB

Ridgeway Path

North Wessex Downs
AONB

READING

BERKSHIRE

BASINGSTOKE

H A M P S H I R E

East Hampshire
AONB

SOUTHAMPTON

PORTSMOUTH

ISLE OF WIGHT

0   10   20   30   40km
0   10   20   25miles

South Central England

1 EMBERTON PARK
Milton Keynes DC 175 acres (71 hectares)
At Olney 4 miles (6½km) N of Newport Pagnell. Entrance on A509 at SP 887501. Open daylight hours. Admission charge.

Emberton Park is in attractive countryside beside the river Ouse on a site worked for gravel in 1956–62. The land was bought by Newport Pagnell RDC in 1965, and the initial development took place before country parks came into existence. The aim has been to promote recreation (other than noisy activities) and encourage wildlife. The entry charge is offset by a greater than average range of facilities and the fact that (except in wet weather) visitors may take their cars almost anywhere in the park.

The lakes form the focus of this carefully landscaped site, and each has a different pattern of uses. Emberton Sailing Club have sole use of one; another is for public sailing on a day or season ticket basis, and there is a boat compound for those wishing to leave their craft on site. (Boats are not available for hire.) The smallest lake is for model-boat sailing. Fishing is available in the lakes and from the river Ouse banks (day and season tickets are available), but the water is not suitable for swimming. There is extensive and secluded provision for caravan and tented camping, and a site for camping-club rallies. Other facilities include a shop, a restaurant, 3 separate play areas for children, and a pitch-and-putt course. A nature trail features particularly the waterside vegetation, and associated bird and other freshwater life.

2 BLACK PARK
Bucks CC 546 acres (221 hectares)
N of A412 between Slough and Iver Heath. Approach from dual carriageway on A412, turning N along Black Park Lane (signs to Wexham Street and Fulmer). Car-park entrance at TQ 005833. Freely open daylight hours. Accessible by bus.

Black Park and Langley Park immediately to the S were purchased by Bucks CC between 1939 and 1945. Both are now Green Belt land; some 700 years ago both formed part of the large Langley Marish estate.

Black Park is an extensive area of woodland surrounding a fine artificial lake, and offers opportunities for walking, riding and free coarse fishing. There is a swimming area with changing huts, but water sports are limited to daylight hours. There are way-marked riding trails and separate entrances for riders, both here and in neighbouring Langley Park. The picnic area is at the S end of the lake beside the café.

The nature trail passes through mixed

woodland (mainly oak, beech and sweet chestnut) as well as acid heathland, with birch and pine. The soils are poor and often waterlogged (podzol soils developed on glacial gravels). A visit to Black Park can well be combined with one to neighbouring Langley Park or to the churchyard at Stoke Poges and Burnham Beeches, a short distance W.

3 LANGLEY PARK
Bucks CC 136 acres (55 hectares)
Off S side of A412 between Slough and Iver Heath. From A412 turn S down minor road (Billet Lane) just W of Iver Heath roundabout, to car-park entrance at TQ 016824. Freely open daylight hours. Accessible by bus.

This country park adjoins Black Park, and includes the NE sector of the Langley Park estate. The main house and outbuildings lie outside the country park, as does the S part of the estate. However, there is a marked farm trail across farmland here, where public access is limited to certain footpaths. This area is part of the ancient Langley Marish estate.

Visitors will particularly enjoy the rhododendrons and flowering shrubs at the N end of the park. Seats on a raised plinth (formerly the base of a monument) look directly across to Windsor Castle. To the left is woodland and a line of Californian redwood (sequoia) trees; to the right there is an old deer park. A nature trail explores this higher sector of the park, where some of the pollard oak trees may be as much as 400 years old. The riding trail enters Langley Park direct from A412, and the adjoining Black Park. Both Black and Langley Parks are situated within the Colne Valley Regional Park.

4 DINTON PASTURES
Wokingham DC 274 acres
(111 hectares) when complete
3 miles (5km) SE of Reading on N side of M329. Approach along B3030 (Davis Street) past Winnersh Station towards Hurst. Entrance by the Black Swan at SU 787717. Freely open daylight hours.

This country park opened in 1979 on an extensive valley site, and it is still at an early stage; more land is being added in 1981. From the car park beside the Black Swan, paths lead down towards a landscaped area of former gravel pits, now converted to provide for a variety of watersports. There are 7 lakes, and the river Loddon flows along the W side of the park. Coarse fishing, sailing, canoeing and wind-surfing are available. A 9-hole municipal golf course is immediately beside the park, and day tickets for both golf and fishing are available at the clubhouse. The extensive areas of open water already attract a large number of birds.

5 MAPLEDURHAM
Oxford CC 25 acres (10 hectares)
1½ miles (2½km) NW of Reading beside the Thames. Approach along B4526 Reading to Goring road, turning W down minor road at sign to village. Entrance at SU 670768. Very limited opening hours, and car-parking charge, which covers entry to house. Open between Easter and 30 September, Saturdays, Sundays and Bank Holidays, 11.30–17.30. (House open on same days, 14.30–17.30, admission charge.)

This is a small area of riverside meadows beside the Thames, with a weir and locks. The setting is attractive (this is part of the Chilterns AONB), but facilities are limited: in essence the country park provides a car park and picnic site on days when Mapledurham House is open. This is an Elizabethan mansion built by the Blount family, and has an interesting collection of pictures. The village itself, the church and almshouses, are also extremely attractive. A 16th-century watermill, the oldest surviving mill beside the Thames, has now been restored to full working order and is open to the public. The river is considered unsuitable for swimming, and fishing and boating are not available to the public. An alternative way of reaching Mapledurham is by motor launch from Caversham Bridge in Reading, on afternoons when the house is open.

6 SNELSMORE COMMON
Newbury DC 126 acres (51 hectares)
3 miles (5km) N of Newbury on B4494 at SU 463711. From M4 Junction 13 take A34 towards Newbury and turn right at sign to Winterbourne. Then turn left on B4494. Freely open at all times. Accessible by bus.

By contrast with the agricultural landscape of the surrounding chalk downland, this patch of higher ground at 450ft (137m) has remained common land and uncultivated. The poverty of its thin and peaty soils is due to underlying patches of Plateau Gravels and London Clay. These low hills are mostly clothed by ling and bell heather, with patches of birch and pinewood. The picnic area is a glade among silver birches, and there is an inviting network of footpaths and bridleways. (No riding permits are required.) An ancient earthwork can be traced across the common. Snelsmore Common provides pleasant open countryside just within the North Wessex AONB. For the driver beset by the traffic of M4, it offers an oasis of calm.

7 WELLINGTON
Stratfield Saye Estate 603 acres (244 hectares)
7 miles (11km) S of Reading, near Junction of A32 and A33. From M4 Junction 11 or M3 Junction 5, follow A32. Entrance on A32 at SU 724626. Park open daily 1 March–31 October and weekends in winter, 10.00 till dusk. Campsite open 1 March–31 October. Admission charge. This is a privately developed country park (tel Heckfield 444). Accessible by bus.

The focus of the main section of this country park is a large lake, developed and landscaped from former gravel workings. There is a café on the lakeside, and fishing, boating and sailing. The lake also attracts wildlife and provides a pleasant setting for picnics. There is a play area for children and a small collection of farm animals, as well as a fitness course and crazy golf. The entrance buildings include a gift shop and the National Dairy Museum.

Part of this large country park is managed woodland which shelters roe deer, foxes, badgers and other wildlife. A series of marked trails explore the wood and meadowland, passing the reconstruction of a charcoal burners' camp. A landscaped camping and caravan site, with full facilities, is part of the park complex.

A further extensive area between the A32 and A33 roads has been developed as a riding centre. Instruction is available at all levels, and there is a show-jumping arena and a cross-country course. Various events are staged in this section. Still further W and off A33, outside the country park, Stratfield Saye House, home of the Dukes of Wellington, is open daily, except on Fridays, between early April and late September (admission charge).

8 YATELEY COMMON
Hants CC 494 acres (200 hectares)
2 miles (3km) W of Camberley on N side of A30. Several car parks (signed) along A30 between SU 819589 and 838594. Freely open at all times.

The part of Yateley Common which was acquired by Hampshire Council in 1964 and became a country park in 1970 lies just E of Blackbushe airfield. Although a large area, it is only a remnant of the former extensive heathland on both sides of the Blackwater Valley. The poverty of soils derived from Plateau Gravels prevented development until large areas were taken for military training, and more recently for roads and housing. Sandhurst, Camberley, Farnborough, Aldershot and Fleet have taken over much of the former heath. What remains provides an extensive area of heather, gorse and scattered birch trees, and several small ponds available for fishing. There are picnic sites and various paths and trackways for walking and riding (but no camping). There is at present no focus to the park, but a nature trail is planned.

Yateley Common was once part of the ancient manor of Crondal, and belonged to Alfred the Great. Long the haunt of highwaymen, it now offers a welcome respite from heavy traffic on A30.

9 FARLEY MOUNT
Hants CC 263 acres (106½ hectares)
3 miles (5km) W of Winchester. Four separate areas of downland along Sarum Road, the Roman road from Winchester to Old Sarum. Car parks and picnic sites between SU 409293 and 433293. Also accessible along minor roads from King's Somborne, Sparsholt or Hursley (on A31). Freely open at all times. No toilets.

This popular and attractive chain of open countryside is linked by the Roman road and a footpath which runs from Crabwood (nearest to Winchester) to Beacon Hill. Pitt Down and Beacon Hill are chalk downland rising to 572ft (174m) with wide views extending to Salisbury Cathedral and the Isle of Wight.

There are roe deer among the birch, hazel, oak and beech trees of Crabwood and Westwood, which lie nearer to Winchester. Some parts here are managed as a nature reserve, but there are also waymarked woodland walks. Most of Westwood is Forestry Commission land outside the country park, but accessible along public bridleways. A mosaic pavement excavated from a Roman villa site in this wood can be seen in Winchester City Museum. The main attractions of the country park are opportunities for walking and riding; there are barbecue facilities as well as picnic tables.

10 QUEEN ELIZABETH
Hants CC 1147 acres (464 hectares)
4 miles (6½km) S of Petersfield on A31. Park centre signed from dual carriageway at SU 718187. Butser Hill separately accessible from A31 further S. Follow signs along minor roads to entrance at SU 711199. Park open every day. Parking charges by meter (season tickets available). Park centre open daily 1 April to 30 September, 10.00–18.00, and Sundays in winter 10.00 till dusk. Café open on same days from 10.30. Butser Ancient Farm open 1 April to 30 September, Tuesdays to Saturdays 14.00–17.00, Sundays and Bank Holidays 11.00–13.00 and 14.00–17.00. Check opening hours and programme of events, (tel Horndean 595040). Accessible by bus.

This large and most interesting country park is described in Chapter 1, and the main features are summarised here. The South Downs are mainly clad in beechwoods E of A31, but are typical chalk downland on Butser Hill to the W. There are excellent views from summits on both sides of A31, and opportunities for picnics, barbecues and walks, including a forest trail and several other waymarked routes. Facilities for pony-trekking, grass-skiing, orienteering or flying kites and model gliders; and a hang-gliding club uses Butser Hill.

The park centre provides an information service and shop, and there are displays on the history and natural history of the park. Close by, the Butser Ancient Farm Demonstration Area has reconstructed Iron Age buildings, and is experimenting with the types of crops and animals important 2,000 years ago. A regular programme of events includes demonstrations of forestry, shepherding and local crafts; various services available for schools and organised groups.

11 UPPER HAMBLE
Hants CC 403 acres (163 hectares) incomplete
The site is just NE of M27 Junction 8, and the present entrance is via Pylands Lane.

The council already owns a large area of farm and woodland beside the river Hamble, at present known as Cricket Camp and open to the public. The country park is unlikely to be fully completed for several years, but the proposals include the creation of Hampshire Farm Museum at Botley Manor Farm, as well as the country park. A range of informal activities will be possible, including riding and camping, as well as facilities for school use and links to the recently opened activities centre for the handicapped.

12 ROYAL VICTORIA, Netley
Hants CC 143 acres (58 hectares)
At Netley on Southampton Water. Vehicle entrance from Victoria Road, Netley at SU 457080, and footpath entrances from N and E. Not yet complete, but freely open daylight hours. Accessible by bus and train.

Royal Victoria Country Park is the grounds and remaining buildings of the famous military hospital. The site is a beautiful one, with fine views across Southampton Water from parkland on a low clifftop. The original hospital buildings were begun immediately after the Crimean War in 1856. Queen Victoria was a regular visitor and laid the foundation stone. The vast size of the building can still be appreciated. Florence Nightingale campaigned unsuccessfully to modify its outdated design, and it became known as the biggest white elephant in the world before all but the chapel was demolished.

The surrounding grassy terraces and mature trees are an ideal setting for picnics, watching shipping, walking or cycling. Two nature-study areas have been defined and there is access to the beach of fine shingle and shells. There is a café and facilities for tennis, cricket and hockey. Visitors by boat can land at Netley, and there is a small public hard outside the park entrance. The ruins of Netley Abbey, maintained by the DOE, are ½ mile (1km) to the NW.

13 LEPE AND CALSHOT FORESHORES
Hants CC 122 acres (49½ hectares)
Two separate sections of Solent foreshore SE of Fawley. Approach Calshot on B3053 from Southampton via Fawley, to car park at Hillhead, SU 480012. Lepe is approached by

The view of the Isle of Wight and the Solent from the cliffs at Lepe, the western section of Lepe and Calshot Country Park. *Hampshire CC*

minor roads from Beaulieu or Fawley; the car park and café are at SZ 456986. A narrow minor road links these two sections. Both are freely open at all times and accessible by bus.

Both of these narrow strips of cliff top and foreshore are popular and readily accessible from Southampton. Most other stretches of this coast have been industrialised or are otherwise closed to the public. At Lepe the country park land is E of the car park; at Calshot it is to the W, and some ¾ mile of private land separates the two sections. This area is an AONB, and backed by the New Forest, but its greatest attraction is the view of the Isle of Wight and the busy Solent shipping lanes. The panorama includes vessels of all sizes: yachts from Cowes and

Beaulieu River, ocean-going vessels, hovercraft and hydrofoil, even (on my first visit) a Sunderland flying boat.

The beaches are shingle rather than sand, but popular for swimming and sea-fishing. At Calshot a shingle spit extends E to the castle (which is not open to the public). At Lepe the coast is backed by rough grassland and wind-swept trees. The attractive slate-clad coastguard cottages are W of the park boundary. Lepe probably stands near an early port developed by the Romans, but long silted up. It may also be on the line of a prehistoric crossing place from the mainland to the Isle of Wight. Finds made on these shores have included Stone Age (Palaeolithic) implements and the bones of elephant buried in estuarine sand.

14 ROBIN HILL
Downend Enterprises Ltd 79 acres (32 hectares)

2 miles (3km) E of Newport, Isle of Wight. The entrance at SZ 533878 is almost at the summit of Arreton Down, close to the Hare and Hounds public house. The approach via minor roads is well signed from Newport and other main roads. Open daily 10.00–18.00. Admission charge. Accessible by bus. This is a privately developed country park (tel Arreton 430).

Opened in 1969 and well advertised, this is a popular country park on an attractive hilltop site, in an AONB. Much is natural wood and grassland, but this has been enhanced by gardens round the main buildings, and a lake and newly established water garden in the valley below. A nature trail explores these natural features and takes in a Roman villa site. Excavations in 1911 revealed a fine mosaic; in 1968 the foundations of an aisled building and bath house were uncovered, but this has mostly been back filled for preservation.

For most visitors a salient feature is the extensive collection of animals and birds, as well as the range of other entertainments. There are more than 100 varieties of animals and birds, native and foreign, a pets corner for children, a large walk-through enclosure housing animals and birds, and a tropical aviary.

Other entertainments at the park include a putting green, a competitive obstacle course, a commando-style assualt course and both pony and donkey rides. At the park centre are a cafeteria and licensed bar, and a gift shop. The barbecue and open-air restaurant are open for lunch from early May and up to midnight in the high season.

15 FORT VICTORIA
Isle of Wight CC 49 acres (20 hectares)

On the coast at Sconce Point, W of Yarmouth. From A3054 turn W (sign) at SZ 344893 to the car park at the ruins of Fort Victoria. Freely open at all times. Accessible by bus or on foot along Coast Path F6 from Yarmouth or Totland.

Although officially designated in 1971, this country park remains incomplete for lack of finance. It has essentially 3 features: the fort, the coast and the wooded cliffs behind. The originally impressive but rapidly outdated fort was built in 1853 on the site of an earlier gun battery of the Napoleonic period. It was intended that this and Hurst Castle would control the Needles Passage, and prevent an attack on Portsmouth. The fort originally had a complement of 60 guns but only ruins remain today. From the upper floor there is an excellent view of one of the busiest seaways in the world, with a café and picnic and barbecue facilities below.

The beach is quiet but dangerous for swimming or boating because of the tide race and wash from passing ships. It is popular for sea-angling. The woodland on the unstable cliff behind is full of interest for the naturalist. The summit is on Bembridge Limestone (Oligocene) overlying sands and clays. Contrasts in rock type have led to varied plant communities, but the whole cliff area is subject to landslips. A nature trail starts from the café and leads up to several good view points. Hurst Castle on the mainland opposite was built by Henry VIII. Charles I was later held prisoner there, after being transferred from Carisbrooke in 1648. The beach is accessible down flights of steps, but the path can be wet.

OTHER SCHEMES
A CHILTERN OPEN AIR MUSEUM

There are plans to open a collection of buildings, rescued from other sites, along the lines of Weald and Downland Museum Country Park, at Singleton in W Sussex. The site will be in Newland Park at Chalfont St Giles, but it is unlikely to be open for some time.

B MEDINA COUNTRY AND WATER PARK Isle of Wight CC

There are proposals for a park on each side of the Medina river between Newport and Cowes. These would include additional access and parking, and the opening of a privately run miniature railway along the former railway track. It is hoped to provide sites for dinghy-launching. There are considerable problems to be overcome, and so far facilities are limited to a nature trail along the E bank, starting from Newport quayside.

South-west England

1 CRICKLEY HILL
Glos CC 148 acres (60 hectares)
The approach road (signed) is off B4070 just N of its junction with A417 (the Gloucester to Cirencester road) and close to the Air Balloon public house. Freely open at all times.

Crickley Hill is an important archaeological site where excavations continue each summer. The park visitor centre contains a small exhibition on local archaeology, geology and natural history. A spur projects beyond the main Cotswold escarpment and at its furthest limit are the remains of a Neolithic rampart. Much more obvious, however, are what survives of an Iron Age settlement. Excavations inside the main rampart have revealed a paved street, much worn by traffic, and the post holes of timber buildings from different periods.

The view over Gloucester to the Forest of Dean and the Malvern Hills is magnificent. When complete this country park should cater for a variety of interests. Cotswold stone (Oolitic Limestone of Jurassic age) has been quarried here and is clearly exposed just below the crest of the escarpment. An interesting collection of downland plants survives on this exposed site and contrasts with woodland and meadow in the Scrubbs (National Trust land) immediately adjoining. The whole area is designated an AONB, and part is also an SSSI.

2 ROBINSWOOD HILL
Gloucester City C 240 acres (97 hectares)
An isolated hill on the S edge of Gloucester. Approach from roundabout where B4072 (Gloucester to Stroud road) crosses the ring road A38. At roundabout take unnamed suburban road (Reservoir Road) which is the turning to left of that to Stroud, and continue through houses to park entrance at SO 836157. Freely open at all times. Information centre open and refreshments available at peak times only. Accessible by bus.

Robinswood Hill rises straight out of housing estates on the edge of Gloucester and provides an excellent viewpoint. The country park includes the summit and W side; the E side is a private golf course. This hill is an outlier of the Cotswolds 650ft (200m) high. Marlstone and beds of sand underlie the summit and upper slopes, forming a natural reservoir from which Gloucester has long obtained part of its water supply. There is an ancient stone cross covering an early well. The silts and clays of the lower slopes have been used for brick-making in the works (now disused) at Tuffley. Contrasted rock and soil types provide a variety of vegetation and wildlife habitats. A nature trail and footpaths lead up to the summit viewpoint. There is also a riding trail, children's play area and provision for camping.

179

The view towards Gloucester from Crickley Hill Country Park on the Cotswold edge. In the foreground the Cotswold Way runs through an important archaeological site. Robinswood Hill Country Park is on the far side of the isolated hill in the middle distance. *Gloucester CC*

3 KEYNES PARK, COTSWOLD WATER PARK
Glos CC 104 acres (42 hectares)

4 miles (6½km) S of Cirencester on the county boundary. Easiest approach from A419 Cirencester to Cricklade road, turning W along new spur road at junction just N of Latton Creamery (sign to park). In 3½ miles (5½km) turn right on Spratsgate Lane towards Cirencester, to the entrance at SU 026957. (Alternative approaches direct from Cirencester or from the W via Kemble village.) Freely open daylight hours.

Keynes park is part of the Cotswold Water Park referred to in Chapter 6, in the wide valley of the Upper Thames quite near its source. The whole area between the attractive villages of Ashton Keynes, Somerford Keynes and South Cerney has been extensively worked for gravel. Because these gravel terraces overlie Oxford Clay, the high water-table ensures that the excavated pits become areas of open water, now much valued for sailing and fishing. At Keynes Park two gravel pits have been landscaped and opened for watersports. Ashton Keynes Angling Club issue day fishing permits on site (or from Mr J. Parker, tel Wootton Bassett 2028). Keynes Park Sailing Club, with clubhouse and facilities at the park, also issue day permits for sailing.

The surrounding banks provide picnic sites with opportunities to watch the sailing or to study the waterbirds which frequent the area. There is ample space for walking and informal games. As gravel extraction proceeds more areas are likely to be added to this country park. The old canal which formerly linked the Severn and Thames is another attraction. It has unusual lock keepers' cottages and is crossed by an interesting bridge at SU 072973.

4 LYDIARD PARK
Thamesdown BC 147 acres (59½ hectares)

At Lydiard Tregoze, 3 miles (5km) W of Swindon. From A420 Swindon to Wootton Bassett road turn N at roundabout just N of M4 interchange, and follow signs. (Present entrance leads to St Mary's church and parking behind the house at SU 104848.) From M4 take Junction 16 on to A420 towards Swindon. Turn left at next roundabout. Park freely open daylight hours. House and church open Sundays 14.00–17.30, other days 10.00–13.00 and 14.00–17.30. House admission charge.

With commendable far-sightedness Swindon Corporation bought Lydiard Tregoze mansion and part of the former estate in 1943. The house and landscaped parkland have been open to the public for many years. Parts of the buildings have been developed as a management training centre; there are also camping and hostel facilities for organised groups. The estate is now to become a country park and some changes in its layout are planned to meet pressures resulting from the expansion of Swindon. Future visitors are likely to enter at the S end of the park. Necessary clearance and replanting of trees is enhancing the beauty of the setting. Lawns and fine trees surround the house, but nothing remains of the original formal gardens. A lake survives from what was formerly a much larger expanse of water; this will be reshaped and improved, but is not available for boating or fishing. A nature trail circles the lake and parkland.

The house, remodelled in the 1740s, has handsome state rooms open to visitors, and the church nearby contains exceptionally interesting memorials.

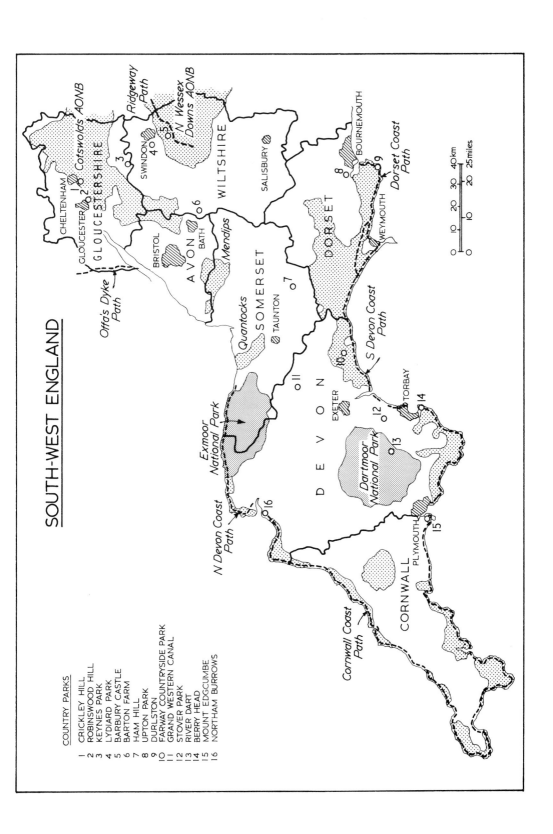

SOUTH-WEST ENGLAND

COUNTRY PARKS

1   CRICKLEY HILL
2   ROBINSWOOD HILL
3   KEYNES PARK
4   LYDIARD PARK
5   BARBURY CASTLE
6   BARTON FARM
7   HAM HILL
8   UPTON PARK
9   DURLSTON
10   FARWAY COUNTRYSIDE PARK
11   GRAND WESTERN CANAL
12   STOVER PARK
13   RIVER DART
14   BERRY HEAD
15   MOUNT EDGCUMBE
16   NORTHAM BURROWS

Barbury Castle on the Marlborough Downs, from the west. This air view shows a Bronze Age disc barrow in front of the ramparts of the magnificent Iron Age hill fort, and the two ancient trackways which it dominates. To the left, the prehistoric Ridgeway descends the chalk escarpment towards Liddington Hill, while the present Ridgeway Path passes through Barbury Castle towards the car park and Smeathe's Ridge at the top right of the picture. *Wiltshire CC*

5 BARBURY CASTLE
Wilts CC 131 acres (53 hectares)

5 miles (8km) S of Swindon. Accessible from M4 Junction 15 and Swindon via A345 or A361, and then B4005 (linking Wroughton and Chisledon). The approach road turns S (at sign) from B4005 to the car park entrance at SU 157761. Freely open at all times.

Barbury Castle is an Iron Age hill fort on the summit of the Marlborough Downs at a height of 879ft (268m). Its double earth ramparts may have supported a wooden pallisade, with the main entrances fortified by look-out towers. It is scheduled as an Ancient Monument but has not so far been systematically excavated. Barbury is one of a series of hill forts linked by a network of ancient trackways. The prehistoric Ridgeway, and its continuation the Icknield Way, followed the general line of the chalk escarpment from Wessex to East Anglia. Barbury Castle stands at the junction between the Ridgeway (which here descends towards Liddington to the NE) and the equally ancient Smeathe's Ridge which runs SE and is now the line of the long-distance Ridgeway Path.

The whole area is rich in prehistoric remains. A disc barrow, probably dating back to 1700 BC (the Early Bronze Age), lies just W of the hill fort. The boundaries of ancient fields (the so-called Celtic field systems) are well preserved E of the approach road and are best revealed by oblique sunlight. Immediately below and to the N of Barbury Castle is the site of a great battle, mentioned in the *Anglo-Saxon Chronicle*, where the Romanised Britons attempted to repel the Saxons in AD 556. The approach road itself was the old coach road from Swindon to Marlborough, and some of the old milestones survive beside the unsurfaced descent towards Rockley.

The other great attractions of this country park are the views N, the fine downland scenery in this AONB, and the freedom to walk and ride along the Ridgeway. A display kiosk in the car park sets out the many possibilities.

6 BARTON FARM
Wilts CC 25 acres (10 hectares)
From A363 in Bradford on Avon and just S of the river bridge, follow the signed approach to car-parking by the station. The park entrance is at ST 823605. Freely open at all times. Accessible by bus and train.

This small country park is a strip of meadowland between the Kennet and Avon Canal and the river Avon itself. At this point the river has cut a gorge through the Jurassic limestones which provide the admirable building stone characteristic of the whole area. The park itself is attractive, but it is its position close to so many interesting buildings which is more important. The magnificent 14th-century tithe barn, which once belonged to Shaftesbury Abbey (and is now maintained by the DOE) lies immediately S. Beside it are the buildings of Barton Farm (now being restored). The farmhouse has a chapel on the upper floor and there is a granary and unmodernised cowsheds. N of the country park and approached by a signed footpath across the 14th-century Barton Bridge, is the famous Saxon Church, founded in the 8th century.

The Kennet and Avon Canal is also worth exploring, although at present it is not fully navigable. (Boat trips are available from the lock at the Frome Road bridge outside the country park.) The canal crosses the Avon on an impressive aqueduct designed by John Rennie and completed in 1804. The aqueduct, old mill buildings and cottages of Avoncliff lie at the W end of the park and are best approached along the towpath.

The meadowland by the river is attractive for picnics and walking. Information boards' provide large-scale maps of the area. Day fishing tickets are available from Bradford on Avon Angling Association. Bradford Rowing Club have premises by Barton Bridge, and small boats may be launched from the river bank.

7 HAM HILL
Yeovil DC 153 acres (62 hectares)
Hilltop 5 miles (8km) W of Yeovil and immediately S of Stoke-sub-Hamdon. Approach along A3088 Ilminster to Yeovil road, turning S at sign in Stoke village. A series of car parks and toilet block around ST 478167. Freely open at all times.

Ham on Hamdon Hill rises dramatically above the levels of S Somerset. It has been important both as a defensive site and as a

Medieval buildings beside the River Avon at Barton Farm Country Park, Bradford on Avon. The farm buildings and magnificent tithe barn are visible beyond the fourteenth-century bridge. The Kennet and Avon Canal is immediately behind the barn. *Wiltshire CC*

source of the fine golden building stone, whose qualities may be judged from buildings in the surrounding villages. Ham Hill stone is a shelly limestone from the Upper Lias rocks of Jurassic age. The hilltop commands much wider views than its mere height (426ft or 130m) would suggest. It is ringed by the impressive ramparts of a large Iron Age hill fort, and there is evidence that the site was occupied during the Neolithic and Bronze Age periods. Part of the summit was later occupied by a Roman garrison to protect the ford where the Fosse Way crossed the river Parrett. (Antiquities of Iron Age and Roman date, excavated from Ham Hill, are in the Somerset County Museum at Taunton.)

Apart from opportunities to walk round the summit or stop at a viewpoint, the extensive quarrying has provided what amounts to a natural adventure playground. A brochure about this park is in preparation but there is no nature trail or other planned activity at present.

Montacute village lies immediately below and E of Ham Hill. Montacute House (National Trust) is a magnificent Elizabethan house of Ham Hill stone. Open daily, except Tuesday, from 1 April to 31 October between 12.30 and 18.00.

186

8 UPTON PARK
Poole BC 54 acres (22 hectares)

On the S side of A35 just W of Poole. The approach from Poole is signed down a slip road from the dual carriageway. Freely open daily 9.00 till dusk. Accessible by bus.

Upton Park is a small but attractive park running down to the shore of Holes Bay, an inlet off Poole Harbour. The present house was built in 1818 by Christopher Spurrier, whose father had been a wealthy merchant and banker in Poole. William Llewellin gave the house to Poole BC in 1957, but the estate has only recently been opened to the public as a country park. The house is a Grade II Listed Building; though structurally sound, it cannot be opened to the public until funds are available for its restoration.

The house stands on a low hill surrounded by gardens, fine trees and meadowland. The picnic and informal games area is in open parkland in front of the house or by the shore. From the terrace is a view S over Holes Bay, framed by fine specimen trees and flowering shrubs. The walled garden is being restored and it is hoped eventually to serve refreshments and develop a riding trail and two bird hides. The bird-watcher can hope to see waders and typical salt-marsh species as well as some of the rarer woodland birds.

9 DURLSTON
Dorset CC 262 acres (106 hectares)

Immediately S of Swanage on the coast at Durlston Head. Approach from centre of Swanage along Lighthouse Road to car park at SZ 032773. Park freely open at all times. Information centre normally open Easter to 31 October, 10.30–17.30. Accessible by bus and on foot from Swanage.

Durlston Country Park is on a stretch of Dorset coast which has long been a favourite with visitors. The area is designated an AONB and SSSI, and is defined as a Heritage Coast. This popularity has been one of the problems: it is a fragile environment, liable to damage through over-use by people or cars. The new information centre is the best starting point for first-time visitors. Displays and the excellent literature on sale here explain the important features of the area. There is also a programme of guided walks. The picnic areas are sited nearby and refreshments are available in the 19th-century Durlston Head Castle.

The great attraction here is the wild and relatively unspoilt character of the coast. The variety of coastal scenery in Purbeck is the consequence of its geological structure. Rocks of the Upper Jurassic period dip N so that a sequence of beds outcrop at the coast, the younger Wealden series at Swanage, the older Purbeck and Portland beds at Tilly Whim and Anvil Point. Softer rocks are eroded to form bays; more resistant rocks stand out as cliffed headlands, Upper Purbeck at Peveril Point, Lower Purbeck and Portland at Durlston Head. In addition folding and faulting has occurred, and can be seen in various cliff sections. The Portland stone is an excellent freestone which has been extensively quarried. Tilly Whim Caves (now dangerous and closed to the public) are old quarry workings. The 40 ton stone globe of the world illustrates the qualities of Portland stone, but is now suffering from weathering. (Visitors should be warned that cliff paths near the globe can be muddy in wet weather.) The Dorset Coast Path, which follows the coast S from Swanage, continues through the country park. There are in addition marked nature trails, a stone trail and a woodland walk.

The cliffs are renowned for their sea-bird colonies and between Durlston Head and Tilly Whim Caves are maintained as a wild-life sanctuary. The cliff top vegetation is rich in uncommon species. Inevitably some of the most interesting plants have largely disappeared from around the coastal footpath, a point which underlines the need for visitors to preserve what has survived. A series of footpaths run inland, while the coast path itself continues W beyond the country park towards Dancing Ledge and St Aldhelm's Head.

10 FARWAY COUNTRYSIDE PARK
Mrs J. M. Forbes 119 acres (48 hectares)
4 miles (6½km) S of Honiton. Approach from Honiton along A375 and B3174 to Roncombe Gate or from the A3052 S coast road along B3174. There are good road signs to the entrance at SY 183932 (avoid descending to Farway village). Open Easter to October, daily 10.00–18.00. Admission charge. This is a privately developed park (tel Farway 224).

Farway Countryside Park has 3 major features. It is part of a working farm (Holnest in the valley below) and offers the visitor a chance to see farm animals at close quarters. More important, there is an extensive collection of rare and ancient breeds of farm animal which visitors can study. The setting is the unspoilt Devon landscape in an area designated an AONB, with fine views from the park centre at 720ft (220m), and contrasts in scenery and wildlife between Strap Common on the summit and woods and farmland below.

Entertainment at the park centre includes

Adam the Brahman bull, one of the rare breeds of cattle to be seen at Farway Countryside Park in Devon. *Mrs J. M. Forbes*

pony and donkey rides, a putting course, a gift shop and a small licensed café. Children can enter the pets' enclosure for the tame rabbits and guinea pigs, peacocks, pheasants, ducks and other favourites. The collection of rare breeds is not only interesting to the casual eye but potentially important in preserving certain genetic qualities. There are 7 breeds of horses and ponies, 7 breeds of cattle, 9 varieties of sheep and the so-called Iron Age pigs (highly entertaining in stripes and spots). In addition to roe deer, which run wild in the area, there are 3 species of deer in enclosures.

There are 3 waymarked nature trails set up by the Devon Trust for Nature Conservation. Two descend from the summit towards the valley below and emphasise the contrast in natural vegetation and wildlife between the poor acid soils above (developed on Clay-with-Flints), the steep slopes of the Upper Greensand outcrop and the softer contours and richer red soils (derived from Keuper Marls) in the valley below.

In 1977 the park was extended to include a new area NW of the entrance. Here there is freedom to wander past Bronze Age burial mounds and a badger sett to an excellent viewpoint. Farway lies on a prehistoric routeway and Bronze Age finds from here are now in Exeter Museum.

11 GRAND WESTERN CANAL
Devon CC 11 miles (17km) of restored canal and towpath, extending from Tiverton to the Somerset border
Main car park, boat hire, etc, signed from the centre of Tiverton and off the minor road to Cullompton at SS 963124. From M5 Junction 27 follow A373 to Tiverton. Freely open at all times. Accessible by bus.

This canal was opened in 1814 and originally intended as part of a network linking the English and Bristol Channels from Topsham, Exeter to Bridgwater. Local stone and lime formed the main traffic and trading finally ceased in 1924. Devon CC bought the canal in 1971 and have now restored both the waterway and the towpath. The canal is accessible wherever roads cross it, but parking is difficult except at Tiverton Basin.

The Grand Western Horseboat Co operates a horse-drawn passenger barge (with bar and refreshments) from Tiverton to East Manley during the summer (late May to 30 September normally, tel Tiverton 3345 for details). In addition rowing boats, canoes and punts are available for hire. Those wishing to use private unpowered craft should write to the County Estates Surveyor, County Hall, Exeter for weekly or season licences. Permits are available locally for fishing between Tiverton and Fossend Bridge. The full length of the towpath is attractive for walking; there are many water birds and wildlife is particularly rich at the N end beyond Waytown Tunnel.

12 STOVER PARK
Devon CC 114 acres (46 hectares)
Close to the Drumbridges roundabout at the junction of A38 and A382 (the Bovey Tracey to Newton Abbot road). Three car parks are being developed, one from A382 at SX 830752. Freely open at all times. Accessible by bus.

Devon CC bought Stover Park from the Forestry Commission in 1979, and this site is gradually being developed. The park is part of the former estate of Stover House, built in 1786 on a hilltop above and now a private school. The woodlands at Stover contain the Granite Lodge (a listed building), a lake and many interesting trees which date back to ornamental plantings in the early 19th century. Once the accumulated silt has been cleared, the large lake will provide an attractive centrepiece to the park and a popular coarse-fishing site (day and weekly permits are available). The woodland undergrowth is also being cleared by men working under the special temporary employment programme, and paths have been opened up around the lake. An adventure playground, nature trail and horse-riding trail will be added soon, and it is hoped later to provide a touring campsite.

Stover Park is well placed to provide peaceful natural beauty beside one of the main holiday routes into the SW, a valuable alternative to the over-popular coast and edge of Dartmoor nearby.

13 RIVER DART
River Dart Country Park Ltd
64 acres (26 hectares)
1 mile (1½km) NW of Ashburton off B3357 Ashburton to Dartmoor road. Approach from A38 at turning on the W side of Ashburton (sign to Ashburton and Dartmoor) and follow B3357. The park entrance at SX 735700 is signed to the left. Open daily 10.00–18.00 throughout the year, but full facilities available only from Easter to 31 October. Admission charge. This is a privately developed country park (tel Ashburton 52511).

Developed in a beautiful setting alongside a mile stretch of the river Dart below Holne Bridge, this country park is within Dartmoor National Park and close to the A38 trunk road. The estate was formerly called Holne Park. It includes attractive gardens, meadowland and fine trees (both native and exotic species). The park has been developed to provide for a wide range of interests and activities and there are plans to add to these. There is fishing for salmon and trout in the Dart; day and season permits are available. A leet carries water to lakes for bathing and to encourage waterbirds. There are nature and forest trails, and an attractive riverside picnic area. Among other facilities available are pony rides, clock golf and a woodland adventure playground for children. Part of the parkland is an AA-listed camp site (3 pennants). Campers and country-park visitors share facilities at the main house, where there is a reception and information office, a shop, a licensed restaurant and self-catering accommodation.

14 BERRY HEAD
Torbay BC 100 acres (40½ hectares)
Headland E of Brixham. The main approach is well signed from the W side of Brixham. Gillard Road leads to the entrance at SX 940562. Pedestrian entrance (accessible by bus) direct from Berry Head Road in Brixham, near Berry Head Hotel. Freely open daylight hours.

Berry Head is a dominating headland at the S limit of Torbay. It offers magnificent views and has many interesting features. This is a local nature reserve and is designated an AONB. The South Devon Coast Path runs round the headland from Brixham into St Mary's Bay and there are other paths and a nature trail which invite exploration. There is also a café and a putting green on the flat summit, and ample space for picnics. There are opportunities for sea fishing at the foot of the cliffs.

Those especially interested in geology, natural history, archaeology or military history will find a wealth of information in the park guide book, obtainable in the display centre at the park entrance or from Torbay Council. Berry Head is composed of Devonian limestone some 300 million years old. Long quarried for building stone, it was used in making steel and underwater cement until recently. Older slates and grits, which underline the limestone, outcrop in St Mary's Bay and form the dramatic caves and stacks round Cradle Rock. The flat summit of the headland is an erosion surface of Tertiary date. A number of rare plants grow on the thin summit soils. Some may be survivals from a late glacial flora; others are more characteristic of S Europe. The conservation of rare species such as wild rock rose and varieties of orchid, stonecrop and autumn squill was a major aim when Torbay Council bought Berry Head in 1968. The sea cliffs provide nesting sites for important seabird colonies, and visitors can see fulmars, kittiwakes and guillemots as well as commoner birds.

The strategic importance of Berry Head has been appreciated from prehistoric times. Much of the archaeological interest was lost when forts were constructed in Napoleonic

The Italian Garden at Mount Edgcumbe Country Park in Cornwall, one of several formal gardens on a beautiful stretch of coast beside Plymouth Sound. Elsewhere there are a thousand camellias, and a deer park above the house itself. *By courtesy of Mount Edgcumbe Joint Committee*

times. The huge rampart of an Iron Age promontory fort survived into the 19th century, and was known as the Berry (from the Saxon *Byri*, fortification). In World War II it was the site of an anti-aircraft battery and Observer Corps post. But the ruins of two forts, constructed between 1803 and 1805, are the most conspicuous man-made feature. A thousand men and 50 horses were protected by a dry moat and gun emplacements; a sentry box and the artillery store also survive. The present coastguard station is built on top of the old magazine building, beside the lighthouse which dates from 1906.

15 MOUNT EDGCUMBE
City of Plymouth and Cornwall CC
759 acres (307 hectares)
The only road approach is from the W along B3247 to the Maker entrance by St Macra's church at SX 447520 or the main Cremyll entrance at SX 454534. Passenger ferry services from Admiral's Hard (off Durnford Street, W of Plymouth centre) to Cremyll. Accessible by bus. The country park is open daily 8.00 till dusk. Mount Edgcumbe House is open on Monday and Tuesday, 14.00–18.00 from 1 May to 30 September. Admission charge.

Mount Edgcumbe is probably the most beautiful country park in England, especially when approached across Plymouth Sound. The main section of the park is a headland opposite Plymouth, but there is also a strip of coast extending W round Penlee Point and Rame Head into Whitesand Bay, along the Cornish Coast Path. The house (rebuilt within the Tudor shell after bombing in World War II) is not part of the country park.

The park and gardens were already famous in the 18th century and drew praise from Dr Johnson. Most visitors today will enter through the Cremyll Gate, passing the café and warden's house. Formal gardens with fountains and statuary in French, English and Italian style stretch down to the water's edge. There is a fine 18th-century orangery. In 1967 the International Camellia Society gave 1,000 camellias to beautify these gardens. The former deer park lies beyond, filled with daffodils and primroses in spring. The natural setting of coastal cliffs and woods has been enhanced by various follies, and seats are placed to take advantage of the panoramic views. The Maker entrance is better placed for those wishing to explore the higher, wilder parts of the park or to continue W along the coast. Three routes of different lengths are waymarked.

16 NORTHAM BURROWS
Devon CC 654 acres (264½ hectares)
On Bideford Bay adjoining Westward Ho! and Northam. Main approach from Bideford via B3236 to Northam and straight down on to the Burrows over a cattle grid at SS 444298. Alternative approach, rougher but signed, from Westward Ho! Open at all times. Toll charge for use of road and car-parking.

This is a magnificent stretch of unspoilt coast. A fine sandy beach is backed by sand-hills and a tremendous pebble ridge some 20ft high (almost 7m) formed of large flat stones brought by the sea from cliffs near Hartland Point. The sandy beach is popular for swimming and surfing, but the currents are dangerous at the N end. Back from the coast is a wide expanse of grassland; part of this area is leased to the Royal North Devon Golf Club and another part is set aside as a horse-riding area. The Commoners of Northam maintain their ancient rights to pasture on the Burrows, and keep cattle and geese here. Visitors are asked not to approach the animals. Camping is not allowed.

Northam Burrows is not yet a fully completed country park. There are plans to increase facilities for informal sports, to improve car parks and provide viewing areas. There is also scope to develop a nature reserve.

OTHER SCHEMES

Ashton Court, Bristol, functions as a country park but has been independently developed by the City Council. The main entrance is at the junction of A369 and the Clifton Suspension Bridge road, B3129. The woods, deer park, gardens and part of the mansion are open to the public.

Dorset CC have developed Avon Forest Park between A31 and A338, 2 miles (3½km) SW of Ringwood, with picnic sites in an area of heath and pine woods.

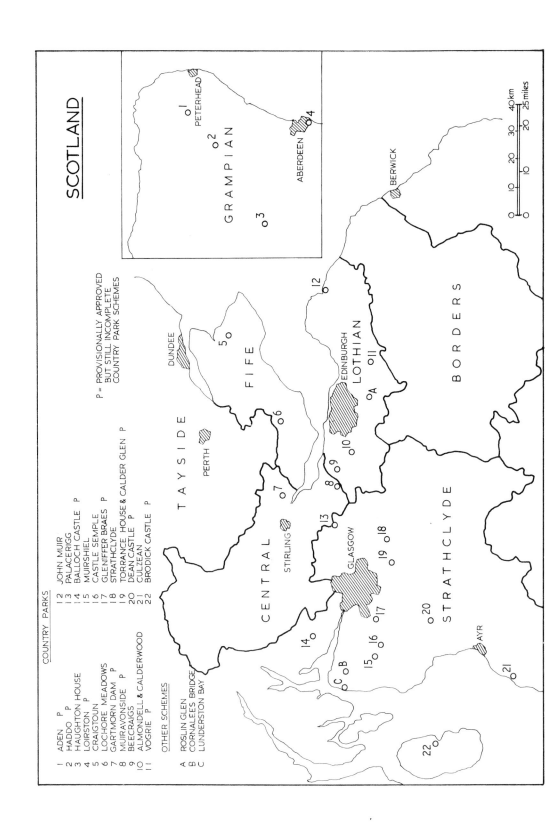

SCOTLAND

COUNTRY PARKS

1	ADEN P	12	JOHN MUIR
2	HADDO P	13	PALACERIGG
3	HAUGHTON HOUSE	14	BALLOCH CASTLE P
4	LOIRSTON P	15	MUIRSHIEL
5	CRAIGTOUN	16	CASTLE SEMPLE
6	LOCHORE MEADOWS	17	GLENIFFER BRAES P
7	GARTMORN DAM P	18	STRATHCLYDE
8	MURAVONSIDE P	19	TORRANCE HOUSE & CALDER GLEN P
9	BEECRAIGS	20	DEAN CASTLE P
10	ALMONDELL & CALDERWOOD	21	CULZEAN
11	VOGRIE P	22	BRODICK CASTLE P

OTHER SCHEMES

A ROSLIN GLEN
B CORNALEES BRIDGE
C LUNDERSTON BAY

P = PROVISIONALLY APPROVED
BUT STILL INCOMPLETE
COUNTRY PARK SCHEMES

Scotland

1 ADEN
Banff and Buchan DC 220 acres (89 hectares)

6 miles (9½km) W of Peterhead. Main entrance from A950 W of Mintlaw at NJ 984484. (Pedestrian entrance beside Old Deer Church.) Freely open at all times.

Aden is the northernmost of the country parks to date. Despite its position on the open lowlands of NE Scotland, this is a sheltered and attractive site, filled with flowers in spring and early summer. The Aden estate was the creation of the Russell family, who were lairds here for almost two centuries. At its greatest extent the estate covered 10,000 acres (4,047 hectares). The country park includes the ruins of the house, the policy (estate grounds), home farm and farmworkers' cottages. Shelter and self-sufficiency were keynotes in the development. Belts of trees were planted and the winding valley of the South Ugie Water became the lower gardens, planted with shrubs and a variety of native and exotic trees. Many mature trees survive, although quick-growing conifers now make up much of the extensive woodland.

Aden House itself was built in 1773 on the site of an earlier home, and surrounded by lawns sloping down towards the river. Behind the house a crescent of farm buildings was erected. There was a walled garden, an ice house and a coal-fired gasworks to light the house. Mounting costs forced the last laird to sell the estate in 1937, and subsequent neglect and a gale in 1952 irretrievably damaged the house, now a picturesque ruin. The farm buildings have fared better and are being reconstructed to provide an information and display centre. A school study centre and café will be added, and a farmworker's cottage reconstructed. The surrounding landscaped grounds are being rescued. Footpaths radiate from the house towards the river and to the pond (originally a source of water power). A riding trail crosses the park and there is fishing for brown trout, sea trout and salmon in the river Ugie. From an observation hide visitors can watch the large variety of birds. A camping site is being developed.

2 HADDO
Grampian Regional C 180 acres (73 hectares)

SE of Methlick and 20 miles (32km) N of Aberdeen. Approach the estate from the S, following signs from B999 at Tarves along a minor road. A long drive (with speed bumps) leads from the entrance at NJ 864325 to both country park and Haddo House (National Trust). Park freely open daylight hours. House open 1 May to 30 September, weekdays 11.00–18.00, Sundays 14.00–18.00. Admission charge. NT members free.

Creating a country park at Aden House in Grampian. The farm buildings are being restored and converted to provide a visitor centre. The house is now a picturesque ruin, but its policy grounds provide beauty and shelter in this most northerly of our country parks.

Haddo House and Country Park were first opened to the public in 1979 and the park is still provisionally registered. The Palladian mansion and its immediate gardens are managed by the National Trust for Scotland and not part of the country park, but most visitors will wish to see both house and country park. The latter is a section of landscaped parkland (the policy) lying E of the house, and including woodland, grassland and a lake. The long drive up from the estate entrance serves as a fitting introduction to Haddo, yet the whole landscape is less than two centuries old. When George Gordon, 4th Earl of Aberdeen inherited Haddo in 1805, the land was bare peat moss. The moss was drained, trees and shrubs planted, landscaped vistas framing architectural features laid out and lakes created. The resulting shelter attracted a

great variety of wildlife, and the park is now the home of roe deer, red squirrel, stoat, mink, fox and many bird species. The picnic site is in grassland E of the house, and paths lead on round the lake. Stable buildings at the house are being converted to provide an information centre and shop.

3 HAUGHTON HOUSE
Grampian Regional C 48 acres (20 hectares)
At Alford, Donside. Turn N (at sign) in Alford village to the entrance at NJ 577167. Freely open at all times. Car-parking charge by meter.

The Howe of Alford is a sheltered lowland beside the winding river Don, and ringed by hills, of which Bennachie is the most

196

striking. At the heart of this lowland stands Haughton House. The Farquharson family bought the estate in the late 17th century, living first at a cottage (now a listed building) near the river. The main part of Haughton House (also a listed building) was erected between 1890 and 1900, a stark 3-storey block of hand-hewn granite which looks E over meadow and woodland. The house and camp site beside it are not strictly part of the country park, although they are accessible to all park visitors. The camp site (AA 4 pennants) is open from 30 March to 1 October for touring campers and cara-vanners. Self-catering accommodation is also available, with a site shop and other facilities in the house (tel Alford 2107 for bookings).

Much of the country park is scattered woodland, typically rowan and silver birch growing among the ling. The gardens by the house have been developed to provide various entertainments including an aviary, an adventure playground, barbecue site, putting green and miniature railway.

The opportunities to walk along the river bank and through attractive woodland extend W from the country park into the adjoining Murray Park. The latter (also part of the Haughton House estate) was given to the people of Alford in 1935 by the poet Charles Murray, who was born and educated in Alford. It includes a pond used in winter for curling. Nature trails in both sections feature the variety of birds and animals living in this woodland sanctuary.

4 LOIRSTON
City of Aberdeen DC 620 acres
(251 hectares)

The coast SE of Aberdeen. An extensive country park in 2 sections, accessible at many points and with no obvious centre. E section, the coast from Torry Battery, Aberdeen, to Cove Bay, is accessible along the coast road linking these two. W section, Kincorth Hill, accessible through Kincorth or at Nigg. Freely open at all times. Accessible by bus.

Loirston Country Park covers a large area and has great potential for the development of informal recreation facilities (the park is provisionally registered so far). A guide book available from the council's Leisure and Recreation Department provides a map, and sets out the range of possibilities. Unfortu-nately, construction work is affecting the whole coastal sector SE of Aberdeen. There is fine scenery with magnificent views all the same. A good starting point for new visitors is the headland E of the harbour and round Girdle Ness to Nigg Bay and St Fittick's church. There are car parks with excellent views near the South Breakwater and in Greyhope and Nigg Bays. This is an opportunity to see Arctic skua, shearwater, cormorant, guillemot and many other sea-birds. Girdle Ness lighthouse was designed by Robert Stevenson (grandfather of the writer). It was built in the 1830s and can be visited at times convenient to the keeper. Walker Park, the greensward behind, is now used for football and other sports but was originally grazing for the keeper's cattle. Balnagask golf course occupies other parts of the headland. St Fittick's church marks the spot where, according to legend, a disciple of St Ninian was shipwrecked and built a simple cell in the 7th century. Visitors can find the leper squint in the N wall of the existing church ruins, and a number of interesting monuments and grave slabs.

The coast S of Nigg Bay is a series of cliffs and coves cut into hard metamorphic rocks, and further modified by glacial action. Small coves once supported fishing communities at

The rocky coast of Loirston Country Park at Aberdeen is an excellent place to study seabirds. *City of Aberdeen Leisure & Recreation Dept*

Altenshaven and Burnbankshaven, and salmon, dolphins and porpoises still visit this coast.

Kincorth and Tullos Hills lie inland and on the W side of the country park. This is a landscape of heather moorland, with boulders left by glacial action. The extensive view from both summits takes in the sites of battle and massacre when Covenanters under Montrose fought the Royalist army and loyal citizens of Aberdeen.

5 CRAIGTOUN
NE Fife DC 49 acres (20 hectares)
2½ miles (4km) SW of St Andrews. On the minor road from Claremont to Pitscottie. From St Andrews approach via Hepburn Gardens; a drive (signed) leads up to extensive car parks by the entrance at NO 478145. Freely open at all times. Entertainments available late March to 30 September 11.00–18.00 (10.00–19.00 in June, July and August). Accessible by bus 1 June–30 September.

Craigtoun has been developed in the gardens and landscaped grounds of Mount Melville House, formerly the home of the Younger family and now a geriatric hospital. The house stands on a shelf of rising ground, looking over St Andrews to the sea. The gardens and parkland were laid out in 1902 and have been well maintained since Fife CC bought the estate in 1947. This is a small but popular country park, offering a considerable range of activities. In addition Craigtoun has a special role in assisting local

198

horticultural organisations and providing display material for local events. (The range of glasshouses for display and propagation is open to the public from Monday to Friday, 10.00–16.00.)

A small stream flowing along the S side of the park has been dammed to provide a lake for boating and fishing. The water attracts a variety of birds and acts as a foil to the buildings known as the Dutch Village. A miniature railway runs round this part of the grounds, and there are bowling and putting greens. Among the beautiful gardens near the house there is a small open-air theatre. Refreshment facilities available include both a café and a licensed restaurant.

A number of animals and birds breed within the informal areas of the park, but the development of a nature trail really requires access to parts of the surrounding parkland. A new countryside centre for interpretative displays and educational use is planned, and the park has a ranger service.

6 LOCHORE MEADOWS
Fife Regional C 919 acres (372 hectares)
Around Loch Ore E of M90. Main entrance from B920 (Lochgelly to Ballingry road) in Crosshill at NT 178959. Also accessible from a car park E of B996 near Kelty. Freely open at all times. Accessible by bus.

Lochore Meadows is at the heart of a remarkable reclamation scheme, the most ambitious so far attempted in Britain. The last coal pits here closed in 1966, leaving a desolation of spoil heaps, derelict buildings and Loch Ore itself, the result of mining subsidence. A visitor today enters the park past the ruins of a 12th-century castle, set amongst recently planted trees and grassland, to reach the new park centre beside the water's edge. The reshaped Loch Ore, complete with specially created islands, occupies a third of the park area and is its central feature. There are facilities for sailing and canoeing (visitors launch their own craft). Day and season permits are available for coarse fishing, and the loch is being stocked with brown trout. In suitable weather the loch is used for curling. New footpaths lead round the shore to a nature reserve developed at the W end, and wildlife is being encouraged to return to the area. Already there are roe deer and many kinds of birds.

A new park centre provides a cafeteria, display space and rooms for meetings or educational use. From the windows, and from the picnic site outside, one looks down the full length of the loch. The winding-gear of the Mary Pit has been retained as a monument to those who worked in the coal mines. It is hoped to establish a mining museum within this framework, but the meadowland at its foot will become a golf course. The Fife Ranger Service is based at the park centre, and there is a programme of guided walks and lectures.

7 GARTMORN DAM
Clackmannan DC Incomplete
Based on the existing reservoir at NS 923941 near Sauchie, Alloa.

Gartmorn Dam is a recent addition to the list of provisionally registered Scottish country parks. A ranger is already in residence, and the reservoir is an important site for wintering wildfowl. It is intended to provide a small visitor centre, picnic area and bird hides.

8 MUIRAVONSIDE
Falkirk DC 151 acres (61 hectares)
3 miles (5km) SW of Linlithgow. Not open to the public at present. Access is likely to be from A825 near NS 960759.

Muiravonside is provisionally registered as a country park but may not open for some time. Stirling CC made the original proposals and at that time Muiravonside House was regarded as an important feature. This has now had to be largely demolished but the farm buildings remain and may be converted into a visitor centre. The surrounding landscaped parkland will be open and there are several special features. The river Avon flows in a deep wooded gorge round the E end of the estate, cutting across the complete sequence of Upper Carboniferous rocks. Part of the valley side is designated an SSSI. The Union Canal, completed in 1822, crosses the valley on an impressive aqueduct, and there are limekilns and other industrial archaeology remains.

9 BEECRAIGS
West Lothian DC 793 acres (321 hectares)
2 miles (3km) S of Linlithgow. Approach along Preston Road, a minor road running S from Linlithgow centre towards Bathgate. At the ridge summit NS 999747 turn left and first right for the reservoir, or continue forward to the barbecue and picnic site at Balvormie NS 998741. Freely open at all times.

Beecraigs is an extensive area of old Forestry Commission plantations on the Bathgate Hills. This group of steep-sided summits, developed on an outcrop of igneous rocks and rising to over 900ft (274m) provides good walking country and some excellent views, especially N across the Firth of Forth.

The attractive picnic and barbecue site at Balvormie is near the centre of the park, and information boards indicate the options. There is also a trim course at this point—an invitation to test agility and balance—and a camping site for youth organisations.

From another car park at the W end of the park, at NS 993743, one can walk beyond the park boundary to an isolated summit viewpoint and hill fort. Beecraigs Reservoir is the focus at the E end of the park, with car-parking at NT 007743. The reservoir is attractively set in woodland and there are observation hides for studying wildlife. The loch and its surrounding woodlands provide a sanctuary for mallard, pochard, widgeon, teal and goldeneye, and interesting flowers include the butterfly and marsh orchid. A trout hatchery has been established beside the loch, and may be visited at times indicated on the notice boards. Day permits are available for fishing and the reservoir is stocked with brown and rainbow trout from the hatchery. Another enterprise with both commercial and educational aims is the establishment of a red-deer farm, which can be visited provided that dogs are kept on a lead. A pony-trekking route and a series of footpaths link the whole country-park area, and an orienteering course has been set out. There is a programme of organised walks on summer Sunday afternoons. It is hoped to complete a display and information centre at Beecraigs in 1980.

10 ALMONDELL AND CALDERWOOD
West Lothian DC 222 acres (90 hectares)
In the Almond Valley 10 miles (16km) W of Edinburgh. N entrance to Almondell is well signed down minor road turning S from A89 at

Broxburn to North Lodge car park and entrance at NT 091698. S entrance to Almondell from A71 at the E end of East Calder village, NT 091681. Entrance to Calderwood from A71 in Mid Calder village. Freely open daylight hours. Accessible by bus.

This is a linear park following the deep and wooded valleys of the river Almond and its tributaries, a quiet retreat but readily accessible. Calderwood, the W section, was formerly owned by Lord Torphichen and acquired by the local council in 1967. It is bounded by the Linhouse Water and Murieston River and is to remain a wildlife refuge in its semi-natural state. Footpaths run through the woods and link this section to the more developed part of the country park at Almondell.

From both the North and South Lodges of Almondell, driveways lead down into the unspoilt and attractive Almond Valley, towards the picnic and barbecue sites. Almondell House, built in 1790 and the home of the Earls of Buchan, stood here until 1969, when its neglected condition made demolition inevitable. The stables are being converted to provide a display and information centre. The mixture of broad-leaved and coniferous woodland with river-side and grassland provides a diversity of wildlife habitats. Four unusual bridges add interest to the scene. The suspension bridge was erected in 1970, the main framework being brought in by helicopter. An aqueduct, built in 1820, carries water from the Almond to feed the Union Canal. The railway viaduct was built about 1885 to carry a branch of the North British Railway and serve industrial works at Pumpherston. The Nasmyth bridge, built about 1800 to the designs of Alexander Nasmyth (a painter whose portraits of Robert Burns are in the

Scottish National Portrait Gallery) is now in poor condition and likely to be demolished.

Local conservation groups and schools have been responsible for making the seats and setting up the picnic and barbecue sites. The 4½ miles (7km) of well-surfaced foot-paths were all constructed by members of International Youth Work Camps, and the visitor can now walk from Almondell to join the towpath of the Union Canal further E. There is a programme of organised walks on Sunday afternoons from March to September.

11 VOGRIE
Midlothian DC 257 acres (104 hectares)
4 miles (6½km) SE of Dalkeith. Not open to the public at present. Access will be from B6372 just S of Dewartown.

Vogrie estate is provisionally registered as a country park, and the first stage of necessary reconstruction work has begun. The landscaping of the parkland dates from the early 19th century, and needs to be rescued from neglect, but in this case the mansion (built in 1875) and stables (Gothic Revival) have been maintained and can be converted to new uses. The land at Vogrie is fertile and agriculture and forestry will continue on part of the estate. The walled garden and conservatory are already being used to raise shrubs and trees.

The first stage of development of the country park is the clearance of paths, rescue of the amenity woodland and establishment of a picnic area. The next stage is to develop a car park, a field-study centre and an area for informal games. The ultimate aim is for Vogrie house to provide accommodation for residential courses, and to develop facilities for sports such as golf.

12 JOHN MUIR
East Lothian DC 1668 acres
(675 hectares)

The coast immediately W of Dunbar. Directly accessible from Dunbar; easiest approach from A1 W of the town, turning NE along A1087. Main car park is well signed off A1087 at NT 651782. Two smaller car parks also approached along A1087 are at Shore Road, Belhaven, NT 663987 and beside Dunbar Castle, NT 678793. Freely open at all times. Accessible by bus and train.

This large and interesting country park is named after John Muir (born in Dunbar in 1838) who went to America at the age of 11 and later became famous as an explorer and naturalist. He campaigned to protect the wilderness areas of America, and it was largely through his efforts that the Yosemite Valley was established as the first National Park of the USA in 1890.

The outstanding feature of the park is the 8-mile stretch of coast extending W from Dunbar Harbour round Belhaven Bay and Tyninghame Sands to beyond Whitberry Point. At both ends are cliffs, stacks, rocky foreshores and a raised beach. There are wide stretches of sand in Belhaven Bay and around the mouth of the Tyne River, and extensive areas of salt marsh in parts of the estuary. The Bass Rock, the Isle of May and the Fife coast are prominent features of the panoramic views. Traprain Law and North Berwick Law are visible inland to the W and, like Bass Rock, are of volcanic origin. The rock structures and landscape features illustrate the consequences of volcanic action here some 300 million years ago, and the effects of subsequent glacial and marine erosion.

Those interested in wildlife will find a range of plants on coastal cliffs, sand dunes and salt marsh. Some 220 bird species frequent the area, both summer visitors like the fulmar and Arctic tern and residents including eider duck, cormorant, shag, gannet, redshank, sandpiper and many more. The whole area is recognised as of great landscape value and designated an SSSI. Because of the importance of the site and the need to protect some parts from over-use, East Lothian DC have published detailed plans for the park, further discussed in Chapter 7.

Effectively there are 3 sections to the park. The large Linkfield car park gives direct access to the sands of Belhaven Bay and the Tyne estuary. The main facilities are concentrated here, at the park centre, and a ranger is based here in the main season. Picnics, a barbecue site and a children's play area are provided for. Sand-yachting takes place on the foreshore, and special events include a kite festival and a sand-yachting regatta. Swimming in the sea is not recommended, but the open sands offer many attractions, including collecting shells. Permits are available for sea-angling and bait-digging, and there are special riding trails.

The cliffs from Shore Road to Dunbar Harbour form the E section of the park and are best explored with the help of the pocket-size guide to the cliff-top walk. This can be joined at various points, or alternatively there are regular guided walks, starting at the Shore Road car park on Wednesdays at 14.00 in summer. The E end of the park also includes the Winterfield caravan site and the council-owned Winterfield golf course.

(opposite page) A badger at Palacerigg Country Park near Cumbernauld, with the park director and Japanese visitors. *Scotsman Publications Ltd*

The W section of the park, beyond the estuary of the Tyne, is accessible down an unsigned minor road off A198, across the Tyninghame estate. This part is being left undeveloped and has restricted car-parking on Tyninghame Links, some distance from the coast. Permits are available for wild-fowling on the Tyne estuary during the winter.

13 PALACERIGG
Cumbernauld and Kilnsyth DC
633 acres (256 hectares)

2 miles (3km) SE of Cumbernauld. Approach following signs along minor road from Cumbernauld station towards Greengairs. Entrance at NS 783732. Park freely open at all times. Countryside centre freely open daily except Mondays, 11.00 to dusk (or 20.00 in summer). No dogs.

Palacerigg is unlike any other country park in Scotland. Though the name is ancient, the park has been developed not from an old estate, but from rundown farmland on an exposed hilltop—what the director terms ecologically degraded marginal land. Reclamation in this case has involved planting mixed woodland and hedgerow species (over 200,000 trees and shrubs) to provide shelter and cover for wildlife.

A special road sign 'Badgers crossing' greets the visitor, and it is the collection of native wildlife which is the feature of Palacerigg. Small mammals such as the fox, wild cat and weasel have generally been hand-reared, and are on display in enclosures with their names in Scots, Gaelic and English. Larger animals, fallow, roe and red deer for example, are in paddocks over a wide area. The number of wild species of birds and animals attracted back to live and breed in the park is growing steadily. To provide food for them, Palacerigg has become a working farm, with a breeding herd of cows, and now produces all the hay and grain it needs. Six miles of nature trails lead through the park, and there are 5 picnic sites, often at excellent viewpoints.

The Countryside Centre includes a cafeteria and a display space, and an information desk selling natural history publications. There are facilities for lectures and audio-visual projection, and a special room for school use (tel Cumbernauld 20047 for bookings). A museum of country life is being established.

The other side of Palacerigg's activities is provision for a range of sports. There is a golf course and clubhouse. Sailing takes place on Fannyside Loch and there is a touring camp and caravan site.

14 BALLOCH CASTLE
Dunbarton DC 200 acres (81 hectares)

At S end of Loch Lomond. Main entrance from B854 in Balloch, beside bus terminus and car park at NS 394821. Pedestrians enter here or 30m further W beside river Leven. Vehicle entrance (well signed) at North Lodge in Mollanbowie Road NS 395830 (may be restricted to disabled drivers). Freely open daylight hours. Accessible by bus and train.

Formerly known as Lomond Park and managed by Glasgow Corporation, Balloch Castle now has provisional recognition as a country park. Dunbarton DC are drawing up management plans for this very accessible and attractive site. At Balloch the built-up area of Clydeside reaches almost to the shore of Loch Lomond and the highland fringe. A tourist information centre in the main car park provides material on the country park and its nature trail, and a visitor centre in the castle itself is now open to the public. It is partly occupied by the regional office of the Nature Conservancy Council and the Ranger Service is already based here. The present imposing castle was built on a site above Loch Lomond in 1808.

There are at present two major attractions for visitors: the opportunity to explore the extensive parkland and lakeshore with magnificent views of Ben Lomond, and the fine walled gardens, shrubs and trees between the castle and the main gate. The rhododendrons and azaleas are splendid in early summer, and the walled garden has herbaceous borders and beds of heathers and roses. A nature trail starting at the main entrance leads past the gardens, out into open grassland and the site of the old castle, and to the lakeshore and river Leven bank. There is a slipway here, and nearby are toilets and a shelter for wet-weather picnics. The best views over Loch Lomond are from the front of the castle and paths N of this. Balloch Castle Country Park welcomes organised parties but it is helpful to contact the ranger service in advance (tel Alexandria 58216).

15 MUIRSHIEL
Strathclyde Regional C 79 acres (32 hectares)

3 miles (5km) NW of Lochwinnoch. From the E end of Lochwinnoch follow B786 initially, but fork left at signs. Park entrance near head of Calder Valley at NS 319628. Freely open at all times. Park centre normally open in summer 9.30–20.30, and in winter 9.30–16.30.

Muirshiel Country Park was opened in 1970 as Renfrew County Council's contribution to European Conservation Year, and the first of 4 recreation areas which together make up Clyde Muirshiel Regional Park. (The other three are Castle Semple Country Park and smaller sites at Cornalees Bridge and Lunderston Bay.) An adventurous singleway road with passing places penetrates up the attractive Calder Valley to a sheltered woodland site in the heart of rolling moorland. A manor house was built here in the 18th century, which later became a hunting lodge. The car park is on the house site, and the surrounding open woodland and rhododendron thickets are the policy grounds of the old estate, now the country park. The information centre is normally manned by a ranger, and features displays on local wildlife and the impact of man on the surrounding area, themes taken up in 2 different trails through the park.

The contrasted habitats of wood, moor and river are reflected in the variety of wildlife. Birds seen locally include buzzard, hen harrier, kestrel, sparrowhawk and red grouse from the moors, and dipper, tree pipit, bullfinch and goldcrest by the river and woods. Man's impact on the area began in the Bronze Age (there is a reconstruction of a Bronze Age hut), and continued through the clearance of the original woodland cover to the rotational burning still practised to regenerate the heather cover for game and grazing.

Muirshiel has sheltered picnic areas, beautifully set in this unspoilt and apparently remote spot. Access outside the park boundaries is strictly limited, however. Visitors are allowed to follow two scenic routes to the waterfall on the Calder River and up to the viewpoint on Windy Hill at 1,038ft (316m) by special access agreements, but dogs must not be taken beyond the park boundary because of grazing animals. The country park is on land leased from the local water board and construction of a reservoir in the valley has begun. This development will alter the facilities at Muirshiel, though additional land will be brought into the park. Day permits for river fishing are available, free, from the ranger (by courtesy of the Renfrew Angling Association).

16 CASTLE SEMPLE
Strathclyde Regional C 341 acres (138 hectares)˙

In Lochwinnoch. Turn off A760 into Lochwinnoch; the entrance is signed from the E end of the town, down to the loch at NS 357589. Open at all times. Accessible by bus.

With the neighbouring country park at Muirshiel and other facilities at Cornalees Bridge and Lunderston (see Other Schemes), Castle Semple forms part of the Clyde Muirshiel Regional Park. This is essentially a water park. The loch is a natural feature with gentle banks, reeded edges, water lilies and overhanging trees. There are some 210 acres (85 hectares) of open water, a good place to learn to sail. The country park facilities include a launching ramp for sailing craft, a pontoon for canoes and rowing boats, a catwalk with mooring rings and a fenced dinghy park. Power boats are not allowed, but visitors may launch their own craft on payment of a small fee, or may hire craft (tel Lochwinnoch 843445). Boat storage is available, and there are changing facilities at the park centre. A number of clubs use the loch and have exclusive use during regattas. Day permits are available for coarse fishing from the N bank of the loch.

Castle Semple itself stood at the N end of the loch but has now been demolished.

Parkhill Wood, part of the policy grounds of the estate, is now being added to the country park, and a nature trail is being developed here. The ruins of the church of Low Semple (listed by the DOE as an ancient monument) are also accessible by public footpath.

The Lochwinnoch Nature Reserve, run by the Royal Society for the Protection of Birds, covers 398 acres (157 hectares) of land on both sides of A760 at the S end of the loch, and 10 minutes' walk from the country park. The reserve is designated an SSSI because of its important wetland plants and birds. A nature centre has been built here at NS 358582, and this and a limited area of the reserve are open to the public on Thursdays, Fridays, Saturdays and Sundays, 10.00–17.15 (tel Lochwinnoch 842663 for details). Dogs are not allowed in the nature reserve.

17 GLENIFFER BRAES
Renfrew DC Area incomplete

Hillside immediately S of Paisley. Most accessible car park and viewpoint adjoins B775 at NS 454605 (known as Robertson Park). Present centre of park facilities is in Glen Park just off B774 and close to the cattle market at NS 480608. (From Paisley follow B774 to where this turns sharply E, and here fork right into Glenfield Road.) Freely open at all times. Accessible by bus.

Gleniffer Braes park is an extensive area of steep N-facing hillside bordering Johnstone, Paisley and Barrhead. The view N covers the whole lower Clyde area and extends into the Highlands. Gleniffer Braes is provisionally registered as a country park; the toilets and park centre buildings are in temporary premises in Glen Park and not well placed for visitors attracted by the impressive views from the higher land, but already there is much to enjoy.

Paisley Glen Park is an area of mixed woodland on the lower slopes. A network of paths lead up the glen past a waterfall and 2 small dams (reservoirs built to supply local industry) and an unexpectedly deep gorge. A natural amphitheatre on the hillside was formerly celebrated for open-air performances by bands and choirs. This Concert Glen and many other parts of Gleniffer Braes commemorate the writings of the weaver-poet Robert Tannahill, who lived in Paisley. There is a nature trail in Glen Park, and facilities for schools at the park centre.

Because of the extensive views, the upper slopes of the park may appeal more to those arriving by car along B775 or the minor Braehead Road. Newly planted trees will provide more shelter, but at present this is rough grass or moorland. The Tannahill way leads round E from the car park on B775, past a direction indicator and across Braehead Road towards the upper end of Glen Park. The country park also extends W of B775, and although part of this land is encumbered with pylons and wirework, there are opportunities for hill-walking with views W. Gleniffer Braes also provides for pony-trekking, flying model aircraft and archery.

18 STRATHCLYDE
Strathclyde Regional C 1601 acres (648 hectares)
Between Hamilton and Motherwell, and bisected by M74. Main entrances to E section, by signed slip road from A725 just E of motorway Junction 5 (best for camping site), or from A723 E Junction 4 (nearer the watersports centre). W section entrance from Muir Street, Hamilton. Freely open at all times. Watersports facilities open 10.00–21.00 or an hour before dusk. Accessible by bus.

Strathclyde Country Park is on a different scale from all others in Britain. Third in terms of area, it offers far the most extensive range of outdoor activities. A multi-million pound project involving reclamation on a massive scale, it was opened in 1978.

The idea of reclaiming the low haugh land beside the Clyde, then disfigured by colliery waste and other tipping, to create facilities for recreation was initially put forward by Professor Patrick Abercrombie in 1946. During the 1960s work was undertaken by the local authorities directly concerned and the main project was completed by the new Strathclyde Regional Council.

A large area of open grassland, attractively planted with young trees and shrubs, but incorporating surviving woodland and hedgerows, surrounds the new man-made loch. There are lochside footpaths and picnic areas with landscaped car parks, and maximum use has been made of the attractive features of the Orbiston Glen (the South Calder Valley). The watersports facilities on the loch are central to the project; powerboats are not allowed, but all other craft are catered for. The loch contours have been designed to provide a 6-lane 2,000m rowing course or a 9-lane canoeing course to international standards, and this is also used for sailing. The watersports centre is available both to the general public and to the specialist sportsman, and has changing facilities, a restaurant, a viewing platform, and boat storage and repair facilities. Major events monopolise the water for limited periods; people can launch their own craft or hire boats at the centre. Fishing is available

207

in the Clyde and Avon, and the loch is now being stocked with fish.

Hamilton racecourse, a fairground and a private golf course were incorporated into the park area, and a council-owned 9-hole golf course has been added. Facilities for team games are concentrated in 3 areas, each with changing facilities, and some pitches can be floodlit. Football, rugby, hockey, cricket, tennis, bowls and putting are all catered for, but the building of an indoor sports centre has had to be postponed. A camping and caravan site for touring campers (AA 3 pennants) has been developed beside the N entrance. This is open throughout the year and has a site shop and other facilities (tel Motherwell 66155, ext 55).

Though so much is new, there are survivals from the past. The existence of a Roman fort at Bothwellhaugh was already known. Excavations for the loch revealed the ruins of a Roman bath-house dating from AD 142 (not yet open to the public). The so-called Roman bridge nearby is a packhorse bridge which probably dates from the 17th century. Bothwellhaugh was also the scene of the celebrated battle between Covenanters and Royalists. The Dukes of Hamilton built and later enlarged Hamilton Palace, on the W side of the Clyde. The palace was demolished in 1927, as a result of mining subsidence, but the extraordinary mausoleum building survives. The South Calder Valley bears traces of early industry and of the ill-fated Orbiston Community. Robert

A view across the western section of Strathclyde Park, looking north over Hamilton Golf Course towards part of the nature reserve area. *S. Reid, Strathclyde Park Director*

Owen was one of the promoters of this early 19th-century social experiment. A nature trail developed beside the South Calder Water explores these sites.

Most visitors would be surprised to learn that nature reserve land at Strathclyde covers an area greater than that of the loch. Flooded land beside the Clyde had already been developed as a nature reserve before the park was created, because of the numbers of waterfowl which winter here. The construction of M74 disturbed the wildlife, but traffic noise now it is completed does not. Parts of the area are now designated an SSSI; there is a heronry and some 130 bird species now visit the area.

Strathclyde Regional Council publish and distribute free literature on the park. There is an information point in the watersports building, and a new interpretation centre in Raith Cottage. Any other inquiries to the park director (tel Motherwell 66155).

19 TORRANCE HOUSE AND CALDER GLEN
East Kilbride DC 373 acres (151 hectares)

1 mile (1½km) SE of East Kilbride. Entrance from A726 signed at NS 650528. Freely open at all times. Accessible by bus.

This country park has provisional recognition and work is in progress to develop the site. There are obvious parallels between this Calder Valley and its namesake at Almondell in West Lothian. Both rivers have deep winding wooded valleys, and both held sites of early industry; both are now country parks with a linear form and an extensive footpath system. At East Kilbride the Calder Valley is narrower and more dramatic, having waterfalls, deep pools and

rock slides. There were two estates here in the past: Calderwood, the home of the Maxwells, and Torrance House, originally the home of the Hamilton family. Several buildings surround a courtyard at Torrance, and both the tower house of 1605 and the 18th-century coach house are listed buildings. However, since East Kilbride Development Corporation moved out of Torrance House in 1966, the fabric has deteriorated badly through neglect, fire and vandalism. It is hoped that some of the buildings will be for an information centre and café.

Parts of Torrance House policies have already been successfully developed to provide sports-club facilities and East Kilbride Golf Club course. A nature trail already exists in the valley below the house (and seasonal guides to this are obtainable from the local civic centre). The first phase of country-park development is to reinstate the lawns and gardens round the house, to improve car parking and to establish a new picnic site and pets' corner. A ranger service operates and East Kilbride are now drawing up further plans.

20 DEAN CASTLE
Kilmarnock and Loudoun DC
200 acres (81 hectares)

In Kilmarnock NE of town centre. From Glasgow approach along A77 and avoid the bypass, taking B7038 into Kilmarnock. Turn left (at sign) along Dean Road to entrance at NS 435392. Country park freely open at all times. Information centre freely open daily 10.00–18.00. Castle open free but for restricted hours during present restoration. Closed November to Easter; guided tours 14.00–17.00 on weekdays and 10.00–17.00 at weekends and public holidays. Accessible by bus.

Dean Castle and the surrounding woodland have provisional recognition as a country park. The fine castle buildings stand in a parkland setting beside the Fenwick Water. The castle was inhabited until it was burned down in 1735, and stood as a ruin until 1905, when restoration was begun. The imposing keep is the oldest part, and probably dates from the 14th century. The castle belonged for a time to the Earl of Glencairn, friend and patron of Robert Burns, and this Burns connection adds a further interest for visitors; the castle is on the Burns Heritage Trail and the garden contains specimens of every plant mentioned in his poetry.

The surrounding land in the valleys of the Fenwick Water and its tributaries is attractively wooded, and there are fine specimen trees of both native and exotic species. There is an extensive network of footpaths, and a nature trail draws attention to the variety of plants and animals. The Dower House next to the castle now contains interpretative displays and a tea room. A regular programme of organised walks starts from here at 14.30 on Saturdays and Sundays from early May to late September.

21 CULZEAN
National Trust for Scotland
576 acres (233 hectares)
On the coast 12 miles (19km) SW of Ayr. Approach on A719 to signed entrance at NS 244098. Country park open always. Park centre and castle open daily 1 April–30 September, 10.00–18.00, and 10.00–16.00 in October. Admission charge to country park and admission charge to castle.

Culzean was Scotland's first country park, and it is certainly the most magnificent in

Britain. The country park is administered by the National Trust for Scotland for a joint committee of local authorities, and aspects of its planning are discussed in Chapter 4. The castle is separately administered by the trust; visitors will wish to see both castle and park.

Culzean (pronounced Khulain) is one of Robert Adam's finest achievements and has been beautifully restored; and a display commemorates General Eisenhower's association with the castle.

The magnificent parkland, gardens and coast surrounding the castle became a country park in 1969. The park centre is in the Home Farm, built by Robert Adam in 1777. This fine and highly functional group of buildings form a square around a courtyard, and now provide a restaurant, shop, and information and exhibition centre with facilities for school use and lectures.

The audio-visual programme and displays are the best starting point for visitors. The 9th and 10th Earls of Cassillis who remodelled the castle were pioneers of agricultural improvement. Case studies based on estate documents have been used to bring the significance of this to life. In similar fashion the local geology is set out below windows looking directly at the main features: Ailsa Craig, the Isle of Arran, the coast of Kintyre. The park centre has won 5 awards since it opened in 1973.

The surrounding wood and parkland is rich in wildlife and offers all sorts of opportunities for walks. These can be extended by using the right-of-way along the former railway line. The old Glenside Station area is now a camping and caravan site. The most beautiful spots include the Fountain Court, a sheltered garden and orangery below the castle, and the walled garden some distance away. The herbaceous borders here were planted in 1962; there is a forestry exhibition here, and plants are on sale. Swan Pond is the largest of several water areas. Many wild birds frequent this artificial lake, and there is a small aviary and children's play area. A cliff path follows the coast, linking the various points where there is access to the beach. To the N of the castle the cliffs are developed in Devonian Sandstone (also used in much of the building). Beneath and to the S of the castle, harder rocks of volcanic origin occur, and semi-precious stones derived from these may sometimes be found on the beach below the castle, by the Bath House. The small sandy beach at Port Carrick is popular for bathing.

The team of rangers and naturalists based at Culzean staff a varied programme of organised walks and evening films throughout the season, with daily activities during the busiest months. (For details of these and other events tel Kirkoswald 269.)

22 BRODICK CASTLE
Joint Committee incomplete
The Brodick Castle Estate on the Isle of Arran.

A country park based on the gardens, woodlands and estate policies of Brodick Castle is likely to be developed by a joint committee of the National Trust for Scotland with Cunningham DC, along the lines of the scheme at Culzean Castle.

OTHER SCHEMES

There are various types of park which should be noted here. Because the Scottish system of grant aid for recreation is different from that used in the rest of Great Britain, private schemes receiving it and having a grant-aided ranger service are not called country parks. Three schemes in particular are comparable to private country parks in England: Hopetoun House near South Queensferry in West Lothian, Finlaystone at Langbank on A8 and Kelburn on A78 between Largs and Fairlie, both in Strathclyde.

Certain picnic sites deserve mention and the two within Clyde Muirshiel Regional Park are separately listed. Brimmond and Elrick Hills, some 6 miles (9½km) W of central Aberdeen are approached by minor roads linking A96 and A944, to a car park at NJ 858101. City of Aberdeen DC describe this site as a country park and publish a good guide to its interesting features. Fife Regional Council have developed two picnic sites with toilets in the Lomond Hills near NO 228063. A study is being undertaken which may lead to further recreation provision here.

A ROSLIN GLEN
Midlothian DC 52 acres (21 hectares)
5 miles (8km) SW of Dalkeith and immediately S of Roslin. Not open to the public at present. Probable entrance from B7003 beside river Esk bridge at NT 268627.

Midlothian has made proposals to develop a country park in Roslin Glen, and a Land Renewal Project is currently being undertaken. At this point the river Esk has cut a deep and winding gorge. In the past the water powered a number of gunpowder mills, and there is scope to open up various sites of interest to the industrial archaeologist. The glen is clothed in woodland and rich in wildlife. The scenery is attractive and it is believed that the river is once again sufficiently pure to allow the return of fish.

Immediately N of the proposed park is another attractive section of the Esk Valley, in part designated an SSSI. Rosslyn Castle, built by the St Clairs in the 14th century (and later enlarged), stands high on a cliff above the river. Still better known, and open to the public, is Rosslyn Chapel, the private family chapel and a celebrated example of 15th-century Gothic architecture.

B CORNALEES BRIDGE
Strathclyde Regional C

SW of Greenock on moorland road from Greenock to Inverkip at head of Shielhill Glen. Information centre and main car park at NS 247722. Freely open at all times.

This is one of the facilities of the Clyde Muirshiel Regional Park. There are 3 main attractions here: the aqueducts built in 1827 to supply Greenock with water for drinking and power, the contrast between heather moorland and wooded glen, and the fine views over Dunoon and the Clyde. A 1½ mile (2½km) trail follows the banks of the Kelly and Greenock Cuts, parts of a scheme developed by Robert Thom and now scheduled as an Ancient Monument. The trail descends into the Shieldhill Glen on a wooden walkway. The surviving remnant of natural woodland, mainly ash, birch, oak and rowan, is designated an SSSI. This trail crosses private land and moorland grazed by sheep, so dogs must be kept on a lead. A longer walk follows the Greenock cut to Overton, above Greenock, returning along a rough track past Loch Thom Cottage.

C LUNDERSTON BAY
Strathclyde Regional C

SW of Gourock on A78 1 mile (1½km) S of Cloch Lighthouse at NS 205740. Freely open at all times.

This is the smallest of the recreation areas within the Clyde Muirshiel Regional Park. It is the nearest beach to Glasgow on the S side of the Clyde. There is a large field, a car park, toilets and drinking water. The beach is stony with patches of sand, and there is a mile-long walk S along the rocky foreshore, with good views across the Clyde.

Appendix 1:
Country Parks in Northern Ireland

More details are available from the Northern Ireland Information Service, Stormont Castle, Belfast.

1 CRAWFORDSBURN
On the S shore of Belfast Lough, 10 miles (16km) from Belfast.

2 ROE VALLEY
Between Dungiven and Limavady in County Londonderry. Approach from B192.

3 THE NESS
Around a fine waterfall, 2½ miles (4km) on N side of Londonderry to Claudy road, 7 miles (11km) from Londonderry.

4 CASTLE ARCHDALE
On the NE shores of Lough Erne, 12 miles (19km) from Enniskillen.

5 SCRABO/KILLYNETHER
Includes Scrabo Tower and Killynether National Trust woodland, 1 mile (1½km) from Newtownards, County Down (incomplete).

6 REDBURN
Close to Holywood, County Down, and still at an early stage of development.

7 THE LAGAN VALLEY REGIONAL PARK
Based on the river Lagan, this is 9 miles (14km) of towpath between Belfast Lough, Lisburn and beyond.

Appendix 2:
Useful Addresses

Countryside commission
Head Office: John Dower House, Crescent Place, Cheltenham.

North Region: Warwick House, Grantham Road, Newcastle.

Yorks and Humberside: Fairfax House, Merrion Street, Leeds.

NW Region: Arkwright House, Deansgate, Manchester.

West Midlands: Auchinleck House, Broad Street, Birmingham.

East Midlands: Cranbrook House, Cranbrook Street, Nottingham.

Eastern Region: Terrington House, Hills Road, Cambridge.

London and SE: 25 Savile Row, London W1X 2BT.

South Central Region: Minster House, Minster Street, Reading.

SW Region: Bridge House, Sion Place, Clifton, Bristol.

Wales: 8 Broad Street, Newtown, Powys.

Countryside Commission for Scotland
Battleby, Redgorton, Perth.

English Tourist Board
4 Grosvenor Gardens, London SW1W 0DU.

Forestry Commission
231 Corstorphine Road, Edinburgh.

Nature Conservancy Council
19–20 Belgrave Square, London SW1X 8PY.

The Country Code

Guard against all risk of fire

Fasten all gates

Keep dogs under proper control

Keep to the paths across farmland

Avoid damaging fences, hedges and walls

Leave no litter—take it home

Safeguard water supplies

Protect wildlife, wild plants and trees

Go carefully on country roads

Respect the life of the countryside

Bibliography

Information in the gazetteer has been based on published park guides or on material supplied by the managing authorities and the park staff. Detailed plans quoted include:

East Lothian Council, *John Muir Descriptive Management Plan* (1976) and *John Muir Prescriptive Management Plan* (1976).

Staffordshire County Council, *Cannock Chase Country Park Plan* (1979).

University of Edinburgh, *TRRU Report No 39 Strathclyde Park, 1977* (1978).

GENERAL SOURCES

Countryside Commission, *Leisure in the Countryside* (1979) (a short useful summary).

Gilg, Andrew W., *Countryside Planning: The First Three Decades 1945–76* (1978).

Newby, Howard, *Green and Pleasant Land? Social Change in Rural England* (1979).

RESEARCH REPORTS AND OFFICIAL PUBLICATIONS

Countryside Act 1968 (reprinted HMSO 1974).

Countryside Commission publications:

Advisory Notes on Country Park Plans (1974).

Annual Reports.

Cannock Chase Country Park Study Vol 2 Interim Report of Survey (1978).

Countryside for All? CRRAG Conference 1978.

Digest of Countryside Recreation Statistics 1978.

Grants to Local Authorities and other Public Bodies for Conservation and Recreation in the Countryside (1979).

Grants to Private Individuals and Bodies for Conservation and Recreation in the Countryside (1978).

Tatton Park Interpretive Study (1976).

Countryside Commission for Scotland publications:

Annual Reports.

A Park System for Scotland (1974).

A Policy for Country Parks (1973).

Scottish Tourism and Recreation Planning Studies,
  1 *Strategic Issues* (1977).
  2 *A Guide to the Preparation of Initial Regional Strategies* (1977).
Dartington Amenity Research Trust reports:
  Interpretation in Visitor Centres (1979).
  Scottish Tourism and Recreation Planning Studies, a report by DART on their contribution (1978).
  Self-guided Trails (1978).

Leisure in the Countryside, England & Wales, Cmnd 2928 (1966) (the White Paper).

PERIODICALS
Countryside Recreation Review.
Recreation News.
Fitton, Martin, 'Countryside Recreation—The Problems of Opportunity', *Local Government Studies (1979), pp. 57–90.*

Acknowledgements

The sources I have used for the general background on the development of our park system are listed in the bibliography. Information on the individual parks comes from published park guides, or from conversations and correspondence with the managing authorities, the local planning departments and (above all) from the park staff.

I cannot separately acknowledge or adequately thank the very large numbers of people who helped me in this way. I owe a great debt to the national and regional offices of the two Countryside Commissions, the National Trust, Nature Conservancy Council, Forestry Commission, water authorities and the tourist boards, as well as to innumerable private individuals whose information—and misinformation—enlivened my adventures.

For the illustrations I am indebted to many local authorities, other organisations and private individuals, and these sources are acknowledged in the captions. Other photographs are from my own collection.

Index

221